CAMBRIDGE LIBRARY COLLECTION

Books of enduring scholarly value

History

The books reissued in this series include accounts of historical events and movements by eye-witnesses and contemporaries, as well as landmark studies that assembled significant source materials or developed new historiographical methods. The series includes work in social, political and military history on a wide range of periods and regions, giving modern scholars ready access to influential publications of the past.

Catalogue of a Collection of Works on or Having Reference to the Exhibition of 1851

C. Wentworth Dilke (1810–69), an influential figure at the Society of Arts, was one of the key organisers of the Great Exhibition of 1851. He played a leading part in planning the event and the catalogue, overseeing the installation of exhibits and managing the PR. The exhibition generated an enormous number of publications, official and unofficial, both in Britain and abroad, ranging from vistors' guides to London and descriptions of individual exhibits to discussions about the long-term future of the Crystal Palace, together with essays, sermons and poems. Dilke acquired several hundred such books and pamphlets, in various languages, and in 1855 privately published this catalogue of his collection, noting that it omits 'mere trade pamphlets' and that his 'departments' of relevant music and engravings are not comprehensive. Alphabetically organised and thoroughly cross-referenced, Dilke's catalogue remains an invaluable research resource for those studying the Great Exhibition and its global impact.

T0364266

Cambridge University Press has long been a pioneer in the reissuing of out-of-print titles from its own backlist, producing digital reprints of books that are still sought after by scholars and students but could not be reprinted economically using traditional technology. The Cambridge Library Collection extends this activity to a wider range of books which are still of importance to researchers and professionals, either for the source material they contain, or as landmarks in the history of their academic discipline.

Drawing from the world-renowned collections in the Cambridge University Library, and guided by the advice of experts in each subject area, Cambridge University Press is using state-of-the-art scanning machines in its own Printing House to capture the content of each book selected for inclusion. The files are processed to give a consistently clear, crisp image, and the books finished to the high quality standard for which the Press is recognised around the world. The latest print-on-demand technology ensures that the books will remain available indefinitely, and that orders for single or multiple copies can quickly be supplied.

The Cambridge Library Collection will bring back to life books of enduring scholarly value (including out-of-copyright works originally issued by other publishers) across a wide range of disciplines in the humanities and social sciences and in science and technology.

Catalogue of a Collection of Works on or Having Reference to the Exhibition of 1851

In the Possession of C. Wentworth Dilke

CHARLES WENTWORTH DILKE

CAMBRIDGE
UNIVERSITY PRESS

CAMBRIDGE UNIVERSITY PRESS

Cambridge, New York, Melbourne, Madrid, Cape Town,
Singapore, São Paolo, Delhi, Tokyo, Mexico City

Published in the United States of America by Cambridge University Press, New York

www.cambridge.org
Information on this title: www.cambridge.org/9781108036610

© in this compilation Cambridge University Press 2011

This edition first published 1855
This digitally printed version 2011

ISBN 978-1-108-03661-0 Paperback

Exhibition of the Works of Industry of All Nations,

1851.

CATALOGUE

OF A COLLECTION OF WORKS ON

OR HAVING REFERENCE TO

THE EXHIBITION OF 1851,

IN THE POSSESSION OF

C. WENTWORTH DILKE.

Printed for Private Circulation.

1855.

This Copy was Printed for

THE UNIVERSITY LIBRARY, CAMBRIDGE.

LONDON: PRINTED BY W. CLOWES AND SONS, STAMFORD STREET.

APPLICATION having been made to me for a Catalogue of the works which I possess relating to the Exhibition of 1851; and it appearing from inquiries that many of the works—temporary, of course, in interest and character—are not, even now, to be obtained, I have been induced to print a Catalogue, believing that it might be acceptable to those who took an active part in the arrangements for the Exhibition, and who received in recognition of their services "Presentation Sets" of the publications from Her Majesty's Commissioners. Few persons, perhaps, are aware of the number of works issued on that occasion, both in this country and abroad.

In nearly all cases the title-page has been copied literally. The only exception is in regard to quotations, which often appear with double inverted commas, whereas in this Catalogue single inverted commas only have been employed— the double commas having been reserved to indicate extracts from the book itself or translations of such extracts.

The publisher's or printer's name, date, and price, when they do not appear on the title-page and could be ascertained, are inserted between brackets; also the size of the work and the number of pages.

The number of pages has been copied from the paging of the book; it being thought better to adopt this system, as a rule. It is requisite, however, to mention that in some instances the introductory pages have been by the Printer of the work included in the continuous paging, whereas in others the Arabic numbers commence from the first page.

A brief explanation—when possible, in the words of the Author, or in literal translations of such words—has been added, when the title appeared not clearly, or sufficiently, to explain the contents of the work or the views of the writer.

In addition to Books and Pamphlets, the titles of such engravings and music as are in the collection have been added; but it is not presumed that either of these departments is complete. Mere trade Pamphlets have not been included.

The Books will be found alphabetically arranged, according to the first word on their title-page, except in the case of general headings—" Exhibition of 1851 "—"Exhibition of Industry of All Nations "—"Great Exhibition of Industry of All Nations "—" Exposition de 1851 "—" Exposition Universelle de 1851 "—" Exposition de Londres "—" Exposition Universelle de Londres "— and " Grande Exposition de Londres "—when not substantive titles.

Cross-references will be found to Authors' names and pseudonyms when they appear on the title-page. When the Author's name appears in the body of the work it has been added in the note.

With regard to cross-references generally, the search is to be made for the first word of the title, the others having been added only to explain precisely the work referred to. Thus, under " Birmingham," reference is made to " Slight sketch of Manipulatory Processes." To find this work the search is to be made under " Slight."

The works marked ⁰ have been seen, but copies have not yet been obtained.

The works marked * are only known by advertisements, and it is doubtful from the inquiries made whether some of them were ever published.

The abbreviations used are those adopted at the British Museum.

w. y. signifies that the title-page is without year.

v. directs to the title under which the description of the work will be found.

CATALOGUE

Of a Collection of Works on

THE EXHIBITION OF 1851.

Account (An) of the Kenilworth Buffet, with elaborately carved relievos, Illustrative of Kenilworth Castle, in the Elizabethan Period, Designed and Executed by Messrs. Cookes and Sons, of Warwick, for the Grand Exposition of Industry of All Nations. By W. Jones.

London: Published by J. Masters, 78, New Bond Street, and 33, Aldersgate Street; Cundall and Addey, 21, Old Bond Street.

Warwick: H. T. Cooke, High Street. 1851.

[Price 3*s.* Royal 4to, pp. 22, with Illustrations. The work was printed by H. T. Cooke, Printer, High Street, Warwick; *v.* also Description of Kenilworth Buffet.]

Account (An) of the Proceedings at the Dinner given by Mr. George Peabody to the Americans connected with the Great Exhibition at the London Coffee House Ludgate Hill on the 27th October 1851.

London. William Pickering. 1851.

[Circulated privately. 4to and 8vo, pp. 114. A Report of the speeches delivered at the parting dinner given by Mr. Peabody, and an Appendix containing Newspaper comments on the dinner and Mr. Paxton's speech at a dinner at Derby, August 6, 1851.]

Ackermann's Pictures of the Crystal Palace, *v.* Rambling Inspiration over.

Adam, Adolphe, *v.* Fête.

Adam, Mons., *v.* Palais de Cristal ou les Parisiens a Londres.

Adams's Pocket London Guide Book: a Complete Historical, Critical, General, and Topographical, Survey of the Metropolis, for the Use of the Resident or Stranger. Giving in a compendious form a full Description of every thing that can be seen within its limits, Corrected up to the latest Period, and arranged in an entirely novel and interesting manner. By E. L. Blanchard, Author of Adams's Descriptive Guides to the 'Environs of London,' 'The Watering Places of England,' &c. &c.

London: W. J. Adams, 59, Fleet Street; and all Booksellers.

[W. y. Price 3*s.* 6*d.* 12mo, pp. xii., xvi. and 241, with engravings. Published in 1851 and contains a short account, 16 pages, of the Building and general arrangements of the Exhibition, with an exterior View.]

Addington, Samuel, *v.* Reports by the Juries.

Address (An) by J. A. Hammersley, Esq., Principal of the Manchester Government School of Design, on the Preparations on the Continent for the Great Exhibition of 1851, and the Condition of the Continental Schools of Art. Delivered at Nottingham on the 15th of October, 1850, At the request of the Local Committee for the Great Exhibition. Reported by Thomas Whitehead, of the 'Nottinghamshire Guardian.'

Nottingham: Printed by T. Forman, 'Guardian' Office, 14, Long Row. 1850.

[Circulated privately. 8vo, pp. 16. "*We must send to the Exhibition,* and *in sending we must* NOT *copy the works that were done years before; we must not copy the works of other countries.* * * * It is a piece of moral turpitude on the one hand, and a piece of national shame on the other, that education has been so long delayed in this country,—an education

that

that shall enable our manufacturers to obtain designers equal to those on the Continent. I do not say that any one is blameable; but this I do say—the cure is coming with this Exhibition. I believe we shall exhibit, but I believe we shall have extensive short-comings, which, however, will be compensated for by redoubled efforts on the part of the manufacturers."]

Address by the Local Commissioners for Sheffield. To the Merchants, Manu-facturers, and Artizans of the Borough of Sheffield.

[Without Publisher's or Printer's name, or date. Circulated gratuitously in 1850. 4to, pp. 3. "Perhaps the greatest benefit the approaching Exhibition will confer upon us will be the opportunity of comparing the productions of the Countries already mentioned with our own. * * * The ends of the Exhibition—so far as Sheffield is concerned—will not be answered unless we show clearly to the world *all* that we can produce in our staple Manu-factures * * * from the cheapest article fabricated up to the most expensive." Signed Wilson Overend, Thomas Dunn, Robert Younge, Commissioners for Sheffield.]

Address of the Bath Local Committee.

Meyler and Son, Printers, Herald Office, Bath.
[W. y. Circulated gratuitously in 1850. Royal 8vo, p. 1. Inviting subscriptions, and urging Bath to "send to the Exhibition specimens of the skill of her operative Workmen." And signed James Tunstall, Wm. Akerman, Hon. Secretaries.]

Adress (En) till Utlandningar som besoka den stora Konst-Expositionen uti London, 1851. Skriften och Sabbaten utí England.

London : Tryckt pa bekostnad af Sallskapet for Christlig kunskaps utbredande ; sald vid dess Depôt, Great Queen Street, Lincoln's Inn Fields, No. 4, Royal Exchange; No. 16, Hanover Street, Hanover Square; och hos alla Bokhandlare.
[W. y. Price 1*d.*, or 7*s.* per 100. 12mo, pp. 10. One of the addresses issued by the Society for Promoting Christian Knowledge.]

Aerial Pontoon Railway Suspension Bridge, Thomas Watts, *v.* Description.

Agricultural Villages, Andrews, R., *v.* Public Meetings in.

Air-Navigation, by means of the Rotatory Balloon. By John Luntley. Pro-visionally Registered, April 26th, 1851.

London : Houlston & Stoneman, Paternoster Row. 1851
[Price 1*s.* 6*d.* 8vo, pp. 20. Dedicated "To Her Majesty's Commissioners of the Great Exhibition." "The Royal Commission of 1851, however, is a commission of peace."]

Akerman, Wm., *v.* Address of the Bath Local Committee.

Albert, Alfred, *v.* Palais de Cristal ou les Parisiens a Londres.

Albrecht, Dr , *v.* Amtlicher Bericht.

Aldis, Rev. J. *v.* Forty-four Sermons.

A l'Etranger dans Hyde Park.

Londres : Dépôt de la Société des Traites Religieux, Paternoster Row.
[W. y. Price 1*d.* 12mo, pp. 12. A translation of the work which will be found under To a Stranger.]

Alexander, William, Electro-Magnetic Telegraph, *v.* Plan and Description of.

Alger, Rapport de Monsieur Fléchey, *v.* Chambre de Commerce.

Allon, Rev. H. *v.* Forty-four Sermons.

Almanacs, *v.* Crystal Palace—Exhibitors'—Furbers—Gilbert's Crystal Palace—Illustrated Exhibitors—Illustrated London—Industrial Exhibition—Perfumed —Ross.

A los Estrangeros que Visitan la Gran Exposicion de las Artes en Londres, 1851. Las Escrituras y el Domingo en Inglaterra.

Londres : Impreso por la Sociedad para Promover los Conocimientos Cristianos ; se Vende en el Deposito, Great Queen Street, Lincoln's-Inn-Fields ; N. 4, Royal Exchange ; y en casa de Todos los Libreros. 1851.
[Price 4*s.* per 100. 12mo. pp. 8. One of the addresses issued by the Society for Promoting Christian Knowledge.]

Alphabet of English Things, *v.* Aunt Mavor.

Alphabet of Foreign Things, *v.* Aunt Mavor.

Alphabet of the Exhibition, *v.* Aunt Mavor.

Alphabetical and Classified Index to the Official Catalogue of the Great Exhibition of the Works of Industry of All Nations, 1851.

Part 1. Alphabetical Index of Contributors and others whose names appear in the Catalogue. Memorandum.—This Index includes the name of every person, and public or other Company, mentioned in the Catalogue, whether as Contributor, Manufacturer, Patentee, Agent, or in any other way connected with Articles in the Exhibition.

Part 2. Alphabetical and Classified List of Articles contained in the Official Catalogue. Memorandum.—Persons consulting this Index will find that the articles contained therein are arranged according to a principle by which the whole of a series of the same species are grouped together as far as practicable. *Ex. gr.*: Under 'Magnesia' will be found 'Magnesia, Bi-Carbonate of,' 'Magnesia, Sulphate of,' and so on. Under 'Railways' will be found 'Railway Axles,' 'Railway Bars,' &c. &c.

London: Spicer Brothers, Wholesale Stationers; W. Clowes & Sons, Printers; Contractors to the Royal Commission, 29, New Bridge Street, Blackfriars, and at the Exhibition Building. 1851. [W. y., but published in 1851. Price 1s. Small 4to, pp. 96 and 99.]

American Superiority at the World's Fair. Designed to accompany a Chromo-Lithographic Picture, illustrative of Prizes awarded to American Citizens, at the Great Exhibition. A compilation from Public and Private Sources, by Charles T. Rodgers, of Louisiana.

'Westward the star of Empire takes its way.'

Philadelphia: Published by John J. Hawkins. 1852.
[8vo, pp. 148. Contains a portrait of Mr. E. Riddle, the American Commissioner. Eight lithographic engravings of objects exhibited. The subjects especially treated of are Yachts—Reaping and Mowing Machines—India-Rubber Fabrics—Astronomical Clock and Spring Governor—Colt's repeating Arms—Hobbs' Locks, &c., &c., with extracts from publications on Triumphs of American skill. The engraving is designed and drawn on stone by Thurwanger Brothers, lithographers of A. Brett and Co, Goldsmiths' Hall, Library Street, Philadelphia, and it is Dedicated to the People of the United States by Mr. Charles T. Rodgers.]

Amtlicher Bericht über die Industrie-Ausstellung aller Völker zu London im Jahre 1851, von der Berichterstattungs-Kommission der Deutschen Zollvereins-Regierungen. Erster Theil. Einleitung: Vorbereitung, Beschickung und Ausführung der Ausstellung. Erste Gruppe: Rohstoffe und Materialien. Zweite Gruppe: Maschinenwesen, Werkzeuge, Gegenstände des Land-, Wege-, Wasser- und Eisenbahnbaues, Schiffe, Waffen und Ausrüstungsgegenstände, landwirthschaftliche Geräthe, naturwissenschaftliche, musikalische, horologische und chirurgische Instrumente und Apparate. Zweiter Theil. Dritte Gruppe: Gespinnste, Gewebe, Häute und Lederwaaren, Papier-, Buchdruck- und Buchbinderwaaren, Farbstoffe und Farben, Dessins, Erzeugnisse der Bleiche, Färberei und Druckerei, Teppiche, Filzwaaren, Wachstuche, Stickereien, Stroh- und Gummiwaaren und fertige Kleidungsstücke. Mit Grundrissen des Ausstellungsgebäudes und der Aufstellungen desselben im Erdgeschoss und dem obern Stockwerk. Dritter und lezter Theil. Vierte Gruppe. Metall-, Glas- und Irdenwaaren. Fünfte Gruppe: Holz- und Steinfabrikate, kurze und gemischte Waaren. Sechste Gruppe: Kunstsachen. Schlussbericht: Verlauf und Schluss der Ausstellung, Gesammtergebnisse derselben. Alphabetisches Verzeichniss der Aussteller. Nachträge und Berichtigungen.

Berlin, 1852–3. Verlag der Deckerschen Geheimen Ober-Hofbuchdruckerei.
[Price R 8. 20 sgr. 3 Vols. 8vo. Theil I., pp. xvi, 943; Theil II., pp. vi, 714; Theil III., pp. viii, 864. "The Industrial Exhibition of All Nations in London was undertaken with the view of showing, by specimens of the productions of the whole world, the actual state of industry and art, and of placing before the nations of the globe the various products of every trade and plastic art, and of affording to the industrial and commercial classes, to their patrons and to Governments, a new basis for furthering the industry and art of their countries. * * * Independently of the agitated times and the necessary preparations, Germany had, in joining this comprehensive undertaking, great difficulties to overcome, owing to the absence of united action, from which other nations were exempt. It was, therefore, a preliminary task how to set the strength of the different states in motion, how to make them work in concert, and how to represent them. * * * We have mentioned in the report the most meritorious exhibitors in all classes of articles, especially those who have been rewarded by Prize Medals; in regard to the names of the producers, only those in the most important branches of industry have been given." The report opens with a general statement of the Exhibition and an account of the principal officers of the English Commission, and the following is a list of the Commissioners who have reported on the different classes. Class 1. F. Schreiber (Bieber). Class 2. Prof. Varrentrapp (Brunswick). Class 3. Prof. Dr. Heeren (Hanover), Dr. Dünkelberg (Wiesbaden), Dr. von Viebahn (Berlin).

(Berlin). Class 4. Dr. von Viebahn, Weyhe (Director of the Agricultural Academy at Poppelsdorf), Prof. Dr. Rau (Heidelberg). Class 5. Commerzienrath Roessler (Darmstadt), Prof. Schneider (Brunswick), Mr. Deninger (Mayence). Class 6. Prof. W. Wedding (Berlin), Prof. Dr. Hülsse (Dresden). Class 7. Regierungs- u. Baurath Stein (Aix la-Chapelle), Oberbaurath Hartwich (Berlin). Class 8. Will. Oechelhäuser (Siegen). Class 9. Prof. Dr. Rau, Dr. Dünkelberg. Class 10. Prof. Dr. Schubarth (Berlin), Conservator Dr. Schafhäutl (Munich). Class 11. Ph. Ellissen (Francfort). Class 12. Ministerialrath Dr. von Hermann (Munich). Class 13. C. Gropius (Berlin). Class 14. Wm. Oechelhäuser, Gustav Kramsta (Freiburg), J. Sonnenthal (Jessnitz). Class 15. S. Weigert (Schmiedeberg). Class 16. Carl Deninger. Class 17. W. Oechelhäuser, Prof. Dr. Hülsse. Class 18. Dr. Kunheim (Berlin), Dr. von Viebahn, Ph. Ellissen, C. Gropius. Class 19. S. Weigert. Class 20. Dr. Albrecht (Director of the Industrial School at Königsberg). Class 21. Director Karmarsch (Hanover). Class 22. Regierungsrath Dr. v. Steinbeis (Stuttgard). Class 23. Ludwig Gruner (London). Class 24. Bergrath Prof. Dr. G. Schueler (Jena). Class 25. Ministerialassessor F. Odernheimer (Wiesbaden). Class 26. Wm. Oechelhäuser. Class 27. Prof. Rühlmann (Hanover). Class 28. Prof. Dr. Schubarth. Class 29. Prof. A. W. Hofmann (London). Class 30. Prof. G. F. Waagen (Berlin). The preface, introduction, and concluding chapter are by Dr. G. W. von Viebahn. The second volume contains two ground-plans.]

Amtlicher Catalog der Ausstellung der Industrie-Erzeugnisse aller Völker, 1851. Deutsch bearbeitet von Edward A. Moriarty.

> " Die Erde ist des Herrn, und was darinnen ist ;
> Der Erdboden, und was darauf wohnet."

London : Gebrüder Spicer, Papierhändler ; W. Clowes u. Söhne, Buchdrucker. Von der Kœnigl. Commission privilegirte Herausgeber, 29, New Bridge Street, Blackfriars, und im Ausstellungs-gebæude, Hyde Park. Price 2s. 6d.
[W. y., but published in 1851. Small 4to, pp. 308. A translation of the "Shilling Catalogue," which will be found under Official. A French translation will be found under Catalogue Officiel.]

Amtliches Verzeichniss der aus dem Deutschen Zollverein und Norddeutschland zur Industrie-Ausstellung aller Völker in London eingesandten Gegenstände. Mit Angabe derjenigen Preise dieser Gegenstände, deren Veröffentlichung freigestellt worden, nebst Reduktionstafeln, alphabetischem Namens-Verzeichniss und Nachweisung der Klassen.

Berlin, 1851. Verlag der Deckerschen Geheimen Ober-Hofbuchdruckerei.
[Price 12½ sgr. 8vo, pp. viii, 378. An edition in English will be found under Official.]

Andrews, R., *v.* Public Meetings in Agricultural Villages.

Anrede an die Fremden welche die grosse Industrie- und Kunst-Ausstellung zu London Anno 1851 besuchen. Die Heilige Schrift und der Sabbath in England.

London : Gedruckt für die Gesellschaft zur Beförderung Christlicher Erkenntniss, zu verkaufen in den Niederlagen, Great Queen Street, Lincoln's-Inn-Fields ; No. 4, Royal Exchange ; No. 14, Hanover Street ; und in allen Buchhandlungen.
[Price 1d., or 7s. per 100. 12mo, pp. 12. One of the addresses issued by the Society for Promoting Christian Knowledge.]

Ansted, Professor D. T., *v.* Lectures [Non-Metallic Mineral Manufactures]— Reports by the Juries.

Answer (An) to ' What is to become of the Crystal Palace ? ' By Greville.

London : John Ollivier, 59, Pall Mall. 1851.
[Price 1s. 8vo, pp. 29. "Pull it down, we say, in conformity with the compact solemnly entered into, upon which alone its erection was tolerated. * * * That such may be the illustrious close of an exhibition, unexampled in its national daring since the world began, is earnestly desired for the honour and welfare of the country !"]

Appeal for a National Expression of Praise at The Close of ' The Great Exhibition.'

[Circulated gratuitously. 12mo, 1 p. A poem signed Martin F. Tupper.
> " When with prayer we well begin,
> And are prospered many ways,
> It were pity, shame, and sin,
> Not to make an end with Praise :"]

*Appel aux Industriels Francais pour representer dignement notre Industrie a l'Exposition Universelle, par M. Charles Dupin 1850.

Appold, J. George, *v.* Centrifugal Pumps.

Arbitrate, Arbitrate, *v.* Placards.

Archer, Rev. Dr., *v.* Forty-four Sermons.

Architectural Ornament, Gibbs, W., *v.* Handbook.

Architectural Quarterly Review (The).
> 'Well Building hath three conditions: Commodity, Firmness, and Delight.'
> Vol. I.—No. 1.   June, 1851.   Price five shillings.

London: George Bell, Next St. Dunstan's Church, 186, Fleet Street.
> [8vo. Contains an article upon the Great Exhibition and its influence upon architecture (pp. 17-27). "The building for the Exhibition is the greatest evidence that the Exhibition affords of the industrial resources of this country. * * * But let it be distinctly understood by all who are carried away by its vastness, or by the splendour, and general effect of its contents, that the building has no claim whatever to be considered as a work of ART, and is no evidence of what the ART of Architecture could accomplish, whether now or at any other time."]

Arenstein, Prof. Dr., *v.* Kurze Beschreibung.

Are you going to the Crystal Palace?   A Plain Question for the present time.
> 'He showed me that great city, the holy Jerusalem, descending out of heaven from God, having the glory of God; and her light was like unto a stone most precious, even like a jasper stone, clear as a crystal.'—Rev. xxi. 10, 11.

London: Wertheim and Macintosh, 24, Paternoster-Row.   1851.   Price One Penny.
> [12mo, pp. 13.   "Dear reader, most persons are going eagerly and anxiously to one Crystal Palace, but there is 'a City of pure gold, like unto clear glass,' unto which the saints only are travelling, that 'City of habitation,' which hath 'foundations whose builder and maker is God.' It is *that* Crystal Palace of which I ask, *Are you going thither?*"]

Argyll, Duke of, *v.* Reports by the Juries.

Arles-Dufour, *v.* Politique Nouvelle—Travaux.

Arnoux, J. J., *v.* Palacio de Cristal.

Arnoux, L., *v.* Lectures [Ceramic Manufactures].

Art and Faith, in fragments from the Great Exhibition of Arts and Manufactures in 1851.   By George Troup.
London: Partridge and Oakey, Paternoster Row.
Edinburgh: Charles Zeigler.   *Glasgow:* Thomas Murray and Son.   1852.
> [Price 2*s.*   12mo, pp. 2 and 354.   This work was originally issued in Numbers at 1*d.* and 2*d.* each, and in Parts at 6*d.*, and this is, apparently, the first collected edition.   It was printed by George Troup, 29, Dunlop Street, Glasgow.]

Art and Faith; or the Harmony of Science and Scripture.   By George Troup.
London: James Blackwood, Paternoster Row.
Edinburgh: J. Menzies.   *Glasgow:* W. Collins.   1852.
> [Price 4*s.* 6*d.*   12mo, pp. viii. and 408, with 8 Illustrations.   "Designed to illustrate the close and intimate connexion between the revelations of Creation, of Providence, and of Scripture, and to vindicate the latter by eliciting its invariable correspondence with things seen.   They were undoubtedly intended to support the opinion of the writer that natural, or rational religion, must agree with the doctrines generally denominated Evangelical, as they are found in the Word of God, and that the assumption of the titles "natural" and "rationalistic," for systems opposed to the great doctrines of Evangelical Protestant Churches, is entirely inconsistent with all the analogies that can be deducted from nature and art. * * * References have been made to the contributions transmitted to the Exhibition of 1851, because the products of art and industry were associated there in a more convenient form for inspection than under any previous circumstances." This edition was also printed by George Troup, 29, Dunlop Street, Glasgow.]

Art-Education at Home and Abroad.   The British Museum, the National Gallery, and the Proposed Industrial University.
> 'The advancement of the Fine Arts and of Practical Science will be readily recognised by you as worthy of the attention of a great and enlightened nation. I have directed that a comprehensive scheme shall be laid before you, having in view the promotion of these objects, towards which I invite your aid and co-operation.'—See Her Majesty's Speech to Parliament, Nov. 11th, 1852.

By G. W. Yapp.   Second Edition, with a Postscript.
London: Chapman and Hall, 193 Piccadilly.   1853.
> [Price 1*s.*   8vo, pp. viii. and 71.   A pamphlet, "the main object of which was to bring into one view the condition of our public establishments connected with popular instruction in Art, and the opinions and views of those who had given most attention to the subject. Dedicated to the Council of the Society of Arts.]

Artists, *v.* Friendly Observations to Sculptors and Artists.

Artizans' College, Organization of an Industrial, *v.* Notes.

Artizans of All Nations, a Poem, *v.* Dedicated to the.

Art Journal (The). Illustrated Catalogue. The Industry of All Nations 1851.
London: Published for the Proprietors, by George Virtue.
[W. y. Price 21*s.* Royal 4to, pp. xxvi. 328, xvi.*, viii.‡, viii.†, viii.**, xxii.*** This volume is a republication of Engravings having relation to the Exhibition which appeared from time to time in 1851 in the " Art Journal." It also contains a short descriptive account of the Exhibition and its arrangements, and Essays on " The Science of the Exhibition by Robert Hunt, Esq., Keeper of Mining Records Museum of Practical Geology" pp. 16. " The Harmony of Colours as exemplified in the Exhibition by Mrs. Merrifield." pp. 8. "The Vegetable World as contributing to the Great Exhibition by Edward Forbes, F.R.S., Professor of Botany in King's College, London, &c." pp. 8. " The Machinery of the Exhibition: as applied to Textile Manufactures. by Lewis D. B Gordon, Regius Professor of Mechanics, University of Glasgow." pp. 8. " The Exhibition as a Lesson in Taste, an Essay on Ornamental Art as displayed in the Industrial Exhibition in Hyde Park, in which the different styles are compared with a view to the improvement of Taste in Home Manufactures. By R. N. Wornum." pp. 22. Mr. Wornum was awarded the prize of one hundred guineas, offered by the proprietors of the " Art Journal," for an Essay on the best mode of rendering the Exhibition practically useful to the British manufacturer.]

Art Journal Prize Essay. Art, Science, and Manufacture as an Unity, an Essay in Four Chapters. What we *have been* doing. What we *are* doing. What we *ought* to do. What we *can* do. By George Wallis, Head Master of the Birmingham School of Design; Principal Superintendant of British Textile Manufactures, and Deputy Commissioner in charge of Group C of Juries, in the Great Exhibition of 1851; formerly Head Master of the Manchester School of Design.
' Nil actum reputans, dum quod superesset agendum.'
Printed for private circulation only. 1851.
[Without Publisher's or Printer's name. Royal 4to, pp. 245–271. This Essay, an excerpt from the " Art Journal," was written in competition for the Prize offered by the proprietors of the " Art Journal," and was awarded a Second Prize. " What we can do " contains suggestions by Mr. Wallis as to the future uses to which he proposed to turn the Exhibition Building, with designs.]

Art-Manufacturers' Institute at Bradford. To Samuel Smith, Esq., Mayor of Bradford, &c. &c.
[Without Publisher's or Printer's name, or date of publication. Circulated privately. 8vo, pp. 8. A pamphlet, dated Kensington, 5th February, 1852, and signed " Henry Cole," on the proposed establishment of an Art-Manufacturers' Institute at Bradford, with estimated receipts and expenses, written on the occasion of a Deputation from the Society of Arts visiting Bradford, *v.* also Society of Arts.]

*Art Manufactures of the World. Drawn by P. H. Delamotte & H. C. Pidgeon. Engraved by J. Thompson & T. Thompson. Described by C. A. Cole.
[Advertised but never published.]

°Art News (The) : An Illustrated Journal of the Great Exhibition of 1851.
[Printed by Richard S. Francis, No. 25 Museum St.]

Ashton, Thomas, *v.* Reports by the Juries.

Association to Promote a Cheap and Uniform System of International Postage for Letters and Printed Papers.
[Without Publisher's or Printer's name, or date. Circulated gratuitously by the Society of Arts. 8vo, pp. 1 & 4. The Association was composed of gentlemen connected with the Exhibition of 1851. The longest Paper is a Report of an interview with Earl Granville, Secretary of State for Foreign Affairs, on the 23d January, 1852. Printed by George Barclay, Castle Street, Leicester Square, London.]

Atmospheric Maps, showing the Direction of the Wind, the Barometric Pressure, and the State of the Weather, at various Places in Great Britain, from Observations collected by the Electric Telegraph Company at the Great Exhibition, Aug. 11 to Oct. 11, 1851.
London: Trelawny Saunders, 6, Charing Cross. 1851.
[Published daily at the Exhibition, price 1*d.* each. Folio. 56 separate maps of England, with the condition of the atmosphere, &c., marked each day by arrows.]

Attempt (An) to define the Principles which should regulate the Employment of Colour in the Decorative Arts, with a few words on the present necessity of an Architectural Education on the part of the Public.

' We

'We should do our utmost to encourage the Beautiful, for the Useful encourages itself.'—*Goethe*.

Read before the Society of Arts, April 28, 1852. by Owen Jones, Fellow of the Royal Institute of British Architects, Corresponding Member of the Academy of S. Fernando of Madrid.

London: 1852.

[Without Publisher's name, but printed by G. Barclay, Castle St., Leicester Sq. Circulated gratuitously. Royal 8vo, pp. 59. "It can scarcely too often be repeated, that amongst the many advantages which must result to England from the gathering of the products of the world's industry in the Great Exhibition, no one is so prominent as that we have thereby learned wherein we were deficient; and although we may gather from the Lectures which have already been delivered before this Society a high idea of the power, wealth, and industry of this great country; of the untiring enterprise which gathers from a distance the products of every clime; of the persevering industry which makes them available to the wants of man; and may further witness the constant struggle to utilise every gift of Nature, till truly it may be said, nothing has been made in vain; yet, side by side with success, we have seen much of labour wasted, much knowledge imperfect, much energy misapplied: and when we leave the field of Science and Industry and turn to Art, we have to learn from the Great Exhibition a fruitful lesson; from leading the van in the march of progress, we must fall into the rear, and suffer to pass before us nations whose efforts we have hitherto but imperfectly appreciated. In that branch of art, the employment of colour, the more immediate subject of this lecture, we were not only behind some of our European neighbours, but, in common with these, were far outstripped by the nations of the East. Let us endeavour to trace the cause of this, and, if possible, discover the principles which in their case have led to so signal a success."]

Aubry, M. Felix, on Lace, *v.* Travaux.

Aunt Busy-Bees Series of 13 Coloured 6*d.* Books—
    The Fine Crystal Palace The Prince Built.

London: Dean and Son, Threadneedle-street.

[W. y. Royal 8vo, pp. 8, with colored engravings. One of a series of books for children, describing the Crystal Palace in verse.]

Aunt Mavor's Picture Books for Little Readers.—
    The Old Cornish Woman.—[8 large Cuts.]
    Alphabet of Foreign Things.—[24 Cuts.]
    Uncle Nimrod's First Visit.—[19 Cuts.]
    Uncle Nimrod's Second Visit.—[23 Cuts.]
    Uncle Nimrod's Third Visit.—[8 Cuts.]
    Alphabet of the Exhibition.—[8 large Cuts.]
    Alphabet of English Things.—[24 Cuts.]
    Ploucquet's Stuffed Animals.—[7 large Cuts.]
    The Exhibition and Grand London Sights.—[16 Cuts.]
    Dolls and Sights of the Crystal Palace.—[8 large Cuts.]
    Old Mother Bunch.—[8 Cuts.]

London: George Routledge & Co., Farringdon Street.

[Price 6*d.* each. W. y. Royal 8vo. Series of children's books, describing in verse and prose the Great Exhibition and the sights of London.]

Austrian Section. By authority of the Royal Commission. Official Catalogue of the Great Exhibition of the Industry of All Nations, 1851.

London: Spicer Brothers, Wholesale Stationers; W. Clowes & Sons, Printers; Contractors to the Royal Commission. City Office, 29, New Bridge Street, Blackfriars.

[W. y. Price 1*s.* Small 4to, pp. 162. The prices of the greater number of articles are given. Contains also a "Map of the Austrian Empire, showing the places which have contributed to the Exhibition, 1851, by Augustus Petermann, F.R.G.S."]

°Auszug des Ersten Berichtes.

Regensburg, 1852.

[4to, pp. 36, *see* Erster.]

Authentic Account (An) of the Chinese Commission which was sent to report on the Great Exhibition; wherein the opinion of China is shown as not corresponding at all with our own The whole from the Chinese Reports now Collated, by Sutherland Edwards, and by him Translated, and put into Rhyme with about enough reason to suit the demands of the Holiday Season.

Printed at 15 and 16, Gough Square, by H. Vizetelly, and sold by him there. To be had of all Booksellers throughout the land, and likewise at each railway book-stall or stand. To suit the occasion the Publisher's willing to charge the merely nominal price of One Shilling.

[W. y.

[W. y. Price 1s. Square 8vo, pp. 32, with Illustrations. A story, as shown by the title, in comic verse.

    " If the affair, we sum up it must be allowed
    To be one of which England may justly be proud;
    It's a barbarous land, but you find there much good,
    Though the uses of opium are not understood."]

Aux Etrangers qui sont Venus visiter la Grande Exposition de l'Industrie, à Londres, 1851. Les Saintes Ecritures, et le Dimanche, en Angleterre.

Londres: Imprimé aux frais de la Société pour la Propagation des Connaissances Chrétiennes; et se trouve au Dépôt, Great Queen Street, Lincoln's Inn Fields, 4, Royal Exchange, et 16, Hanover Street, Hanover Square; et chez tous les Libraires. 1851.
    [Price 1d., or 7s. per 100. 12mo, pp. 12. One of the Addresses issued by the Society.]

Aveling, Rev. T., *v.* Forty-four Sermons—Great Sights.

Avenir Probable de l'Europe, *v.* Bourse.

Babbage, Charles, *v.* Exposition of 1851—Letter to the Board (Sheepshanks).

Ballads, Street. [One Halfpenny and One Penny each.]

    Come let us go and see the Exhibition for a Shilling.—E. Hodges Printer, 31, Dudley Street, Seven Dials.
    National Exhibition.—Do.
    The Great National Exhibition of 1851.—Do.
    The Exhibition and Foreigners.—Do.
    Crystal Palace.—Do.
    Crystal Palace.—Do.
    Wonders of the World.—Do.
    Lamentations of the Exhibition.—Do.
    London Exhibitions.—Do.
    Exhibition Fashions.—Do.
    Queen Victoria's Welcome to the City Banquet.—Disley, Printer, 16, Arthur Street, Oxford Street.
    °Wonders of the Great Exhibition.—Do.
    °The Opening of the Great Exhibition.—Do.
    °Uncle Ned's Description of the Exhibition.—Do.
    I'm going to see the Exhibition for a Shilling.—Do.
    Downfall of the Exhibition.—Do.
    The Exhibition Songster for 1851. The Great Exhibition of 1851.—C. Paul, Printer Gt. St. Andrew-street, Broad Street Bloomsbury.
    The Queen's Visit to the City Banquet.—Do.
    °The Wonders of the Exhibition.—Do.
    The Downfall of the Exhibition.—Do.
    Have you been to the Chrystal Palace.—Birt, Printer, 39, Great St. Andrew Street, Seven Dials, *London.*
    The Great National Exhibition of 1851.—Do.
    The National Exhibition.—On the same sheet as the Cholic. [No printer's name.]
    The Big Show Coming.—T. King, *Birmingham.*
    All Serene.—Do.
    Exhibition of All Nations.—W. Pratt, Printer, 82, Digbeth, *Birmingham.*
    Exhibition of All Nations.—Do.
    The New Exhibition Sights and Wonders!—Do.
    John Bull and the Exhibition.—Do.
    Uncle Ned's Visit to the Exhibition.—Do.
    See the Exhibition for a Shilling.—Do.
    The Great National Exhibition of 1851.—Do.
    The Great National Exhibition.—John Harkness, Printer, 121 and 122, Church Street, *Preston.*
    Exhibition of All Nations.—On the same sheet as Kendal Fair. No Printer's name, but printed by Mr. Harkness, of *Preston.*
    °A Broadside of.—Printed by R. E. Leary, Printer, &c. 19, Strait, *Lincoln.*

Ball at Guildhall, *v.* Brief Historical account of Guildhall—Grand Procession.

Balloon, Rotatory, *v.* Air-navigation by means of, John Luntley.

Balloon View of London (A) taken by the Daguerreotype Process, (size of Engraving 43 by 25 inches,) Exhibiting eight Square miles, shewing all the Railway Stations Public Buildings, Parks, Palaces, Squares, Streets, &c., with their Names clearly Written, forming a complete Street Guide.
London: Appleyard & Hetling, 86, Farringdon Street. In Sheet, 1s.; In Case for the Pocket, 1s. 6d.
[W. y. A Map on a large scale, with a view of the Building.]

Banking, *v.* Gilbart—Prize Essay.

Banville, Theodore de, *v.* Fête.

Bard, M. J., *v.* Semaine a Londres.

Baring, Thomas, London Institution, *v.* Illustrations presented to.

Barlow, H. C., *v.* Industry on Christian principles.

Barrière, Th., *v.* English Exhibition Comédie-Vaudeville.

Basingstoke, Address to Mechanics' Institute at, *v.* Card.

Bath, *v.* Address of the Local Committee.

Baxter, John, *v.* Brief Description of two models of improved Farmyard.

Baxter's Gems of the Great Exhibition. Dedicated by Special Command to His Imperial Majesty the Emperor of Austria, by His most Obedient and Obliged Servant, George Baxter.
London: Published at the Offices of the Patentee, 11 & 12, Northampton Square.
[W. y. Price 1l. 11s. 6d. Small folio. Nine engravings printed in oil-colours, with letter-press description.]

Baxter's Pictorial Key to the Great Exhibition (forming a Companion to the Official Catalogue), and Visitors' Guide to London. In English, French, and German.
London: Published at the Patentee's Offices, 11 & 12, Northampton Square. Price three shillings.
Thomas Harrild, Printer, Silver Street, Falcon Square, London.
[W. y. Small 4to, pp. 16, with two illustrations in oil colours and a ground-plan divided by figures, to which references are made in the short catalogue which forms part of the key.]

Bayley, F. W. N., *v.* Little Folks' Laughing Library—Rambling Inspiration.

Bazley, Thomas, *v.* Lecture upon Cotton—Lectures on the Results.

° Beale's Universal Broadsheet and Family Companion of Science, Literature, Romance, Wit, Humour, and Utility. Price One Penny.

Beasland's London Companion during the Great Exhibition; 1851. Containing much important information, and a carefully compiled account of the Sights and Wonders in the Metropolis, being a Stranger's Hand-Book and a Londoner's Remembrancer. Illustrated by a superb Engraving of the 'Crystal Palace.'
London: Published by R. Donaldson, 52 Holywell Street. And Sold by all Newsvenders in the Metropolis and the Country. Also to be had at every Railway Terminus in London. Price Twopence.
[W. y. Royal 12mo, pp. 24. Pages 7–9 contain an account of the Crystal Palace.]

Beaumont, Rev. Dr., *v.* Forty-four Sermons.

Beautes (Les) Architecturales de Londres. Edition Poliglotte. En Francais, Anglais et Allemand.
H. Mandeville, *Paris.* Ackerman & Co. & Read & Co. *London.*
[W. y. Price 21s. Oblong 4to. Contains besides other engravings twelve interior and exterior views of the Exhibition Building, which views also appear in the Gallery of Arts.]

Beggs, Thomas, *v.* Exhibition and the People.

Be Just before you are Generous, *v.* Industry of All Nations.

Belgian Report, *v.* " De l'Enseignement "—Industrial Instruction in England.

Belgian Sale at close of Exhibition, *v.* Catalogue of.

Belgravia. a Poem.
London: Charles Westerton, 20, St. George's Place, Hyde Park Corner. 1851.
[Price 2s. 6d. 8vo, pp. 79.
"See the vast wonder of the opening year!
The Crystal Palace—like a dream appear!"]

Bell, Jacob, v. Lectures [Chemical processes].

Belshazzar's Feast in its application to the Great Exhibition. Daniel 5.
London: Houlston & Stoneman, Paternoster Row.
Dublin: F. Cavenagh, Wicklow Street. 1851.
    [Price 3*d.* 12mo, pp. 24. "The present moment may surely thus remind us of Belshazzar's
Feast. Gods of gold and of silver, of brass, of iron, and of wood, are praised—the resources
and capabilities of the world are displayed,'thoughtless of its rejection of Christ. * * *
The Exhibition is therefore in full collision with the mind of God. Christ *exposes* the
world; the Exhibition *displays* it. Christ would *alarm* it, and call it to a sense of judgment;
the Exhibition *makes it on better terms with itself than ever.*"]

Bengal, v. Catalogue of East Indian Productions collected in—List.

Bennett, John, v. Circular on Watch and Clock Makers' Meeting.

⁰Beobachter (Der) und Berichterstatter in London, seiner Umgebung und seinem
    Kristallpalaste, oder Beschreibung Londons, seiner Umgebung und des seiner
    Art grössten menschlichen Werkes der Welt, nämlich der grossartigen Welt-
    Industrieausstellung des neunzehvten Jahrhunderts im gläsernen Tempel
    der Künste aller Nationen unserer Erde. Mit dem Bildnisse des Kristall-
    palastes. Herausgegeben von Robert Wunderlich. 1851.
Druck von T. T. Heer in Töss, bei Winterthur.
    [8vo, pp. vi., 154.]

Bericht der Königlich Grossbritannischen Kommissäre, v. Erster.

Bericht über die Abtheilung der Baumwollengewebe und Garne an der allgemeinen
    Industrieausstellung in London im Jahre 1851. Von Paul Kirchhofer, Sohn,
    Schweizerisches Mitglied des Preisgerichts in der Section XI.
St. Gallen. Scheitlin und Zollikofer. 1852.
    [Price 2 sgr. 8vo, pp. 27. The author regrets that the particular branch of industry on
which he reports (cotton) was so inadequately represented at the Exhibition, and that, with
the exception of several parts of Switzerland and some districts of Great Britain, none of
the contending countries had furnished a true picture of their cotton-manufactures.]

Bericht über die englische Landwirthschaft und die zu London 1851 ausgestellten
    Landwirthschaftlichen Geräthe und Maschinen. Von Dr. Fr. X. Hlubek.
    Mit 1 lithographirten Tafel. (Der Ertrag dieser Brochure ist dem Unter-
    stützungsfonde für bedürftige Techniker am Joanneum zu Gratz gewidmet.)
Gratz, 1852. In Commission und zu haben in der F. Ferstl'schen Buchhandlung. (Johann Lorenz
Greiner.)
    [Price 20 sgr. 8vo, pp. vi, 56. A report on English agriculture to the Agricultural
Society of Styria. It contains the results of Dr. Hlubek's observations during his journey
to Scotland, undertaken in conjunction with Prof. Herrmann of Munster and Dr. Thomae.]

Bericht uber die Industrieausstellung, v. Amtlicher Bericht—Erster Bericht.

Bericht über die Landwirthschaftlichen Maschinen und Geräthe welche von dem
    Königl. Ministerium für landwirthschaftl. Angelegenheiten in London
    angekauft sind. Von Dr. C. F. Schneitler, Civil-Ingenieur.
Berlin. Verlag von Wiegandt und Grieben. 1852.
    [Price 7½ sgr. 8vo, pp. 35, with Illustrations. A detailed account of the English agri-
cultural machines and implements, bought by the Prussian Government at the Exhibition,
with the English and German prices. These machines were gratuitously exhibited at the
engine-manufactory of Mr. Wohlert, at Berlin, for the purpose of promoting their adoption
by German agriculturists.]

Bericht über die Weltindustrieausstellung zu London im Jahr 1851, erstattet im
    Auftrage der Industriekommission in der Hauptversammlung der St. Gallisch-
    Appenzellischen gemeinnützigen Gesellschaft zu Wattwil, den 23. Oktober 1851,
    von G. Delabar, Professor, in St. Gallen.
St. Gallen und Bern. Verlag von Huber und Komp, 1852.
    [Price 15 sgr. Post 8vo, pp. 182. Contains a comparative list of all the exhibitors, and a
special one of those of Switzerland, to whom Prize Medals have been awarded, and who have
been honourably mentioned, by means of which the author arrives at the conclusion that
Switzerland in general, and St. Gallen-Appenzell in particular, have reason to be satisfied
with the results of the Exhibition as far as their honour is concerned.]

Bericht über landwirthschaftliche Maschinen und Ackergeräthe, welche sich in
    dem Industrie-Ausstellungs-Gebäude zu London befanden von Th. Labahn in
    Greifswald.

                                         Besonderer

Besonderer Abdruck aus den Eldenaer Jahrbüchern.
Greifswald, 1852.   In Commission bei L. Bamberg.   Preis 12½ Sgr.
[8vo, pp. 38. A report to the Agricultural Society at Eldena. The author, after giving a description and awarding praise to the English agricultural implements, regrets that many of the ablest engineers of Germany had sent no contributions, the more so, as he is of opinion that their productions would have successfully competed with the best English ones.]

Berlioz, Hector, *v.* Great Exhibition and London in 1851.

Berlyn, Peter, *v.* Crystal Palace—Industrial Instruction—Popular Narrative.

Bernoville, M., on Printed Woollen Goods and Clothing, *v.* Travaux.

Besuch (Ein) in London während der grossen Industrie-Ausstellung.   Ein verlässlicher Führer und Wegweiser für den deutschen Reisenden, aus den besten Quellen bearbeitet.
Mit einer Aussenansicht und einem Plane des Innern des Ausstellungsgebäudes.
Wien, 1851.   Aus der kaiserl. königl. Hof- und Staatsdruckerei.
[Price 18 sgr. 12mo, pp. 128, with two Illustrations. A guide to London, with a cursory glance at the Exhibition.]

Beta, *v.* Crystal Palace and Crystal Palaces.

B., E., Tiny Exhibition, *v.* By the authority of the Inventors.

Bevington, J. B., *v.* Reports by the Juries.

Bible (The) the Great Exhibition For All Nations.   By the Rev. A. Fletcher, D.D.
' For every House is builded by some man : but he that built all things is God.' Heb. iii., 4.
London : Hanbury & Co., 70, Edgeware Road ; Partridge & Oakey, Paternoster Row.   1851.
[Price 1s. 6d. 32mo, pp. iii. 138. " The design of the Author in presenting the Bible as the ' Great Exhibition for All Nations,' was suggested by the ' Exhibition for All Nations ' erected in the western portion of our Metropolis. We may justly consider the philanthropy, which gave origin to an object so august and comprehensive, as an emanation flowing from the religion of that sacred and inspired volume, which teaches, by the highest sanctions, the great lessons of universal love, fellowship, and peace."]

Binney, Rev. T., *v.* Forty-four Sermons—Royal Exchange.

Birch, Rev. Henry, *v.* Great Exhibition Spiritualized.

Birkin, Richard, *v.* Reports by the Juries.

[Birmingham, Correspondence between Local Committee and the Royal Commissioners.]
[Without Publisher's or Printer's name or date, but issued April, 1850. Fol. pp. 4. Relates to the name of the Manufacturer being attached to every article.]

Birmingham, *v.* Catalogue of Exhibition of 1849—Preparations for the Exhibition —Slight Sketch of Manipulatory Processes—To H. R. H. Meeting of Clerks.

Bishop, Sir Henry, *v.* Reports by the Juries.

Blackwell, S. H., *v.* Lectures [Iron].

Blackwood's Edinburgh Magazine.   No. 419.   September, 1850.
Edinburgh : William Blackwood & Sons, 45 George Street ; and 37 Paternoster Row, London. To whom all communications (post paid) must be addressed. Sold by all the Booksellers in the United Kingdom. Printed by William Blackwood and Sons, Edinburgh.
[Price 2s. 6d. 8vo. Contains an article on the then proposed Exhibition of 1851 (pp. 278–290) : " Upon many grounds, therefore—none of them being of a trivial description —we object to the proposed Exhibition, and earnestly hope that, unsupported as it is by the public at large, it may be allowed quietly to drop into the limbo of exploded schemes."—A reply to this article will be found under Exhibition of 1851 and the Objections thereto.]

Blaise, Ad. (des Vosges) *v.* Politique Nouvelle.

Blanchard, E. L., *v.* Adams' Pocket London Guide.

Blandydash, Barnabas, *v.* Trip to the Great Exhibition.

Blanqui, *v.* Briefe—Lettres.

Bleekrode, Dr. S., *v.* De Tentoonstelling.

[Bolton, Resolutions of Local Committee of, on 17th September 1851, respecting the erection of a Statue to Prince Albert.]
[Without Publisher's or Printer's name or date, but issued September, 1851. 4to, 1 p.]

Bombay, *v.* Tabular and Descriptive Lists of Articles from.

Bontemps, G., Verres, Vitraux, Cristaux, *v.* Examen Historique.

Book of Wonders.

'Prodigious !!'

London John J. Griffin & Co.
and R. Griffin & Co. *Glasgow.*

[W. y. Price 1*s.* 24mo, pp. 104, with view of the Building, and other Engravings, and on the title-page a representation of Dominie Sampson uttering the word Prodigious. A little book for young people. An account of the Crystal Palace is contained in the first thirteen pages. The book was printed by Bell and Bain of Glasgow.]

Bosc, Aristide, *v.* Ouvriers.

Bouchard, Emile, *v.* Mois a Londres.

Bourse (La) et le Palais de l'Industrie; ou, l'Avenir probable de l'Europe et du Monde. En Trois Parties.

'La terre est au Seigneur avec tout ce qui la remplit,
Le monde avec tous ses habitants.'

Londres: William Jones, 56, Paternoster-Row, et 164, Piccadilly. 1851.
[Price 2*s.* 12mo, pp. viii., 184. A translation from the English, *v.* Royal Exchange. A German translation was also published, *v.* Königliche Börse.]

Boyer, Jules, *v.* Voyage a Londres.

Bradford (Yorkshire) Schools, *v.* Art-Manufacturers' Institute—Society of Arts.

Bradford, Yorkshire, letter of Mr. John Horsfall, *v.* Great Industrial Exhibition.

Bradford, Yorkshire, *v.* Report of a Meeting of Foremen.

Bramah Lock Controversy (The). Extracts from the Press.
London: Printed by T. Brettell, Rupert Street, Haymarket. 1851.
[8vo, pp. 30. Also several other editions with slight variations.]

Brannon, Philip, *v.* Park and the Crystal Palace.

Bref Exposé de la Grande Exposition des Produits de l'Industrie de Toutes les Nations en 1851. Suivi d'un Guide Complet de l'Etranger a Londres, contenant tous les renseignments necessaires a un voyageur qui visite pour la premiere fois la Capitale. A translation, *v.* "Home Circle."

Brentano, Dr., *v.* Briefe.

Brewer, Mrs., *v.* On the Gathering of the Nations.

Brief Description (A) of Two Models of Improved Farm-Yard and Buildings, with their advantages. Shown at the Industrial Exhibition in 1851, (now added to the Library of Agricultural Knowledge,) by John Baxter, of Lewes and Oaklands Farm, Sussex, the Designer.
Lewes: Printed and Published at the Sussex Agricultural Express Office, by Baxter and Son.
London: Simpkin and Marshall, Stationers' Court, and Ridgway, Piccadilly. 1852.
[Price 2*s.* 6*d.* Royal 8vo, pp. 13, with designs.]

Briefe über die Welt-Industrie-Ausstellung in London von M. Blanqui, Mitglied des franz. Instituts, Professor am Conservatorium der Künste und Gewerbe, Director der höhern Handelsschule in Paris, etc. etc. Aus dem Französischen von Dr. Brentano, Lehrer an der Königl. Gewerb-und Handelsschule in Fürth.
Fürth: J. Ludw. Schmid's Buchhandlung, 1852.
[Price 24 sgr. 8vo, pp. xiv, 186. The translator observes in the preface: "Having personally visited and studied the Industrial Exhibition, I am bound to say that M. Blanqui's opinions with regard to it are based upon facts, and in the main correct. I can, however, not subscribe to all the conclusions he comes to, nor can I admit that the London Exhibition is a criterion of the industrial powers of nations, many countries having more or less abstained from exhibiting, and the Zollverein, in particular, having not been very felicitous in its choice." The translator seems to incline towards a moderate system of protection.]

Brief Historical Account (A) of the Guildhall. Presented on the occasion of the Grand Ball, given by the Corporation of London, to celebrate the opening of the Exhibition of the Works of Industry of all Nations, honoured by the presence of Her Most Gracious Majesty the Queen, 9th July, 1851.
Thomas Harrild, Printer, Silver Street, Falcon Square, London.

[W. y.

[W. y. Privately circulated. Sm. 4to, pp. 12. With song at the end entitled "London," since, it is said, set to music.]

Brief Survey (A) of the Objects of Graphic Art exhibited by the Imperial and Government Printing Establishment at Vienna, at the London Exhibition, 1851.

London : Samuel Bagster and Sons, 15, Paternoster Row.
[W. y. Circulated gratuitously. 8vo, pp. 16. A detailed catalogue of the articles exhibited by the Imperial Establishment at Vienna, with an introduction relating to that establishment.]

Briggs, Thomas, *v.* Essay on the Advantages to be gained by Working Men.

Bristol Working Men's Association in connexion with the Great Exhibition of 1851. Rules.
[Mathews Brothers, Engravers & Printers, Broad Quay. W. y. Circulated gratuitously. Small 8vo, pp. 2.]

British Advertizer (The). An illustrated Hand-book of the Great Exhibition. First Issue, August 1st 1851.
London : Jackson and Cooper, 300 Strand and 190, High Holborn.
[12mo, pp. 56. Contains a history and description of the Exhibition, illustrated with several woodcuts.]

º British Guiana Catalogue.
[Without Publisher's or Printer's name, year, or price. 8vo, pp. 33. Signed "W. H. C. Campbell, Honorary Secretary. By order of the Central Committee of British Guiana," and dated "George-town, Demerary, March 12th, 1851."]

British Metropolis (The) in 1851. A Classified Guide to London ; so arranged as to show, in separate Chapters, every object in London interesting to special tastes and occupations.

> 'Let your book be a fact bag without confusion.'—*An eminent living American.*
>
> Myriads of streets, whose river windings flow
> With viewless billows of unweary sound ;
> Myriads of hearts in full commotion mixed,
> From morn to noon, from noon to night again,
> Through the wide realm of whirling passion borne,
> And there is London !—*Robert Montgomery's 'Satan.'*

London : Arthur Hall, Virtue & Co., Paternoster Row. 1851.
[Price 5*s.* Royal 12mo, pp. xx. and 299, with maps and engraving of Crystal Palace. An account of the "Great Industrial Exhibition" is contained in the xx. pages of introduction.]

British Museum, G. W. Yapp on, *v.* Art Education.

British Quarterly Review (The). Nos. 31, August 1, 1852 (and 33, February 1, 1853).
London : Jackson & Walford, 18, St. Paul's Churchyard ; and Simpkin, Marshall and Co., Stationers' Hall Court.
Edinburgh : W. Oliphant and Sons. *Glasgow :* J. Maclehose. *Dublin :* J. Robertson. Price Six shillings. Savill & Edwards, Printers, 4 Chandos Street, Covent Garden.
[8vo. No. 31 contains an article on "Industrial Instruction" (pp. 133-152) written generally in the spirit of the following extract: "We have now given, from dissimilar sources, the evidences which prove the growing feeling that English industry must be properly sustained by industrial instruction. Great as our advances in the arts of peace have been, we have learnt from the Great Exhibition that there are numerous points in which we are inferior to the foreigner, and in some, as in the principles of design, and the science of coloured harmony, we are lamentably ignorant." No. 33 (pp. 203-220) has an article on the "Industrial College :" "Any hot-house system, in which well-salaried professors and Government officials labour merely to maintain the appearance of usefulness, by forcing up a few fine plants, would soon degenerate ; and having produced a few abnormal and useless growths, would moulder and decay. But a system, in which every member should be made to depend directly upon the public for support, would be certain of existing in all activity, and of producing the best possible results for industrial Britain."]

Brock, Rev. W., *v.* Forty-four Sermons.

Brodie, B. C., *v.* Chemical Society.

Bronno-Bronski, Major Count De, *v.* Recueil.

Brown, *v.* Mr. and Mrs. Brown.

Brown, Rev. J. B., *v.* Forty-four Sermons.

Brunel, I. K., *v.* Reports by the Juries.

Bucher, L., *v.* Kulturhistorische Skizzen.

Buckingham, James Silk, *v.* Earnest Plea for Temperance.

Building for the Exhibition of Industry of All Nations in 1851. Statement of
advantages of Mr. Paxton's plan.
[Without Publisher's or Printer's name, or year. Privately circulated. 4to, p. 1. This
statement, the first separate announcement of Mr. Paxton's idea, accompanied an engraving
of the proposed Building from the "Illustrated London News."]

Building (The) erected in Hyde Park for the Great Exhibition of the Works of
Industry of All Nations, 1851. Illustrated by Twenty-eight large plates,
embracing plans, elevations, sections, and details, laid down to a large scale
from the working drawings of the Contractors, Messrs. Fox, Henderson, and
Co. By Charles Downes, Architect. With scientific description by Charles
Cowper, Assoc. Inst. C. E.
London: John Weale, 59, High Holborn. 1852.
[Price 1*l.* 11*s.* 6*d.*   4to, pp. 69.]

Burgess, William, *v.* Great Exhibition, 1851.

Burnet, Rev. J., *v.* Forty-four Sermons.

Burnet, Richard, *v.* To Her Majesty's Commissioners.

Burrows, Rev. H. W., *v.* Great Exhibition. A Sermon.

Bush and Day, MM., *v.* Merveilles de Londres.

Bye-Laws, Society of Arts, *v.* Constitution.

°By Authority. Exhibition of 1851. The only Commissioners' Report, for the
better protection of Strangers and the Public generally, against every descrip
tion of Fraud committed in London, arranged under the following heads:—
Pickpockets Gaming and Flash Houses Swell Mob Ring Droppers Change
Ringers Duffers Cut Purses Houses of Ill-fame Hocussing Night Houses Play
Houses Box and Bundle Men Magsmen Housebreakers Haunts of Thieves
Flash Notes, bad Money, with every precaution to enable Strangers to avoid
being robbed, (the whole authorized to be published) and sold at one penny each.
[12mo, pp. 12.]

°By the authority of the Inventors. Official Catalogue of the Tiny Exhibition, of
Individual Industry, June, 1851.
Richmond: printed and published for the proprietor. 1851
[Twenty-five copies only printed and privately circulated. Sm. 4to, pp. 12. With a
circular of one small side explanatory of the Tiny Exhibition, which says, "it is intended to
place within the compass of 12 square feet, a space requested but not granted, in Hyde Park,
this year 1851, some trifling Models formed from Sticks and Stones: first the Arms of
England, composed of portions of Oak, grown in the Parks and Royal Gardens in the
locality of Richmond—producing the Portraits of King Henry VIII and Queen Elizabeth,
from trees planted and existing in their glorious reigns; representations of Life, Death, and
Sleep, with other objects to be more fully explained hereafter. But for a few days after
May-day, there will be a Tiny Exhibition appear at the IVY HOUSE, at Richmond, to be
viewed by *Tickets only,* when obtained of E. B., gratis, if applied for at the said Ivy House."
It is signed E. B. There is also a Circular announcing the closing of the Exhibition and a
card of admission.]

Cab Fares, *v.* Stradametrical Survey of London.

Calico Printing as an Art Manufacture. A Lecture read before the Society of
Arts, April 22, 1852, by Edmund Potter, Reporter to the Jury on Printed
Fabrics, Class 18, in the Exhibition.
London: John Chapman, 142, Strand.
Manchester: Johnson, Rawson, and Co., Corporation Street. 1852.
[Price 1*s.*   8vo, pp. 63, with three plates of design. Mr. Potter also wrote the Article on Class
18 in the Reports of the Juries.]

Calico Printing, Edmund Potter, *v.* Letter on teaching Design as applied to.

Canada, *v.* Few Words upon.

Canning, Viscount, *v.* Reports by the Juries.

* Cantata par Romainville.
  Rue St. Denis 290.
          [8vo. Advertised in Journal de la Librarie.]

Card on the subject of the Great Exhibition of 1851, addressed to the Members of
the Basingstoke Mechanics' Institute, by the President.
  S. Chandler, Printer, Basingstoke.
          [W. y. or price. Folio, p. 1. Signed Edward Lefroy, and dated West-ham, May 20, 1850.]

Casabianca, M., Speech of, on distribution of Prizes, v. Exposition Universelle.

Catalogue (A) of the highly important and by far the greater portion of the valuable
and interesting Collection as exhibited by the Honorable the East India Company at the Great Exhibition in 1851, representing articles from the whole
extent of territory within the limits of the four Presidences of Bengal, Agra,
Madras, and Bombay, and extending from Singapore on the South to Lahore
on the North, and from Assam on the East to Aden on the West, giving a very
general view of the vast resources of the country, the habits and customs of the
people, and displaying some of the most interesting, costly, and beautiful specimens of native skill, ingenuity, and industry; which will be sold by auction by
Messrs. Hoggart, Norton, & Trist, at the Auction Mart, opposite the Bank of
England, the First Section on Monday, the 7th day of June, 1852, and Four
following days; The Second Section on Monday, the 28th day of June, 1852,
and Five following days; Each day's Sale commencing at One o'clock precisely.
Each Section may be viewed five days preceding the Sale, and Catalogues had
(at Two Shillings each, to admit two persons) at the Mart, and of Messrs.
Hoggart, Norton, and Trist, 62, Old Broad Street, Royal Exchange.
  Cox (Brothers) and Wyman, Printers, Great Queen Street, Lincoln's Inn Fields.
          [4to, pp. vii. 118.]

Catalogue (A) of American Minerals, Fresh-water Shells, Fossils, Coals, Ores,
Indian Relics, Etc. exhibiting at the World's Industrial Exhibition, in London,
A.D. 1851, under the auspices of the State of Massachusetts, and with the
sanction of the Central Committee of the U.S. The collection of Dr. Lewis
Feuchtwanger, Chemist, 141 Maiden Lane, New York, U.S.A.
  New York: Published for the Proprietor. 1851.
          [Privately printed. 8vo, pp. 22. This collection " will be offered for sale on the closing
  of the Exhibition."]

* Catalogue de l'Exposition Universelle de 1851.
  [Benard.
          Advertised in Journal de la Librarie.]

Catalogue of Articles in the Swiss Department of the Great Exhibition in London.
  St. Gall. Scheitlin & Zollikofer. 1851.
          [Price 8 sgr. 8vo, pp. 25, 14, 28, 7. It has in many instances the prices of the articles;
  v. also Section III. and Switzerland.]

Catalogue of a Valuable Collection of Miscellaneous Goods and Works of Art, in
the Belgian division of the Great Exhibition. Which will be sold by auction,
by Messrs. S. Leigh Sotheby & John Wilkinson, at their house, 3, Wellington
Street, Strand, On Thursday, 16th of October, 1851, and following Day, at one
o'clock precisely. May be Viewed at the Exhibition only, on and after the 10th
instant, and Catalogues had at the Place of Sale.
  Printed by J. Davy & Sons, 137, Long Acre.
          [8vo, pp. 16.]

Catalogue of East Indian Productions collected in the Presidency of Bengal, and
forwarded to the Exhibition of Works of Art and Industry to be held in
London in 1851. Compiled by A. M. Dowleans.
  Calcutta: Printed at the Englishman Press, by J. F. Bellamy, 1851.
          [Price 2s. 6d. 4to, pp. 81, and Appendix, pp. 9. More or less details of 3613 articles are
  given; v. also List of Articles.]

Catalogue Officiel de la Grande Exposition des Produits de l'Industrie de Toutes
les Nations, 1851. Rédigé et Traduit de l'Anglais par G. F. Duncombe et
F. M. Harman. Deuxième Edition, entièrement revue et corrigée sur la
                                                                    dernière

dernière Edition Anglaise, et augmentée d'une Introduction Historique, d'une Notice descriptive du Bâtiment, etc.   Par F. Hilaire D'Arcis.

> ' La terre est au Seigneur, ainsi que tout ce qu'elle contient :
> L'étendue du monde et ceux qui l'habitent.'

Londres : Spicer Frères, Papetiers ; W. Clowes et Fils, Imprimeurs, Éditeurs Privilégiés de la Commission Royale, 29 New Bridge Street, Blackfriars, et à l'Exposition, Hyde Park.   Price 2 shillings and 6 pence.
[W. y. Fcp. 4to, pp. 327. A French edition of the small Catalogue, known as the Shilling Catalogue. It has a few pages more of introduction than the English volume, which will be found under Official. A German edition was also published, *v.* Amtlicher Catalog.]

Catalogue of the Articles in the Exhibition of Manufactures and Art, in connexion with the Meeting of the British Association for the Advancement of Science, at Birmingham.   September, 1849.

Birmingham : Printed at M. Billing's Steam-Press, Newhall Street. 1849.
[Price 6*d.* 8vo. pp. 96.   Several calculations for the Exhibition of 1851 were based on the Birmingham Exhibition.]

Catalogue of the Spanish Productions sent to the Great Exhibition of the Works of Industry of All Nations.   1851.

London : Printed by Schulze and Co., 13, Poland Street. 1851.
[Price 1*s.*   Small 4to, pp. 52.   A detailed Catalogue, with the prices affixed to the greater part of the articles.   An edition also said to have been printed in French.]

Catalogue of Turkish Section of the Great Exhibition of the Industry of All Nations. 1851.

[Without Publisher's name or date, but printed by McKewan and Co., 46, London Wall, and published in 1851. Sm. 4to, pp. 25.   More detailed than the Illustrated Catalogue.]

Catalogue Raisonné des Produits de la France a l'Exposition Universelle de Londres Rédigé sur des Documents Authentiques.   Explication des Produits en Français et en Anglais ; Vue du Palais de Cristal, Plans du Rez-de-Chaussée et de la Galerie, Plan détaillé de chacune des Cinq Divisions occupées par les Produits de la France avec l'emplacement des principaux Groupes d'Industrie. Dédié aux Producteurs de la Richesse Universelle.

> ' Aide-toi, le Ciel t'aidera !'

Paris Librairie Scientifique-Industrielle, de L. Mathias (Augustin), Quai Malaquais, 15, 1851.
[Price 2 francs. Royal 8vo, pp. xx., 96. The introduction signed Michel Chevalier.]

Catalogue's Account of itself (The).   [Extracted from ' Dickens's Household Words,' August 23rd, 1851.]

[*London :* William Clowes and Sons, Stamford Street, Printers of the Official Catalogues. W. y. Circulated gratuitously. Sm. 4to, pp. 4.]

Catalogues [of Sale of Timber at the Crystal Palace by Mr. Lerew, 2 March 1852] [of Old Materials on Monday the 26th of April 1852 and following day.] [On Wednesday the 5th of May and two following days.]
[4to, pp. 12 and 23.]

Catalogues, *v.* Amtlicher — Amtliches— Art-Journal—Austrian Section—British Guiana — Clarke's Critical — Department — Indicateur — List — Official — Official Descriptive—Russian Section — Saxon Section—Wurtemburg Section.

Caveda, José, *v.* Memoria Presentada.

Cawood, Martin, *v.* Notes on the Woollen Manufactures of Belgium, &c.

Cazalet, Rev. W. W., *v.* On the Musical Department.

°Centrifugal Pumps (The) in the Exhibition of the Industry of All Nations.   The Public Press and Mr. J. Stuart Gwynne.

Office of the Direct Acting Balanced Centrifugal Pump, 1, Agar Street, Strand, London. 1851.
[8vo, pp. 12. A pamphlet relating to the differences between Mr. Gwynne and Mr. Appold.]

° Ceremonial of the opening of The Great Exhibition, 1851.   With Illustrations of the contributions of All Nations.

London : Published by Henry Beal, 3, Shoe-Lane, Fleet Street.
[W. y. A broadside of facetious woodcuts.]

Chaff; or, The Yankee and Nigger at the Exhibition. A Reading Farce, in two Acts.

London: Edward Stanford, 6, Charing Cross. 1853.
    [Price 1s. 8vo, pp. v., 80. "The fun of the plot hinges on Major Silas Washington Doodle and Gumbo Jumbo happening to take each a bed, in a double-bedded room, of a Mrs. Extra, who lets lodgings during the Exhibition time."]

Chalmers, Rev. W., *v.* Forty-four Sermons.

Chambre de Commerce d'Alger. Extrait du Rapport de M. Fléchey, délégué de la Chambre de Commerce d'Alger, a l'Exposition Universelle de Londres. Alger, le 15 Octobre 1851.

Alger.—Imprimerie Rey, Delavigne et Cie., 37 Rue de l'Etat-Major.
    [W. y. 4to, pp. 12. M. Fléchey chiefly treats of the Raw Material Division.]

Cham, *v.* Exposition de Londres Croquis Comiques.

Chamerovzow, Louis Alexis, *v.* Industrial Exhibition, Observations on.

Charley, William, *v.* Reports by the Juries.

Charter of Incorporation of Society of Arts, *v.* Royal.

Charriere *v.* Ouvriers.

Chart of the Great Exhibition, *v.* Statistical.

خطاب للغرباء الزائرين مدينة لندره لاجل عرض بدائع الصنائع سنة ١٨٥١ في الكتب المقدسة ويوم السبت في انكلتره طبع في لندره لجمعية انتشار المعارف المسيحية يباع في مخزن الجمعية وفي غيره سنه ١٨٥١

    [Price 1d., or 7s. per 100. 12mo, pp. 12. One of the addresses issued by the Society for Promoting Christian Knowledge.]

[Chemical Society. Circular to Exhibitors inviting them on the termination of the Exhibition, to deposit specimens in the Museum of the Chemical Society. Dated June 23, 1851. Signed B. C. Brodie, Secretary.]

    [Without Publisher's or Printer's name. 8vo, p. 1.]

Chemistry of the Crystal Palace: a popular account of the Chemical Properties of the Chief Materials employed in its construction. By Thomas Griffiths, late Professor of Chemistry in St. Bartholomew's Hospital, Author of 'Chemistry of the Four ancient Elements,' 'Recreations in Chemistry,' etc.

London: John W. Parker & Son, West Strand. 1851.
    [Price 5s. 12mo, pp, xvi., 236. The author in his preface says, " A magnificent structure has been raised rapidly, and as if by a kind of enchantment, destined for the reception and display of the products of the 'Industry of all Nations,'—and it justly excites universal interest and attention."]

Chess-men and Table, *v.* Graydon's Crusader Chess-men.

Chester, Harry, *v.* Letter to the Society of Arts.

Chevalier, Michel, *v.* Catalogue Raisonnée—Exposition Universelle de Londres, and Great Exhibition and London in 1851.

Chevreuil, M., on Carpets, *v.* Travaux.

Chinese Commission, *v.* Authentic account of.

Christern, J. W., *v.* Pudelnärrische Reise.

º Christian Visitor's Hand-Book to London (The) ; comprising a Guide to Churches and Chapels, a Companion to Religious and Benevolent Societies, Ragged Schools, Suburban Cemeteries, with a Select List of Public Amusements, and other useful information, specially adapted to Strangers in London, at the present time of the World's Exhibition. To which is added, spare moments with Christian Authors.

London: Partridge and Oakey, Paternoster Row; and 70, Edgeware Road, (Hanbury & Co. Agents.) and to be had by order of all booksellers.
    [W. y. Price 6d. 12mo, pp. 107.]

Christy, T., *v.* Reports by the Juries.

[Circular letter of Mr. John Bennett, followed by Report of a Meeting of Watch
    & Clock Exhibitors, held at the Freemasons' Tavern, Octr., 7th. 1851, extracted
    from the Morning Chronicle of Octr 8th.   Commences " I am directed."]
      [Without Publisher's or Printer's name, or date. 4to, pp. 2. A remonstrance from some
    of the watch and clock makers against the proceedings of the Sub-jury.]

Circular of the Executive Committee of the United States, on the Industrial
    Exhibition of 1851.   Dated, Washington, 22nd October, 1850.   Signed, Peter
    Force, Chairman.   Jos. C. G. Kennedy, Secretary Ex. Committee.
      [Circulated gratuitously. 4to, p. 1.]

° Circulator (The).   Classified Register of Hotels, Boarding Houses, Apartments,
    Lodgings, Furnished Houses, &c., for the period of the Great Exhibition.
    Price 6d. Stamped.
      [Printed and Published by John Cassell, of 35, Acacia-Road, St. Johns-Wood, Middlesex,
    at his Printing-Office, 335, Strand, in the parish of St. Mary-le-Strand, London. W. y. 8vo,
    pp. 16.]

City Ball, v. Brief Historical Account of Guildhall.

Clairville, M., v. Palais de Cristal ou les Parisiens a Londres.

Clarke's Critical Catalogue and Synopsis of the Great Exhibition of the Industry of
    All Nations, for 1851.
    London : H. G. Clarke and Co., 4, Exeter Change.   Price Sixpence.
      [W. y. Sm. 4to, pp. 45. In the "Introduction," which is signed "William Humphreys,"
    the author says :—"Curiosity, the mere desire to see that which has formed the theme of all
    men's thoughts and words for so long a period, will undoubtedly be the power that brings
    most of us to this temple of man's industry. Not so, however, with all ; more special, even
    higher impulses, will have moved many to examine the contents of the Crystal Palace.
    And with those who come to philosophize on man's progress, on the connection of industry
    and industrial advancement with moral advancement, or perchance even on the relations
    of man's power over nature with eternity ; with those who come to search out, to analyze
    the distinctions between nations and sections of nations ; with those who come to criticize
    and to observe on the discrepancies between man's intentions and his achievements, it were
    well to lay down some system whereby a result may flow from his observations, and the
    labour of examining so huge a treasure may not be a mere fruitless toil."]

Classifications des Produits de l'Iudustrie, D. Potonie, v. Des Diverses.

Classified Index to the Official Catalogue, v. Alphabetical.

Clayton, B., v. Great Exhibition of Doings in London.

Clayton, John M., v. Letters.

Clayton, Rev. George, v. Great Exhibition, its dangers—Forty-four Sermons.

Clock and Watch Trade, Report of a Meeting, v. Circular.

Close (The) of the Great Exhibition.   By Miss M. A. Stodart, author of ' National
    Ballads,' &c.   From ' Morning Herald,' ' Record,' ' Bell's Weekly Messenger,' &c.
    [Dated] Hampstead, October 13th, 1851.
      [Without Publisher's or Printer's name. Privately printed. Sm. 4to, 1 p. A Poem.
              " The hour hand pointed unto five ;
                  The final stroke was given,
           When instant from the organs rose
                A solemn sound to Heaven ;
           In transept, nave, and galleries,
                Those well-known strains arise
           O'er waving hats, o'er beating hearts,
                Bare heads and glistening eyes,
           God save the Queen, our Gracious Queen !
                She well deserves our love ;
             Invoke best blessings on her head
               From him who reigns above ;"]

Closing of the Exhibition, Poem by Robert Snow, v. On.

Closing of the Exhibition (The).   Extracts from a Sermon, Preached in the Church
    of St. Stephen, Walbrook, October 12th, 1851.   By the Rev. George Croly,
    LL.D., Rector of the United Parishes of St. Stephen, Walbrook, and St. Benet.
    London : John Kendrick, 27, Ludgate Street, St. Paul's, and 4, Charlotte Row, Mansion House.
    Price Threepence.
      [W. y. 12mo, pp. 12. " The results of the Exhibition must still be matter of conjecture ;
                                                    but

but without indulging in the exaggerated hope that it is destined to harmonize the world, there can be no doubt that it was eminently the offspring of peace, and that it could not have existed in a period of war. There can be as little doubt that its tendency must be to conciliate; that the gentle rivalry of the arts of peace is the most effective antidote to the rude rivalry of war; that if the distant sight of the prosperity of nations is often a source of jealousy, the nearer sight of its causes is a source of friendship; that association is, in itself, a mean of smoothing down the asperities of national prejudices—the gentle current that rounds the pebble, not the torrent that tears away the shore; and that, to witness the talents and virtues even of an enemy, is an advance towards the hallowed conviction, that 'God hath made of one blood all nations of men, for to dwell on all the face of the earth.' "]

Club [Prospectus], v. International.

Cobden, Richard, v. Illustrated London Almanack—Speech. [At Marylebone.]

Cocqueil, v. De L'Enseignement—Industrial Education.

Cole, Henry, v. Art Manufacturers' Institute—Illustrated London Almanack—Lectures [International Results] — Observations—Report made to Prince Albert.

Colladon, M. D., v. Rapport.

Collection of Printed Documents and Forms used in carrying on the business of the Exhibition of 1851, together with some others issued without authority, but bearing upon the subject of the Exhibition; Classified into various Departments.
> [In 8 folio vols.]

Collier, William, v. Sights of London.

Colour, Owen Jones on the Distribution of Form and, v. Gleanings.

Colsey, Thomas, A poem, v. Record.

Comical Creatures from Wurtemburg (The), Including the Story of Reynard the Fox. With twenty Illustrations, drawn from the stuffed animals contributed by Herrmann Ploucquet, of Stuttgart to the Great Exhibition. Third Edition.
> *London:* David Bogue, Fleet Street, 1851. [Price 3s. 6d. Fscp. 4to, pp. 96. "Every one, from her Majesty the Queen down to the least of the charity boys, hastens to see the Stuffed Animals from the Zollverein; every one lingers over them and laughs at them as long as the crowd will allow; and every one talks of them afterwards with a smile and a pleasing recollection. That these clever productions of Ploucquet's talent may be long perpetuated, we have had daguerreotypes of them taken by Mr. Claudet, and engravings made from them on wood as faithfully like as possible."]

Comical People illustrated with sixteen Pictures taken from the embroidered Tapestry contributed by Maria Fusinata, of Belluno, to the Great Exhibition. Drawn and Grouped from the designs of J. J. Grandville.
> *London:* David Bogue, 86 Fleet Street. 1852. [Price 3s. 6d. plain, 6s. coloured. Fscp. 4to, pp. vi., and 56. In the preface we are told that "Grandville in these delineations of the faculties of animals, is quite equal to Kaulbach." This work was advertised before it was published, under the title of "Comical People Met with in the Exhibition."]

Comic-eye, v. What I saw at the World's Fair.

Commerce.
> Charles Macintosh & Co., Patentees of the Vulcanized India Rubber, *London* and *Manchester.* May 1st 1851.
> [A Poem printed in embossed letters on Vulcanized India Rubber.
> "The band of Commerce was design'd
> T' associate all the branches of mankind;
> And, if a boundless plenty be the robe,
> Trade is the golden girdle of the globe."]

Commerce, W. Felkin, v. Exhibition in 1851.

Commission Française pour l'Exposition de l'Industrie de toutes les Nations qui doit avoir lieu à Londres in 1851:—
> °Indications addressées a MM. les Producteurs et Manufacturiers sur les produits qu'on doit désirer de voir paraitre a l'Exposition. Signé par M. Charles Dupin.　Extrait du 'Moniteur Universel,' du 4 Juin 1850.
> Typografie Panckoucke, Rue des Poitevins, 8.
> [8vo, pp. 32. A translation was published, v. Suggestions.]

°Le

°Le Nombre des Industriels Inscrit dans les Bureaux de la Commission Française.
Extrait du ' Moniteur Universel,' du 4 Decembre 1850.
Typographie Panckoucke, Rue desPoitevins, 8.
[8vo, pp. 8.]

°Instructions relatives au Catalogue Général.
Extrait du 'Moniteur Universel,' du 28 Janvier 1851.
Paris: Typographie Panckoucke, Rue des Poitevins, 8, 1851.
[8vo, pp. 8.]

°Liste complete des Jurés Anglais telle qu'elle a été definitivement arrêtér a la dernière séance des Commissaires Royaux.
Extrait du ' Moniteur Universel,' du 7 Mai 1851.
Paris.—Imprimerie Panckoucke, Rue des Poitevins, 8–14.
[8vo, pp. 8.]

°Compte Rendu des Travaux de la Commission Française instituée pour l'Exposition Universelle de 1851, présenté par le Baron Charles Dupin, Sénateur, Membre de l'Institut, President de la Commission, A. S. M. l'Empereur des Français, le 13 Juin 1853.
Extrait du ' Moniteur Universel,' du 17 Juin 1853.
Typographie Panckoucke, Rue des Poitevins, 8 et 14.
[8vo, pp. 32.]

Travaux de la Commission, *v.* Travaux.

Commissioners, Her Majesty's, *v.* Minutes of Proceedings—Reports.

Companion to the Official Catalogue. Synopsis of the Contents of the Great Exhibition of 1851. By Robert Hunt, Keeper of Mining Records. Second Edition.
London: Spicer Brothers, and W. Clowes & Sons, Official Catalogue Office, 29, New Bridge Street, Blackfriars; and at Hyde Park. Price Sixpence.
[W. y.: but published in 1851. 16mo, pp. 95.]

Compte Rendu des Travaux de la Commission Française, *v.* Commission Française.

Concanen, E., *v.* Gems of Art.

Constitution—Bye Laws. [Society of Arts.]
Printed by C. Whittingham, Chiswick.
[W. y. Small 4to, pp. 20.]

Contract between the Society of Arts and Messrs. Munday, *v.* Copies.

Conway, Rev. W., *v.* Great Exhibition, An Opportunity to promote the Glory of God.

Cooke, Rev. Dr., *v.* Forty-four Sermons.

Cookes and Sons, Kenilworth Buffet, *v.* Account of—Description of.

Copies of the Contracts between the Society of Arts and Messrs. James Munday and George Munday for carrying out the Exhibition. Tooke, Son & Hallowes, Solicitors for the Society of Arts. Geo. H. Drew, Solicitor for the Contractors.
[Without Publisher's or Printer's name, or date. Printed for private circulation. 8vo. pp. 43, including the subsequent correspondence between Colonel Phipps and Mr. Drew. An edition in folio was also published, pp. 8 and 5.]

Copy of a Letter addressed by the Commissioners of the Exhibition of 1851 to the Lords of the Treasury, enclosing Memorandum as to the Site of the Exhibition Building in Hyde Park. (Lord John Russell.) Ordered, by the House of Commons, to be Printed, 1 July 1850. 489. Under 1 oz.
[Folio, pp. 7.]

Copy of Warrant authorising the Commissioners for the Exhibition of 1851 to enter upon a piece of ground in Hyde Park, and to erect buildings thereupon for purposes of the Exhibition:—And, Deed of Covenant from the Commissioners to Her Majesty, to observe and perform certain Terms and Conditions mentioned in the said warrant, and to reinstate and yield up the site granted for the purposes of the Exhibition. (Mr. Stafford.) Ordered, by the House of Commons, to be Printed, 22 July 1851. 573. Under one oz.
[Folio.]

Corbaux, Miss Louisa, *v.* Sculpture.

Cordier, Jules, *v.* Palais de Cristal ou les Parisiens a Londres.

Corporation of London, *v.* Brief Historical Account of Guildhall.

Correspondence with the Commissioners of Sewers on the Establishment of Public Water-closets & Urinals.
　　[Without Publisher's or Printer's name. Dated 8th November, 1850. Circulated gratuitously. Folio, pp. 4.]

Cosmopolitan Exhibition of Arts (The) in 1851. From the Spectator of October 13, 1849.
　　[Without Publisher's or Printer's name, or date. Circulated gratuitously. An article reprinted from the 'Spectator.' 8vo, p. 1.]

Cosson, L. A., Guide de l'Etranger à Londres, *v.* Grandiose Exposition Nationale.

Cotton Manufactures of Dacca, *v.* Descriptive.

Country Visitors' Guide (The) to the Great Metropolis and the World's Exhibition of 1851; Containing an account of London, its Streets, Sights, Parks, Public Buildings, &c.; a Description of the Crystal Palace and of matters connected with the Exhibition of 1851; with a well-executed Map of the Streets of the Metropolis; forming a complete Guide to the Visitor in London.
　　London: Published by W. H. Smith & Son, 136, Strand; and sold at all the Railway Stations.
　　[W. y. Price 1*s.* 18mo, pp. 72. Contains a short account of the Exhibition. The work was printed by Alice Mann, Printer, Central-Market, *Leeds.*]

Cowper, Charles, *v.* Building erected in Hyde Park.

Cox, Rev. Dr., *v.* Forty-four Sermons.

Crace, J. G., *v.* Reports by the Juries.

Cristaux, Verres, et Vitraux, G. Bontemps, *v.* Examen Historique.

Crochet Books, *v.* Ingram's Exhibition Knitting and Crochet Book—Royal Exhibition.

Croly, Rev. Dr., *v.* Closing of the Exhibition.

Cros-Mayrevieille, *v.* Lettre sur L'Exposition.

Crouch, Guide de l'Etranger à Londres, *v.* Grandiose Exposition Nationale.

Cruikshank, George, *v.* 1851. [One thousand Eighteen Hundred and Fifty one.] Also Engravings.

Cruikshank, Percy, *v.* Palace of Glass, or London in 1851 — Wanderings of Mrs. Pipe—What *is* to be done with the Crystal Palace.

Crystal College, W. Cave Thomas, *v.* Suggestions for a.

Crystal Hive (The); or, the First of May, 1851. By C. T. W.
　　London: W. H. Dalton, Cockspur Street. 1852.
　　[Price 1*s.* 6*d.* 16mo, pp. 23. A Poem.
　　　　　" 'Twas thought a vision so sublime
　　　　　Would ne'er be realized in time:
　　　　　A thousand obstacles might rise
　　　　　To hinder it, from earth and skies
　　　　　If realized, some said, 'twere worse,
　　　　　A great and multiplying curse,—
　　　　　'Twould bring us feuds, and socialism,
　　　　　And many another fatal *ism!*
　　　　　In short, ' it was a senseless plot,
　　　　　Replete with evil,' it had—*not.*
　　　　　Thus spake the timid spirits all;
　　　　　The braver ones scarce fear'd at all,
　　　　　Or said, with him of southern skies,
　　　　　' Beset with risks of various size,
　　　　　Each glorious palm man fain would boast,
　　　　　And he shall ne'er attain the prize
　　　　　Who first encounters not the cost.' "]

Crystal Labyrinth (The).   A Puzzle.   Drawn by Jno. Eyre.   Price 6d Plain.
   1s Stout Paper Col^d.
   London, Published by T. Dean & Son, 35, Threadneedle Street, May, 1851.
      [A game for children, the centre represents the interior of the Exhibition Building.]

Crystal Palace Almanack (The) For the Year of Our Lord 1852, being Bissextile,
   or Leap Year.
   London : Published by W. M. Clark, 17, Warwick-Lane, Paternoster-Row; and sold by all Book-
      sellers. Price Threepence.
      [4to, pp. 40. Contains a short history and description of the Exhibition, and numerous
      Illustrations.]

°Crystal Palace a Sketch.
      [12mo. The first edition of the work which appears in this Catalogue under the title
      of "A Day in the Crystal Palace."]

Crystal Palace as seen from Kensington Gardens.
      [Price 3s. A Puzzle.]

Crystal Palace Described and Illustrated by Beautiful Engravings, *v.* Tallis.

Crystal Palace.   Intercepted Letters to Mr. Punch.   Letter the First.   Entered
   at Stationers' Hall.
   Printed by C. Strutt, 16, Church-street, Kensington. 1851.
      [Price 3d. Post 8vo, pp. 8. Only one letter was ever published.]

Crystal Palace of Industry (The) ; A Poem, on the Opening of the Exhibition of
   the Works of all Nations by Her Majesty the Queen, May 1st, 1851. By
   Rev. T. K. De Verdon.
   London: Partridge and Oakey, Paternoster Row; and 70, Edgeware Road (Hanbury and Co., Agents).
      [W. y. Price 1s. Post 8vo, pp. 12.
                  " Celestial Peace the plan designed,
                     Her snow-white banner she unfurled ;
                  Love oped the gates to all mankind,
                     And hailed the workmen of the world."]

Crystal Palace Puzzle (The).
   London. Published by Simmon's & Co. 14 St. John Sqr.
      [W. y. Price One Penny. A Labyrinth, with an interior view of the Building in the
      centre.]

Crystal Palace, Retention of, *v.* Preservation.

Crystal Palace (The).   A Little Book for Little Boys, for 1851.
   London : James Nisbet and Co., Berners Street. 1851.
      [Price 1s. 18mo, pp. 83. A story with a religious moral relating to the Great Exhibition.]

Crystal Palace (The), and Crystal Palaces. A proposition for the appropriation of
   a portion of the Glass Building in Hyde Park to a purpose of public benefit,
   and the Erection of Buildings of the same kind in other parts of the country.
   By Beta.
   Seeleys, Fleet Street, and Hanover Street. *London :* 1852.
      [Price 1s. Imp. 8vo, pp. 15. With sketches. "The plan suggested by the writer is the
      provision of an artificial climate, not liable to sudden changes and alternations of tempera-
      ture, by enclosing a number of houses within a covering of glass, resembling in its structure
      the Crystal Palace."]

Crystal Palace (The), and its Contents : being an Illustrated Cyclopædia of the
   Great Exhibition of the. Industry of all Nations. 1851. Embellished with
   upwards of Five hundred Engravings. With a copious analytical Index.
   Published by W. M. Clark, 16 & 17, Warwick Lane   1852.
      [Price 5s. 4to, pp. viii. and 424. A periodical which appeared weekly.]

Crystal Palace (The) and the Crystal City.   By Rev. C. T. Davies, Rector of
   Ecton.   Second Edition.
   Northampton : R. Harris, (late Walesby).
   London : Hamilton, Adams & Co. 1852. Price 2d. each.
      [12mo, pp. 23. "Of this Palace we have all heard, and most of us have beheld its
      wonders. But, in the text, we have brought before us a Crystal *City*—the everlasting abode
      of the blessed. * * * We will consider: I. The Construction of the Crystal Palace. II. The
      Objects for which it was Erected. III. The mode of admission into it." It was printed
      by Lea, Gold Street, *Northampton.*]

Crystal Palace (The), and the Great Exhibition ; An Historical Account of the
   Building, together with a descriptive synopsis of its contents.
                                                      London :

London: H. G. Clarke and Co., 252, Strand. 1851.
>[Price 2*s.* 6*d.* Post 8vo, pp. 182. With woodcuts. The author, in the introductory chapter, says: "Such a microcosm as that of the Exhibition of 1851, is certainly a great and beneficent idea. It is as practical as poetical." &c.]

Crystal Palace (The); a sequel to 'The Country and London.' By the Author of 'Aids to Development,' 'Memorials of two Sisters,' 'Gift at Confirmation,' &c. &c.
London: Francis & John Rivington, St. Paul's Church Yard, and Waterloo Place. 1852.
>[Price 3*s.* 6*d.* Square 18mo, pp. iv., 176. With three woodcuts. A book for young people.]

Crystal Palace (The): Its Architectural History and Constructive Marvels. By Peter Berlyn, and Charles Fowler, Jun.
London: James Gilbert, Paternoster Row. 1851.
>[Price 7*s.* 6*d.* 8vo, pp. viii, 92, and xix. Illustrated with 72 engravings. "If, therefore, the authors cannot lay claim to novelty or originality in the execution of the pleasurable work which they have undertaken, they are not without hopes that, from their having been connected with this gigantic undertaking during the greater part of its progress, they will be enabled to trace in a more detailed and consecutive manner than has yet been attempted the history of the design and execution of the building up to the period of its completion." The Appendix contains the list of the architects who sent in designs, and exterior and interior views of the designs sent in by Messrs. Hector Horeau, and R. and T. Turner, with a copy of the Parliamentary Return called the "Memorandum on the Site." This work was afterwards sold to Mr. Field, bookseller, 65, Regent's Quadrant, and advertised by him for 5*s.*, and with the name of Measom as engraver.]

Crystal Palace (The): its Origin, Construction, Dimensions, and General History. With the authorised arrangements of admission.
>'Earth's distant ends our glories shall behold,
>And the new world launch forth to meet the old.'

London: W. J. Adams, Bradshaw's Railway Publication Office, 59, Fleet Street, City. Price Twopence.
>[W. y. 12mo, pp. 16, with engraving of exterior. "The old barrier of distance has been broken down by railways and steamboats, and the still more formidable barrier of national prejudices and national misconceptions must be for ever destroyed by the recurrence of such meetings as these."]

Crystal Palace (The). Report of the Meeting at Mr. Oliveira's, March 29th, 1852. etc. etc. etc.
London: James Ridgway, Piccadilly. 1852.
>[Circulated privately. 8vo., pp. 58. Report of one of the meetings to promote the Preservation of the Crystal Palace.]

Crystal Palace (The) that Fox Built. A Pyramid of Rhyme, With Nine Illustrations by John Gilbert.
London: David Bogue, 86 Fleet Street. 1851.
>[Price 1s. Square 8vo, pp. 30.
>"These are the Workmen, a busy array—
>Two thousand and more, as I have heard say,
>Who readily, steadily, toiled away,
>And finished before the first of May
>The Crystal Palace
>That Fox
>Built."]

Crystal Palace (The). The London Season. Two Satires for 1851. By E. M. G.
London: John Ollivier, 59, Pall Mall. 1851.
>[Price 1s. 8vo, pp. 23.
>"It is a glorious sight, when all may see
>Assembled nations as one man agree;
>But much I fear the bond of this great farce
>Is just as frail as its component glass.
>No doubt they'll come, in countless numbers too,
>For they've one common object, gain, in view.
>And even Moses with his bard in pay,
>Can't match the advertisement of the day.
>But as for doing good to English trade,
>I think a slight mistake therein is made;
>These foreign gentry sell, but are not sold,
>And lack, not English goods but English gold."]

Crystal Palace, *v.* Elegy—Fate of the—Placards—Preservation of the Building—Reminiscences of—Shall the Crystal Palace Remain—Shall we keep the?—Spare the—Tallis's History and Description of—Walk through the—What is to become of the

Cubitt, Sir William, *v.* Report of the Commissioners.

Cumming, Dr., *v.* Great Exhibition, Suggestive and Anticipative.

Cutch, Articles from, *v.* Tabular and Descriptive Lists of.

Cyclopædia of the Industry of All Nations, *v.* Knight.

Cyclorama, *v.* Description of Series of Tableaux of Crystal Palace.

Daily News, Extract from, *v.* Times.

D'Arcis, F. Hilaire, *v.* Catalogue Officiel.

Daudel, Mons., *v.* Palais de Cristal ou les Parisiens a Londres.

David's Songs of Praise for the Exhibition in 1851.

> ' On Earth thy will be done,
> As it is done in Heaven ! '

To Her Most Gracious Majesty, the Mighty Queen of Great Britain, and His Royal Highness Prince Albert, and the Right Honourable Her Majesty's Commissioners of Works of Industry of all Nations in 1851. These lines are most respectfully Dedicated by their most obedient Servant, J. C. David. Dec. 16, 1850. Price Twopence. Communications, by letter, to 14, Tavistock-Row, Covent Garden.

[Without Publisher's or Printer's name, or date. Post 8vo, pp. 3.

> " Sons of Britain !
> Remember this great and mighty congregation
> Freely came
> From all the earth at thy invitation ;
> Now cast off all suspicion,
> Put forth the friendly uncovered hand,
> Boldly and brotherly,
> Frankly and nobly,
> Meet each man :
> Show your kind hospitality,
> And join in one vast fraternity."]

Davies, Rev. C. T., *v.* Crystal Palace and the Crystal City.

Day (A) in the Crystal Palace. By the Rev. T. B. Murray, M.A. Published under the Direction of the Committee of General Literature and Education, appointed by the Society for Promoting Christian Knowledge. Second Edition.

London : Printed for the Society for Promoting Christian Knowledge ; Sold at the Depository, Great Queen Street, Lincoln's Inn-Fields; 4, Royal Exchange ; and 16, Hanover Street, Hanover Square; and by all Booksellers.

[W. y. Price 2*d.* 16mo, pp. v. and 24. A poem, illustrated with a view of the Centre Transept. The first edition was published in a square form under the title of " Crystal Palace, a Sketch."

> " I saw a Palace, glorious to behold ;
> The wealthy world had heap'd its treasure there ;
> Its pictur'd silver-work, its breathing gold,
> Robes of delight, and gems of beauty rare."]

Day et Bush, MM., *v.* Merveilles de Londres.

Decorative Art, Owen Jones, *v.* Attempt to define.

Decourcelle, Mons., *v.* English Exhibition Comédie-Vaudeville.

Dedicated to the Artisans of All Nations, by the Association held at the ' Marquis of Lansdowne,' Thomas Street, Hackney Road, for promoting the Great Exhibition of 1851, Hyde Park.

[Without Publisher's or Printer's name. Folio, p. 1. A poem signed A., and dated June 18th, 1850.

> " A world of wonders here salutes our gaze,
> Too vast for rapture !—too sublime for praise !
> All Nations here unite their social hands
> From Greenland's wastes to Afric's glitt'ring sands."

v. also Lansdowne Association.]

Delabar, Professor G., *v.* Bericht über die Weltindustrieausstellung zu London.

De la Beche, Sir H. T., *v.* Lectures [Mining, &c.].

De la Rue, T., *v.* Reports by the Juries.

De la Rue, Warren, *v.* Reports by the Juries.

De l' Enseignement Industriel et de la Limitation de la Durée du Travail en Angleterre. Rapport à Monsieur le Ministre de l'Intérieur par Ch. de Cocquiel, Docteur en Droit.

    Bruxelles. Librairie Polytechnique D'Aug. Decq, Rue de la Madeleine, 9.
        [1853. Price 2 francs. 8vo, pp. viii, 124. "During the Great Exhibition of 1851, two nations, England and Belgium, found that all the great competing nations of Europe, except themselves, had established systems of industrial instruction for those engaged in production. * * * Hence we find both countries immediately after the close of the Exhibition setting themselves with earnestness to the realization of that which they had thus neglected. On the 14th of December, 1851, a commission of thirteen members, consisting of eminent manufacturers and politicians, was appointed in Belgium, and the results of their labours have appeared under the title '*Rapport sur l'Organisation de l'Enseignement Industriel*,' in which most extensive measures are proposed to remedy the past neglect of industrial instruction. In the meantime the Belgian Government had sent to England the Chevalier de Cocquiel, a political economist of much promise and great intelligence, to report on the effects produced in this country by the absence of means of industrial instruction."—Extracted from a published translation, *v.* Industrial Instruction.]

Delepine, *v.* Guide du Visiteur.

De Luynes, Duc, on Precious Metals, *v.* Reports by the Juries—Travaux.

De Mauley, Lord, *v.* Reports by the Juries.

De Morgan, Professor, *v.* Exposition of 1851.

Dempsey, G. D., *v.* Machinery of the Nineteenth Century.

Denarius, *v.* Shall we keep the Crystal Palace?

Denham, Rev. J. F., *v.* Sermon.

Deninger, Karl, *v.* Amtlicher Bericht.

Denison, E. B., *v.* Reports by the Juries.

Department of Practical Art. A Catalogue of the Articles of Ornamental Art, selected from the Exhibition of the Works of Industry of All Nations in 1851, and purchased by the Government. Prepared at the desire of the Lords of the Committee of Privy Council for Trade. With an Appendix.

    London: Published for the Department of Practical Art, by Chapman and Hall, 193, Piccadilly. Price 6*s.* each.
        [W. y. 8vo, pp. 102. The prices of the articles are given; and in the Appendix will be found extracts from Mr. R. Redgrave's Report on Design and Manufactures, Mr. J. R. Herbert's Evidence before the House of Commons, Mr. W. Dyce's Report on Foreign Schools of Design, made in 1839, and the Prospectus of the Department of Practical Art.]

Derby, Earl of, *v.* Lord Stanley.

Description (A) of the Series of Tableaux of the Crystal Palace, exhibited in the Royal Cyclorama, Albany Street, Regent's Park; including a brief account of the origin of the Great Exhibition of the Industry of All Nations in 1851, and of the construction of the Building in Hyde Park.

    London: Printed by E. Carrall, Milford-Lane, Strand. 1852. Price Sixpence.
        [8vo, pp. 28. With plan of the Crystal Palace, and woodcuts.]

*Description de l'Edifice, Mode de Classification des Produits, Récompenses aux Exposants, Garantie contre les Contrefaçons, Commission Belge pour l'Exposition, Commission Belge pour le Jury, Catalogue des Produits Belges Envoyés à l'Exposition, suivi d'une Liste, par Ordre Alphabétique, des exposants.

    Bruxelles, G. Stapleaux.
        [Price 1 franc. 8vo, pp. 44.]

Description of a Model of an Aerial Pontoon Railway Suspension Bridge, from England to France, Exhibited at the Grand Exposition, 1851. By Thomas Watts. With an Appendix.

        [Without Publisher's or Printer's name, date, or price. 12mo, pp. 12. "The bridge is to be composed of preserve timber and wire cord, as being the strongest and most effective in economy for its construction. It is to be supported by aerial supports, and moored by means of anchors; each girder to be 300 feet in length, and trussed with the king-posts and wire cord; the end of each girder to be connected by morticing, and bolted at the joint."]

Description of the Kenilworth Buffet, designed and executed by Cookes and Sons, upon their premises in Warwick, and now exhibiting in the Northern Fine Arts' Court (H, 30), at the Crystal Palace, Hyde Park. Abridged from the Illustrated 'Account of the Kenilworth Buffet,' by W. Jones, Esq.
[H. T. Cooke, Printer, High Street, Warwick. W. y. Circulated gratuitously. Folio, 1 p. The larger work from which this is an excerpt will be found under Account.]

Descriptive Account (A) of the Great National Exhibition of 1851. With a View of the Great Building of Glass and Iron now erecting by Messrs. Fox and Henderson, from Designs by Mr. Paxton.
London Published by H. Beal, 3, Shoe Lane.
[W. y. Price 1*d.* 12mo, pp. 10, with two engravings.]

Descriptive and Historical Account (A) of the Cotton Manufacture of Dacca, in Bengal. By a former Resident in Dacca.
London: John Mortimer, 141, Strand, 1851.
[Price 3*s.* 6*d.* 12mo, pp. 152. Dedicated to the Council of the Society of Arts. "But whatever may be the result of a comparison of the Dacca muslins with similar productions of the looms of Europe, it will be admitted that the great celebrity, which these fabrics have for so many centuries possessed, imparts to the history of their manufacture a degree of interest which hardly pertains to any other branch of industrial art in India."]

Descriptive Key to Mr. H. C. Selous' Picture of The Inauguration of the Great Exhibition of 1851.
Lloyd, brothers & Co., 22, Ludgate Hill.
[W. y. Privately circulated. 8vo, pp. 19, with an outline Key to the picture.]

Des Diverses Classifications des Produits de l'Industrie a l'Occasion de l'Exposition Universelle de Londres en 1851 par D. Potonié, Commerçant Parisien.
Extrait du 'Journal des Economistes,' Revue mensuelle. Livraison du 15 Octobre 1850.
Paris Au Bureau du Journal des Economistes, chez Guillaumin et C*e*, Libraires-Editeurs, Rue Richelieu, 14.
Londres, Chez Delizy et C*e*, 15, Regent Street. Imprimerie de Hennuyer et C*e*, Rue Lemercier, 24, Batignolles. Prix: 50 cent. ou 6 pence.
[Royal 8vo, pp. 8, with a Plan. M. Potonié recommended a different system of classification to that announced by Her Majesty's Commissioners. He called his "Classification commerciale," and this pamphlet contained an exemplification of his idea.]

Design of God (The) Traced in the Great Exhibition, and our duty as Christians in reference to it. By the Rev. J. W. Milner, M.A., late of Lincoln College, Oxford.
London: Thomas Hatchard, Piccadilly.
Liverpool: Deighton and Laughton, Church Street, Arthur Newling, Bold Street.
[W. y. Price 2*s.* 12mo, pp. x., 96. "It has been our endeavour in the present little production, to point out, generally the moral and religious bearings of the Great Exhibition, together with the circumstances with which it stands connected." The book was printed by D. Marples, Liverpool.]

Despléchin, Mons., *v.* Fête.

°Deux Lettres Sans Adresse.
Amiens, Typographie de E. Yvert, Rue Sire-Firmin-Leroux, 24. 1851.
[These letters, signed V. S., were privately printed. Royal 8vo, pp. 32.]

De Verdon, Rev. T. K., a Poem, *v.* Crystal Palace of Industry.

Devoir, Mons., *v.* Palais de Cristal ou les Parisiens a Londres.

Dial of the World (The). 1851. By Excelsior.
London: Ward and Co., 27, Paternoster Row. 1851.
[Price 6*d.* 16mo, pp. 31. "Evil *may* arise from it, perhaps much evil. We do well to watch. An experiment so novel may also be hazardous; and if on any side danger be apprehended, timely warning may prove of incalculable service. In the present mixed state of being in this world of conflict and collision, occasions of evil are never wanting, and agents of evil are always numerous and industrious. But *the idea* itself of *such* a congress of all nations, is noble and exalting."]

Dickensons' Comprehensive Pictures of the Great Exhibition of 1851, from the originals painted for H.R.H. Prince Albert, by Messrs. Nash, Haghe, and Roberts, R.A. Published under the Express Sanction of His Royal Highness Prince Albert, President of the Royal Commission, to whom the work is, by permission, dedicated. Vol. 1—(Vol. 2).

London:

London: Dickenson, brothers, Her Majesty's Publishers, 114, New Bond Street. 1854.
  [Price 18*l.* 18*s.* Royal Folio. Fifty-five Plates. Each picture is accompanied by a letter-press description of the View.]

Didot, Ambroise Firmin, *v.* Imprimerie—Reports of the Juries—Travaux.

Dilke, C. Wentworth, *v.* Illustrated London Almanack.

Dinner at Richmond, *v.* Selection of Music.

Dioramic Sketches : Ancient and Modern.

> '—— Should this verse, my leisure's best resource,
> When through the world it steals its secret course,
> Revive but once a generous wish supprest,
> Chase but a sigh, or charm a care to rest;
> In one good deed a fleeting hour employ,
> Or flush one faded cheek with honest joy;
> Blest were my lines, though limited their sphere—'

London: Hope & Co., Great Marlborough Street. 1853.
  [Price 5*s.* Post 8vo, pp. 107. Poems on various subjects, including the "Crystal Palace," pp. 71–78.

> "But sketch like this dare not attempt to dwell,
> Of the 'World's Fair' devoted volumes tell;
> For all that nature, all that art could bring,
> From mute creation, and from living thing,
> All human knowledge of earth, air, and sky,
> And aqueous treasures met the wondering eye."]

°Discours prononcé par M. Charles Dupin, Président de la Commission Française pour l'Exposition Universelle, a la distribution des prix aux Exposants Français, le 25 Novembre 1851.

Paris Typographie Plon freres, Rue de Vaugirard, 36.
  [8vo, pp. 4. "Afin d'acquitter cette dette, que la France prend à sa charge, c'est avec la croix d'honneur que vous proclamerez la perfection des chefs-d'œuvre de tissus dont la beauté, la variété, l'élégance et la richesse ont jeté, sur le Palais de Cristal, un éclat qui donnait un nouveau prix aux flots de lumière circulant de toutes parts, dans ce temple de la féerie." This Speech is also printed at the end of "Industries Comparées."]

Dixon, Rev. Dr., *v.* Forty-four Sermons.

Dohm, E., *v.* Kladderadatsch in London.

Doings in London, *v.* Great Exhibition of.

Dolls and Sights of the Crystal Palace, *v.* Aunt Mavor.

Doubly Great Exhibition (The)!! Or, John Bull Physicking Popery—with a Parliamentary Pill! And the Rumish Conversion of the Crystal Palace!—from—A Great Exhibition of the Choicest of Goods!—into—A Greater Exhibition of the Greatest of Ills! Price One Penny.

London: Published for the Proprietor, by George Osborne, 20, Change Alley, Cornhill.
  [W. y. Oblong Folio. A large sheet containing a Poem and allegorical Engraving directed against the Roman Catholic Religion.]

Dowleans, A. M., *v.* Catalogue of East Indian Productions.

Downes, Charles, *v.* Building erected in Hyde Park.

Doyle, John, on proposed National Gallery, *v.* Letter to Lord John Russell.

Doyle, Richard, *v.* Overland Journey to Great Exhibition.

Drew, George, Correspondence with Prince Albert, *v.* Great Exhibition of Industry.

Drugs, *v.* List of.

Drury, Miss Anna Harriet, *v.* First of May.

Dublin University Magazine (The) : No. 265, January, 1855.

Dublin, James McGlashan 50 Upper Sackville-Street.
William S. Orr & Co. *London and Liverpool.* John Menzies, 61 Princes-Street, *Edinburgh*—Sold by all Booksellers Price 2*s.* 6*d.*
  [8vo. Contains an article (pp. 110–117) entitled "Gossipping Recollections of the Old Crystal Palace. Perils of Peeping." A Tale in Connexion with Dr. Azoux's anatomical preparations.]

Dufour, Arles, *v.* Politique Nouvelle—Travaux.

Dufrenoy, M., *v.* Reports by the Juries.

Duncombe, G. F., *v.* Catalogue Officiel.

Dünkelberg, Dr., *v.* Amtlicher Bericht—Landwirthschaftlichen Geräthe (Die).

Dunn, Thomas, *v.* Address by the Local Commissioners for Sheffield.

Dupin, Baron Charles, *v.* Appel—Commission Française—Discours—Exposition Universelle de Londres—Great Exhibition and London in 1851—Industries Comparées — Reports by the Juries—Six Discours—Suggestions—Travaux, "Hommage a l'Empereur."

Dupont, Paul, Etablissement Typographique, *v.* Notice concernant.

Duty (The) for the Crisis of 1851, in England: The time of its Invasion by Rome, and its Invitation to All Nations.
London: J. Nisbet and Co., Berners Street.
Winchester: Jacob & Johnson, & H. Wooldridge. *Wonston:* James Shayler. Price 1*d.* 7*s.* per 100.
[W. y. 18mo, pp. 23. Printed by Mr. Shayler, Wonston, Andover Road. "Especially, at this time, we would pray that the progress of Romanism may be checked and prevented in this nation."]

Dyce, William, *v.* Department of Practical Art—National Gallery, its formation—Reports by the Juries.

Earnest Plea (An) for the Reign of Temperance and Peace, as Conducive to the Prosperity of Nations; submitted to the Visitors of the Great Exhibition, in which are Collected the Rich Treasures of Art and Industry from all Quarters of the Globe. Accompanied by Documents in Proof of the Statements and Principles involved. By James Silk Buckingham. Of all the causes that are most destructive of human life, and most injurious to Health, Wealth, Morality, and Happiness, Intemperance and War may be numbered as the most powerful: while National and Individual Prosperity, and the highest interests of Education, Commerce, Industry, Science, Art, and Religion—in short, the most perfect enjoyment of the Life that is, and the fittest preparation for the Life that is to come,—are all promoted by Temperance and Peace.
Peter Jackson, late Fisher Son, & Co. Angel Street, St. Martin's-le-Grand, *London.*
[W. y. Price 2*s.* 6*d.* 12mo, pp. xli., 144. The Introduction (pp. v.–xli.) is addressed "to the British and Foreign Visitors of the Great Exhibition." The remainder is an "Appeal to the British people, and especially to the opulent and influential, on the greatest reform yet to be accomplished," followed by a speech of Mr. J. S. Buckingham—Parliamentary Report on Intoxication—Poem on the "Horrors of War," and an "early proposal for a mutual interchange and exhibition of the productions of England and France." The book has an allegorical print, with explanation.]

Echoes of the Great Exhibition.
'Hears not also mortal life

Voices?'—*Wordsworth.*
'Not by might, nor by power, but by my Spirit, saith the Lord of Hosts.'—*Zech.* iv. 6.
By Joseph Turner.
London: William Pickering. 1851.
[Price 6*d.* 16mo, pp. 20. Eighteen sonnets on the subject of the Great Exhibition.]

Eclectic Review (The). New Series. Vol. 1, June, 1851. Vol. 2, November, 1851.
'A good book is the precious life blood of a master spirit, imbalmed and treasured up on purpose to a life beyond life.'—*Milton.*
London: Ward and Co., Paternoster-Row.
W. Oliphant and Son, *Edinburgh:* R. Jackson, *Glasgow:* G. and R. King, *Aberdeen:* and J. Robertson, *Dublin.* One Shilling & Sixpence.
[8vo. The June Number contains an article (pp. 7397–58) on "The Great Exhibition." "We scarcely think there was one person in that wonderful congregation that did not feel, for awhile, that he was in a temple rather than a palace. Such was our own case. Such was the case with all with whom we have compared remembrances. In one short sentence we may say—The *opening* of the Exhibition was worthy of the *Exhibition* itself." The November Number contains an article (pp. 623–641) on "The Religious Aspects of the Great Exhibition." "This unparalleled Exhibition has not been the work of government—has not been sustained by public revenues—has not been the result of political or party schemes. We rejoice sincerely in the favour it has received from royalty, and we are not loath, but glad to join the most loyal of our fellow-subjects in the heartiest congratulations on this account: we know nothing in the history of our monarchy, or of any other, so graceful, so endearing, so sure to win and to keep the love of a great and a free
people,

people, so likely to read a wholesome lesson to the princes of the earth, and to the heads of its republics, as the earnest and enlightened interest which her Majesty and Prince Albert have taken in this most popular affair."]

Edinburgh Review (The), or Critical Journal: No. 192 October 1851.

' Judex damnatur cum nocens absolvitur.'—*Publius Syrus.*

Longman, Brown, Green, and Longmans, *London:*
and Adam and Charles Black, *Edinburgh*, 1851.
[Price 6s. 8vo. Contains an article, pp. 557-598, on the history and progress of the Exhibition. " To seize the living scroll of human progress, inscribed with every successive conquest of man's intellect, filled with each discovery in the constructive arts, embellished with each plastic grace of figured surface or of moulded form, and unroll this before the eyes of men * * * this is, indeed, no mean design, no infelicitous conception."]

Edmond, A., Poem by, *v.* **Reminiscence.**

Edwards, Sutherland, *v.* **Authentic Account of Chinese Commission.**

Einige vergleichende Zusammenstellungen, Bemerkungen und Betrachtungen, die Londner Industrie-Ausstellung von 1851 betreffend.

Regensburg, gedruckt bei Fr. H. Neubauer.
[Privately printed. 4to, pp. 12. Remarks on the Exhibition, with comparative tables of the successful competitors. Particular mention is made of the distinction obtained by the Bavarian exhibitors, to whom, next to France and Algeria, the greatest number of Council Medals were awarded.]

Elegy (An) for the Crystal Palace, adapted from Gray. Supposed to be written in Hyde Park, 31st May, 1852.

' Wilful waste makes woeful want,
And all may live to say,
We wish that we had never let
This Building pass away.'—*Old Saw.*

London: Houlston & Stoneman, 65, Paternoster Row,
and Gall & Inglis, *Edinburgh.* 1852.
[Price 2d. 18mo, pp. 15.
" The Curfew tolls the knell of fading May,
The Crystal Palace we no more shall see,
The Lord of Public Works has had his way,
And left the Park to darkness and to me."]

Ellis, Hercules, *v.* **Rhyme Book.**

Ellissen, Philipp, *v.* **Amtlicher Bericht.**

Emerton, Rev. Dr. J. A., *v.* **Great Exhibition Prize Essay—Moral and Religious Guide.**

Enchanted (The) Hive ; or, the Island of the Bees. A Fairy Tale of Home.

London: G. Brown, Charlotte Place, Goodge Street; F. R. Butler, 20 B, Huntley Street, London University; and may be had of all Booksellers.
[W. y. Price 1s. 24mo, pp. 69. A tale based on Industry, Art, and Science. " But the Island of the Bees had now become the most powerful of all the world ! and the good fairies, Industry, Art, and Science, had so spread their powerful influence over all the Island, and, indeed, the whole Universe, that the good queen and her consort resolved to do honour to the fairies, by establishing a gala in their dominions, and inviting the industrious bees of all nations to send their products to this great fête."]

England and her Palace of Peace. A Poetical Dialogue between the Czar and his Double. By Thomas R. J. Polson, Author of ' The Fortune-Tellers' Intrigue,' etc. etc.

London: published by John F. Shaw, 27, Southampton Row; and Paternoster Row. 1854.
[Price 1s. 12mo, pp. iv. and 30.
" England gives an invitation,
To the world to come and see;
Proudly welcoming each nation,
That her guest consents to be.
Distant nations of strange manners,
Rendezvous upon her soil;
And 'neath Art's embroidered banners
Render homage to King Toil."]

England's Doom ; or, the Fatal Exhibition of 1851. An Essay showing the disastrous consequences of the Exhibition to the Working Men of England. ' Beneath the Grass a hideous reptile lies.' By Junius.

London:

London : J. James, 44, Holywell Street, Strand. And all Booksellers in Town and Country.
[W. y. Post 8vo, pp. 16. "How then, if I tell you that the effect of this Exhibition will
be to increase the numbers of our own poor, and to fill, not only the metropolis, but all
England with swarms of foreign poor? Alas! I not only affirm this, but I will prove it—
prove it so clearly that no man can refute me."]

England's Lament over the Destruction of the People's Palace. A Poem. By R.
C. Soper.
London : Printed and Published for the Author, by Thomas Hardy, 69, Mortimer Street, Cavendish
Square. 1852.
[Price 3*d*. Post 8vo, pp. 4.
"Let not a clique, hostile to a people's cause,
A nation's rights, her liberties, and laws,
This rare Temple of Industry deface,
Or load their country with such foul disgrace ;"]

England's Welcome to The World. By the Author of 'Proverbial Philosophy,' &c.
Printed by T. Brettell, Rupert Street, Haymarket.
[W. y. Circulated gratuitously. Folio, 1 p. A poem signed Martin F. Tupper, and dated
Albury.]
"A Voice of happy greeting to the Nations of the World!
A Flag of Peace for every shore, on every sea, unfurl'd!
A Word of Brotherhood and love to each who hears the call,—
A Welcome to the World of Men, a Welcome, one and all !"]

English and Continental Guide to London (The), in English and French, with an
improved map. Published expressly for the Grand National Exhibition.
London : W. & T. Piper, and Houlston & Stoneman, Paternoster Row. 1851.
[Price One Shilling. 12mo, pp. 88. Contains a very short account of the Exhibition.]

English and French Guide (The) to the Great Exhibition of All Nations for 1851 :
With an Engraving of the Building in Hyde Park, from designs by Mr.
Paxton. Entered at Stationers' Hall. Wood's Edition.
London : J. T. Wood, Publisher, Holywell-Street, Strand. Price One Penny.
[W. y. 12mo, pp. 16. In French and English.]

English Exhibition Comédie-Vaudeville en Deux Actes, par MM. E. Grangé, Th.
Barrière et Decourcelle, Représentée pour la première fois, à Paris, sur le
Théâtre de la Montansier, le 12 Juillet 1851.
Paris Beck, Libraire Rue des Grands-Augustins, 20 Tresse, successeur de J. N. Barba, Palais-
National, 1851. Prix: 60 centimes.
[Imperial 8vo, pp. 18. The scene is laid in London during the period of the Exhibition.]

Engravings on Cotton.
°A small square pocket handkerchief with an outside view of the building,
placed diagonally, within a flowered border. [Price one halfpenny.]
°Another with figures, and Explanations in words, headed 'The Great Exhibition Wot is to be.' [Price 2*d*.]
°Another large square one printed in blue and white with medals, me-
dallion portraits of Prince Albert, and a view, with description in words,
of the Great Exhibition. [Price 3½*d*.]
°Another printed with figures and descriptions in comic verse, and a view in
the centre of 'The Crystal House which Albert built.' [Price 1*d*.]

Engravings on Gelatine.
Exterior general View—(P) J. T. Wood.
Ditto, Another—(P) J. T. Wood.
Ditto, Another—(P) J. T. Wood.
South-East View—(P) J. T. Wood.
End of Transept (Exterior)—(P) J. T. Wood.
View from Kensington Gardens—(P) J. T. Wood.
View from the Serpentine—(P) J. T. Wood.
Interior—(P) J. T. Wood.
Interior of Transept—(P) J. T. Wood.

Engravings on Paper. Described by : Title or Subject—Size in Inches—(A) Artist's
Name—(E) Engraver's or (L) Lithographer's Names—(P) Publisher's Name.

Trihedral View—32 × 19—(A) C. B. P. Shelley and H. H. Treppass—(E) Thomas Jeavons—(P) Ackermann—10*s*. 6*d*.

Exterior View, surrounded by views of Public Buildings—27 × $17\frac{1}{4}$—(A) Thomas Flemming—(E) Thomas Flemming—(P) Ackermann—5*s*.

Exterior View, on the back a ground-plan—10 × $3\frac{3}{4}$—(P) Ackermann.

Palace for the Exhibition—$17\frac{1}{2}$ × $6\frac{1}{4}$—(A) L'Enfant, (P) W. Ward.

Exterior View—$16\frac{1}{2}$ × $5\frac{1}{2}$—(P) G. Berger—3*d*.

Mr. Paxton's Crystal Palace. Printed in gold on blue ground—$13\frac{1}{4}$ × $7\frac{1}{2}$—(P) H. Beal.

Palace of Industry during Winter—18 × $7\frac{1}{2}$—(A) Le Bihan, (L) Le Bihan, (P) Ackermann—1*s*. 6*d*.

Palace of Industry from North-west—18 × $7\frac{1}{2}$—(A) Le Bihan, (L) Day & Son, (P) Ackermann—1*s*. 6*d*.

Palace from the Bridge—18 × $7\frac{1}{2}$—(A) Le Bihan, (L) Day & Son, (P) Ackermann—1*s*. 6*d*.

Palace from the Cascade—18 × $7\frac{1}{2}$—(A) Le Bihan, (L) Le Bihan, (P) Ackermann—1*s*. 6*d*.

View of the Building, with ground-plan, &c.—16 × 10—(L) T. Dean & Son, (P) T. Dean & Son—6*d*. plain, 1*s*. tinted.

View of the Building—19 × 16—(E) W. Gibbs, (P) Elliot—2*d*. colored.

View of the Crystal Palace—20 × $7\frac{1}{2}$—(E) W. Gibbs, (P) Elliot—1*d*.

Exterior (colored)—$9\frac{1}{2}$ × $6\frac{1}{2}$.

Art Palace—$10\frac{1}{2}$ × $7\frac{1}{2}$—(A) Madeley, (L) Madeley.

Exterior—10 × $6\frac{1}{2}$—(P) J. Gilbert—6*d*. tinted, 1*s*. colored.

Exterior—$18\frac{1}{2}$ × $25\frac{3}{4}$—(A) G. Dorrington, (E) G. Dorrington, (P) W. Strange.

View—$9\frac{1}{4}$ × $6\frac{1}{2}$—(P) H. Wettone.

A Sheet containing 4 Exterior Views—$9\frac{1}{2}$ × 7—(P) R. Canton.

Exterior—$12\frac{3}{4}$ × 7—(A) F. C. Robinson, (L) F. C. Robinson, (P) J. Harwood.

Opening (Exterior)—14 × 9—(A) Aug. Butler, (L) Aug. Butler, (P) Stannard and Dixon.

Exterior—19 × $6\frac{1}{2}$—(A) E. Walker, (E) E. Challis, (P) Ackermann—1*s*.

Exterior—21 × $8\frac{1}{4}$—(E) Read & Co.

Exterior from the Serpentine—9 × $6\frac{1}{4}$—(E) Read & Co.

Exterior—$19\frac{1}{2}$ × $7\frac{1}{2}$—(E) Read & Co.

Exterior—18 × 12.

Exterior—7 × $4\frac{3}{4}$—(P) Rock & Co.

Exterior—13 × $8\frac{1}{4}$—(P) Read & Co.

Exterior—6 × $3\frac{1}{2}$—(P) Rock & Co.

Exterior—19 × $6\frac{1}{2}$—(L) Day & Son, (P) Ackermann.

Exterior—9 × $6\frac{1}{4}$—(P) V. Brooks.

Exterior—$13\frac{1}{2}$ × $7\frac{3}{4}$—(P) A. Flude.

Exterior—$16\frac{1}{2}$ × $5\frac{3}{4}$—(E) Boyd & Cannavan, (P) J. H. Woodley.

Building—38 × 13—(L) Geo. Hawkins, (P) Ackermann—7*s*. 6*d*.

Bird's-eye View—32 × 15—(A) G. F. Sargent, (E) T. Bolton, (P) "Weekly Times."

Exterior, Looking across the Serpentine—17 × 9—(L) V. Brooks, (P) V. Brooks.

Exterior, from Kensington Gardens—$17\frac{1}{4}$ × $9\frac{1}{2}$—(L) V. Brooks, (P) V. Brooks.

Exterior, on Day of Opening—27 × 17—(A) George F. Bragg, (L) V. Brooks, (P.) V. Brooks.

Exterior—$19\frac{1}{4}$ × $8\frac{1}{2}$—(L) Day & Son, (P) Ackermann.

Exterior, surrounded by Medallions, &c.—$12\frac{1}{2}$ × $9\frac{1}{4}$—(P) Harris.

Exterior, in an Ornamental Border—9 × 7—(L) R. Canton, (P) R. Canton.

Exterior—16 × 5—(P) J. Allen.

Exterior—$17\frac{3}{4}$ × $9\frac{1}{4}$—(E) H. Vizetelly, (P) James Gilbert.

Exterior—20 × 14—(P) V. Brooks.

Exterior—18¾ × 11—(A) George F. Bragg, (L) V. Brooks, (P) V. Brooks.
Crystal Palace from Knightsbridge Road—14½ × 9½.
Exterior—16½ × 5¾—(E) Boyd & Cannavan, (P) Boyd & Cannavan.
Exterior (Col^{d}.)—7 × 5—(E) C. & E. Layton, (P) C. & E. Layton.
Transept, External View—28 × 14—(A) Chas. Burton, (L) Day & Son, (P) Ackermann—*5s.*
Transparent View, Exterior—8 × 5—(P) Vickers.
Gilbert's View—6½ × 3¾.
Bird's-eye View of Crystal Palace and Surrounding Neighbourhood—36 × 16½.
Exterior View—18¼ × 8½—(A) N. B. Stocker.
Exterior—17 × 12—(A) M. Rouge, (E) M. Rouge, (P) W. Winn—*2d.*
Exterior, South-East View—36¾ × 6¼—(P) "Illustrated London News."
Exterior, 4½ × 2—(P) G. Berger.
Exterior—4½ × 2½—(P) J. T. Wood.
Exterior—6 × 3¾—(P) W. Rogers.
Exterior—4¼ × 2½—(P) A. Walkley.
Exterior—3¾ × 2½—(E) J. King, (P) J. King.
Exterior, looking West from Dante's Temple—17 × 10—(A) Chavanne, (E) R. H. Mason, (P) Read & Co.
Exterior—36 × 9¼. [Supplement of Illustrated London News.]
Exterior, from the Serpentine—16 × 10 (A) Chavanne, (P) Read & Co.
Interior (Empty)—6½ × 3½—(E) S. Lacey, (P) J. Mason.
Interior—18 × 5¼—(E) Macquarie & Co., (P) J. Allen.
Interior, North Transept—9½ × 6½—(A) Chavanne, (E) Chavanne, (P) Read & Co.
Interior, Russian Department—8¾ × 6¾—(A) Read, (E) Chavanne, (P) Read & Co.
Interior, South Transept—9 × 6½—(A) Read, (E) Chavanne, (P) Read & Co.
Interior, Ceylon, Malta, and Canadian Departments—9 × 6¾—(A) Read, (E) Chavanne, (P) Read & Co.
Sectional View of Interior—17½ × 9—(P) G. Berger—*3d.*
View of Interior—17¾ × 9—(P) G. Berger—*3d.*
Perspective View of Interior (colored)—10 × 6½—(L) Mitchell, (P) J. Gilbert.
Interior, Opening Scene—18 × 12—(L) V. Brooks, (P) V. Brooks.
The Nave 39¼ × 28½—(A) Edmund Walker, (L) Day & Son, (P) Ackermann—*12s.*
View of Interior—18 × 9—(P) G. Berger—*3d.*
Interior of Transepts—7 × 10¼—(A) Saddler, (E) Saddler, (P) C. & E. Layton.
Transept—19½ × 25—(L) V. Brooks, (P) V. Brooks.
Nave and Transept—17 × 11—(L) V. Brooks, (P) V. Brooks.
Colored Interior—19 × 13½—(A) Augustus Butler, (L) A. Butler, (P) Stannard and Dixon.
Machinery Department—24 × 15¼—(L) Charles Burton, (L) Day & Son, (P) Ackermann.
The Opening—15¾ × 10¼—(A) George Cruikshank, (P) David Bogue.
Interior looking West—18½ × 25¾—(A) R. Hind, (E) G. Dorrington, (P) W. Strange—*3d.*
Interior View of Design for Winter Garden—18¼ × 6—(P) G. Berger—*3d.*
Transept, looking North—25 × 33½—(A) Edm. Walker, (L) E. Walker, (P) Ackermann & Co.
Transparent View, Interior—8 × 5¼—(P) Vickers.
Interior looking West—17½ × 14¼—(L) Durond, (P) Summers.
Five Views in Interior—(A) H. Sharlet.
Interior—4 × 2½—(P) Rock & Co.
Interior, from the Transept—looking West—17 × 10—(P) Office of the "Mighty London Illustrated."

Interior—Opening Scene—26 × 11¼—(A) E. Le Bihan.
Interior—42½ × 30. [Supplement of the Illustrated London News.]
Chinese Department—20 × 13½.
   [A colored advertisement of Mr. Hewett of Fenchurch Street. The original plate,
   we believe, served as one of "Dickensons' Comprehensive Views."]
Allegory of the Great Exhibition—23 × 16¾—(A) Benedict Masson, (L) F.
   Sorrieu, (P) Ch. Hiltbrunner, Paris.—5 francs.
Musical Emblematic Clock — 25 × 18¼ — (P) Ackermann.
Plan of Estates purchased by Her Majesty's Commissioners—(E) J. & C.
   Walker.
The Ionian Counter—18¼ × 14¾.
Proposed Monument to Prince Albert—19 × 12—(A) Edw. Bennett, (L)
   Day & Son.
Four Views, Exterior and Interior, on a sheet—17½ × 10¾—(P) Dean.
Group in Interior—4 × 12—(A) H. Sharlet.
Crystal Fountains and Group—8 × 12—(A) H. Sharlet.
Group in Interior—7¾ × 12—(A) H. Sharlet.
Group in Interior—7 × 10½—(A) H. Sharlet.
State Opening (Interior)—17 × 10—(P) Read & Co.
State Opening—27 × 19½—(A) Louis Haghe, (L) L. Haghe, (P) Ackermann
   & Co.—12s.
Opening (colored)—10½ × 7—(P) W. Ward.
"London"—37½ × 28½—(A) G. Thomas, (E) J. Williamson. [Supplement
   of Illustrated London News.]
"Great Exhibition"—43¼ × 28—(A) J. L. Williams, G. Thomas, William
   Harvey, (E) J. Williamson. [Supplement to Illustrated London News.]
Design for converting the Crystal Palace into a Tower 1000 feet high—
   9¼ × 13¾—(A) C. Burton—(P) Ackermann—2s.
Ford's Illustrated Memorial—21 × 14¼ — (A) W. A. Dellamotte, (L) T.
   Meyer, (P) William Simpson Ford—Tinted 1s.
Inauguration—30½ × 24—(A) Edmund Walker, (L) E. Walker, (P) Acker-
   mann—21s.
Precious Stones, or Gems. Exhibited by Mr. Tennant.

Engravings on Silk.
   A large square handkerchief, with an Interior View of the Transept.
      [Price 4s. 1d.]
   Another large square one, with a view of the interior, surrounded by por-
      traits of Her Majesty and Prince Albert, and flags of all nations printed
      in colours. [Price 4s.]
   The same, but with the engravings not in colours. [Price 4s.]
   A large square one, with an exterior view and groups of foreigners. [Price 4s.]
   Another large square one, with views of the exterior and interior, and with
      various groups, portraits, views of public buildings, and devices. [Price 4s.]
   A large silk handkerchief with an Allegorical picture, representing a Statue
      of Mercury on a pedestal, encircled by Natives of All Nations joining
      hands, and surmounted by a Medallion portrait of Her Majesty and Prince
      Albert, all within a border ornamented with various devices. The back-
      ground of the picture represents the building.

Epsom National Derby Day Open to All Nations. 1851.
   Ackermann & Co. 96., Strand.
      [W. y. Price 3s. 6d. A long sheet of facetious engravings, representing the visitors of
      all nations going to the races, and the race itself run by animals of various countries.]

°Erinnerung an die Berichterstattungskommission der Deutschen Zollvereins-
   regierungen bei der Industrie-Ausstellung aller Völker zu London im Jahr
   1851.
   Berlin 1853. Gedruckt in der Deckerschen Geheimen Ober-Hofbuchdruckerei.
      [8vo, pp. 20. Letters of thirteen of the Zollverein's Commissioners, on their departure,
      with replies of H.R.H. Prince Albert and the Royal Commissioners.]

F

°Errinnerer der Exhibition der Arbeitsamkeit. Das Gebaude wardgemchtet in
Hyde Park, und sich geoffenet May 1st. 1851.
[The same as Industrial Exhibition Remembrancer and Moniteur de l'Exhibition.]

Erster [und Zweiter] Bericht der Königlich Grossbritannischen Kommissäre für die
Londner Industrie-Ausstellung im Jahre 1851, an den R^{t.} Honble. Spencer
Horatio Walpole etc. etc. Ihrer Majestät der Königin Staatssecretär des
Innern. Auf Königlichen Befehl beyden Parlamentshäusern überreicht. Im
Druck erschienen bei W. Clowes & Sons, London, im Sommer und November
1852. Aus dem (265 Seiten starken) Original-Berichte entnommen und ins
Deutsche übertragen im November 1852 und im Januar 1853 von B. J.
Schubarth, Ritter des K. B. Verdienstordens vom h. Michael, korrespondirendes
Ehren-Mitglied der Society of Arts in London, Ehrenmitglied des Polytech-
nischen Vereins in Würzburg, und Mitglied des Polytechnischen Vereins für
Bayern. Zweite Auflage.
Regensburg, 1852-3. Verlag von G. Joseph Manz.
[Price 11¼ sgr., 8vo, pp. 56, 44. Extracts from the First and Second Reports of the Royal
Commissioners. See also Auszug des Ersten Berichtes.]

Essay (An) explanatory of the Tempest Prognosticator in the Building of the
Great Exhibition for the Works of Industry of All Nations. Read before the
Whitby Philosophical Society February 27th, 1851. By George Merry-
weather, M.D. Whitby, The Designer and Inventor.
London: John Churchill, Princes Street, Soho. To be had of all Booksellers. 1851.
[Price 3s. 8vo, pp. vii. and 63. The Tempest Prognosticator is a contrivance by
which leeches, acted on by the electricity of the atmosphere, are supposed to foretell storms.]

Essay on the Advantages to be gained by the Working Men attending the
Exhibition of 1851. By Thomas Briggs, Millwright.
Bolton: Printed by J. T. Staton, Exchange-Street East. 1850.
[12mo, pp. 8. "In conclusion, I would earnestly urge my fellow working men to consider
the prospective results of this Exhibition, and to examine into its merits, confident that
such examination will result in their enthusiastic support and earnest determination to
attend it; for amongst the many good influences that are, and have been at work in improving society, they will find none more powerful or diffusive in its agency; for independently
of the great good to our commerce and manufactures that will be gained by attending
the Exhibition, the moral effects alone will compensate a thousand fold all the outlay it will
incur; and many a working man will be able to date his starting in the onward progress of
morality and intellectual knowledge, from the day he attended the Nations' Exhibition of
Eighteen Hundred and Fifty-one."]

Etonian, *v.* Our Heartless Policy by an.

Etranger, *v.* A l'Etranger—Aux Etrangers.

Examen Historique et Critique des Verres, Vitraux, Cristaux, Composant la
Classe XXIV. de l'Exposition Universelle de 1851, par G. Bontemps, Fabri-
cant de Verres, Chevalier de la Legion-d'Honneur.
Paris Chez L. Mathias, Libraire Quai Malaquais, 15.
Londres Chez J. Weale, Libraire 59 High Holborn. 1851.
[Price 5s. Royal 8vo, pp. 125.]

Excelsior, *v.* Dial of the World.

Executive Committee, *v.* Public Testimonial to.

Exhibition and Grand London Sights, *v.* Aunt Mavor.

°Exhibition Broad Sheet (The)
[Printed and Published by T. Goode, 30. Aylesbury Street, Clerkenwell. W. y. or price,
pp. 4. A large sheet of facetious engravings, with accompanying letter-press.]

Exhibition de Londres, (Le) Poème en Trois Chants, par A. Le Maout.
'Fraîche nymphe des eaux, qu'un ciel d'azur couronne,
Et dont le front se livre aux baisers des zéphyrs,
Jersey veut célébrer le Jubilé que donne
Sa grande métropole aux valeureux martyrs
Qui suivent du travail la bannière sacrée . . . .
Ce livre est l'*Hosannah* de l'humble Césarée.'
Jersey: Richard Gosset, Imprimeur-Libraire, 20, Queen Street.
Londres: Houlston et Stoneman, Paternoster-Row. 1851.

[Price

[Price 1s. 8vo, pp. 23. Song the first is called Hyde Park, Song the second, Le Palais de Cristal, and Song the third, Les Peuples, followed by a short address to Jersey, in which place the author lived. The spirit of the Poem may be judged of by the opening lines of the second Part—

> " Arts, prêtez à ma muse un rayon de chaleur;
> Eclairez mes tableaux d'une vive couleur;
> Faites qu'en célébrant cette grande merveille
> Mes vers charment l'esprit et caressent l'oreille,
> Et que, sans trébucher au milieu du chemin,
> Je guide mes lecteurs du début à la fin:
> Voilà l'unique vœu d'un timide poète . . ."]

Exhibition Lay (The).
London: Groombridge & Sons, Paternoster Row, 1852.
[Price 1s. 18mo, pp. 32.

> " Few who beheld will e'er forget
> the grandeur of that day,
> The sunbeams flashing on the glass,
> the banners fluttering gay.
> The spring in all its loveliness,
> the gleam on every face,"]

Exhibition London Guide (The), and Visitor's Pocket Companion, describing, on a new plan, the Great Metropolis and its environs. By the Rev. John Richardson, LL.B. Editor of 'Branche's Principia Legis,' etc., etc.

> ' Tot Colles Romæ, quot sunt Spectacula Trojæ,
> Quæ septem numero, digna labore tuo.
> Ista manent Trojæ Spectacula: Busta, Gigantes,
> Histrio, Dementes, Struthiones, Ursa, Leones.'—Barnabæ Itinerarium.

[Entered at Stationers' Hall.]
London: Simpkin, Marshall & Co., Stationers' Hall Court. 1851.
[Price 1s. 18mo, pp. xxiv., 228. Contains an account (pp. 22-24) of the Crystal Palace.]

Exhibition of 1851 (The), and the Objections thereto. (Reprinted from the Blackburn Standard of Wednesday, September the 11th, 1850, at the recommendation of the London Executive Committee.)
[Without Publisher's or Printer's name. Circulated gratuitously. Folio, p. 1. A reply to an article in Blackwood's Magazine, v. Blackwood.]

Exhibition Puzzle (The).
London: Published by Simmon's & Co. 14 St. John Sqr.
[W. y. Price One Penny. Sm. 4to. A Labyrinth, with a view of the Building in centre.]

Exhibition (The) and the People. The Temperance Cause in its relation to the Condition of the Working Classes. By Thomas Beggs, Author of ' An Inquiry into the Extent and Causes of Juvenile Depravity.'
London: Charles Gilpin, 5, Bishopsgate Without. Price 1d. each; 5s. per 100; or 35s. per 1000.
[W. y. 12mo, pp. 16. A Temperance Address, with a short introduction relative to the Exhibition.]

Exhibition (The) in 1851, of the Products and Industry of All Nations. Its Probable Influence upon Labour and Commerce. By W. Felkin, Esq., F.L.S.

> ' If there is any pledge of concord and real progress which Europe can give to the world, it is assuredly the Universal Exhibition, which will speedily collect together in London, the wonders effected by art, science, and human progress.'—Journal des Debats.

London: Arthur Hall, Virtue, and Co., Paternoster Row.
[W. y. Price 6d. 8vo, pp. 30. Mr. Felkin was Mayor of Nottingham in 1851, and one of the Local Commissioners. " This influence may most probably operate—1. By communicating information in the most practical and unquestionable form, to producers and manufacturers; showing their exact relative position, in regard to the quality, style, and price of goods, the one towards the other. * * * The more goods are asked for, the better is the price. Yet from the greater quantity required the cost may be kept down, although wages may be raised." The work was printed by H. Hudston, Borough Printing Offices, Nottingham.]

Exhibition (The) Riddle Book
London: Ryle & Co., Printers 2 & 3, Monmouth Court, Bloomsbury.
[W. y. 48mo, pp. 8. Not otherwise relating to the Exhibition than by its title.]

Exhibition Tracts. No. I. How to Reward all the Exhibitors. No. II. How to Appropriate the Surplus Funds. No. III. How to Commemorate the Exhibition. By Stephen Geary, Architect, (Exhibitor—Class VII.) Author of ' The British Sacred Banner,' a National Hymn adapted to the Times.

[London;

London: Published by W. J. Adams (Bradshaw's 'Railway Guide' Office), 59, Fleet-Street, London, & 47, Brown-Street, Manchester; and to be had of all Booksellers, and at all the Railway Stations throughout the kingdom. Price Fourpence. [Entered at Stationers' Hall.—1851]
[8vo, pp. 16. Only the first of these Tracts, "How to Reward all the Exhibitors," was ever published. The purport of this particular Tract was the propriety of a very wide distribution of honors and rewards.]

Exhibition, 1851.
[Without Publisher's or Printer's name, date, or price. 32mo. A short poem, on a card, signed Universal Brotherhood.
"What might be done if men were wise—
What glorious deeds, my suffering brother,
Would they unite,
In love and right,
And cease their scorn of one another ? "]

Exhibitor, *v.* Illustrated Exhibitor.

Exhibitors [Address on their exclusion from the opening ceremony] *v.* To the.

Exhibitors' Almanac (The) For 1852, being Bissextile, or Leap Year; containing the Calendar; Moon's Changes; and Eclipses; an Alphabetical List of the Prizeholders of the Great Exhibition, Giving their Names and Localities, a Description of the Articles for which Prizes were Awarded, and the Classes in which they were Exhibited; the whole forming a complete and perfect record of the Crystal Palace. Together with a Mass of Useful Information, and the Ordinary Contents of an Almanac.
London: Simpkin, Marshall, and Co., Stationers' Hall Court. 1852. Price Sixpence.
[8vo, pp. 165. Contains a short account of the Exhibition, a list of the awards of the prizes, and an exterior view.]

Exhibitors Exhibited, *v.* Real Exhibitors.

Experiments on the strength of Portland & Roman Cements, conducted at the Great Exhibition Building, Hyde Park, extracted from a communication on the subject of cements, made to the 'Institute of Civil Engineers,' by John Bazley White & Sons, of Millbank Street, Westminster.
London: Printed by Royston & Brown, 40 & 41, Old Broad Street. 1852.
[8vo, pp. 19. Illustrated with engravings.]

Explanatory Catalogue of Models & Specimens illustrative of the Manufacture of Flint Glass, contributed to the Great Exhibition of All Nations, 1851. By Apsley Pellatt & Co., Flint Glass Manufacturers, Holland Street, Blackfriars, & 58, Baker Street, Portman Square, London.
[Printed by W. Clowes and Sons, Stamford Street, Blackfriars, and 14, Charing Cross. W. y. Privately circulated. 12mo, pp. 23. A short account of glass-making, illustrated with woodcuts.]

* Exposition de Londres a MM. Les Imprimeurs.
Thunot, Imprimeur, Rue Racine, No. 26.
[4to. Advertised in Journal de la Librairie.]

Exposition des Produits de l'Industrie Française, under the direction of M. Sallandrouze de Lamornaix, Ancien Deputé, Membre du Conseil General des Manufactures, &c. &c. &c. Private view, Saturday, November 17, 1849.
W. S. Johnson, "Nassau Steam Press," 60 St. Martin's Lane.
[Privately printed. W. y. 4to, pp. 12. A short account of the Exhibition opened by M. Sallandrouze in George Street, Hanover Square, *v.* also Memorandum.]

° Exposition (Le) de Londres Croquis Comiques Par Cham.
Paris au Bureau du Journal le Charivari, 16, Rue du Croissant. Imprimerie Langé Lévy et Comp., 16, Rue du Croissant, à Paris.
[W. y. 4to, pp. 16. Entirely woodcuts.]

* Exposition (Le) Universelle de Londres, signé Ollivier Roland.
Carre, Imprimeur, Rue St. Spire, Impasse a la Grosse Tête No. 5.
[Advertised in Journal de la Librairie.]

Exposition Nationale des Produits de l'Industrie, Agricole, et Manufacturière. 1849. (Catalogue Officiel.)
Imprimerie administrative de Paul Dupont Rue de Grenelle-Saint-Honoré, 55.
[Price 1 franc. 8vo, pp. xi., 317.]

Exposition Nationale 1849, *v.* Plan-Guide.

Exposition of 1851 (The); or, Views of the Industry, the Science, and the Government, of England. By Charles Babbage, Esq. Corresponding Member of the Academy of Moral Sciences of the Institute of France.

London: John Murray, Albemarle Street. 1851.
[Price 6s. 6d. 8vo, pp. xvi. and 231. This work treats of "Error Respecting the Interchange of Commodities" "Societies" "Origin of the Exposition of 1851" "Object and Use of the Exposition" "Limits" "Site and Construction of Building" "Prices" "Prizes" "Juries, etc." "Ulterior Objects" "Intrigues of Science" "Calculating Engines" "Position of Science" "The Press" "Party" "Rewards of Merit" · With this volume is bound up, as relating to the subject, "The Eleventh Chapter of the History of the Royal Society. By C. R. Weld, Esq. Assistant Secretary of the Royal Society. Reprinted with the permission of the proprietor. London: Richard Clay, printer, Bread Street Hill. 1849." 8vo, pp. 369-391. "Professor De Morgan's Review of Weld's History of the Royal Society. [Reprinted from] The Athenæum, London, Saturday, October 14, 1848, pp. 11." And "A Letter to the Board of Visitors of the Greenwich Royal Observatory in reply to the Calumnies of Mr. Babbage at their Meeting in June 1853, and in his book entitled The Exposition of 1851. By the Rev. R. Sheepshanks."]

Exposition Universelle de Londres considérée sous les Rapports Philosophique, Technique, Commercial et Administratif, au point de vue Français Ouvrage dédié aux Producteurs de la Richesse Universelle.
' Aide-toi, le Ciel t'aidera !'
Aperçu Philosophique Lettres Ecrites de Londres, par M. Michel Chevalier Membre de l'Institut, Ingénieur en Chef, etc., etc.

Paris Librairie Scientifique-Industrielle, de L. Mathias (Augustin), Quai Malaquais, 15. 1851.
[Price 2 francs. Royal 8vo, pp. 32. Only this part was published. At the end is printed the speeches made, on the occasion of the distribution of the French prizes, by The President of the Republic; M. Casabianca, Minister of Finance; and M. Charles Dupin.]

Exposition Universelle par M. Arles-Dufour, v. Politique Nouvelle.

*Exposition Universelle, Participation de la France.

Expositor (The): an Illustrated Recorder of Inventions, Designs, and Art-Manufactures.

London: Joseph Clayton, Jun., 265, Strand; and all booksellers and newsmen. 1850.
[Price 1l. 1s. 6d. Folio, pp. iv. and 416. A weekly periodical. The Introductory Address says "Every day there is increased anxiety expressed as to the Great Exhibition. Every one is eager to learn what is being done in all directions: what is France about?— what are the Germans doing?—what do the Americans mean to send?—what things are to come from India?—what is going on in all our cutlery and hardware, iron and glass, porcelain and pottery, silk, woollen, cotton, stuff, hosiery, and carpet districts?—what are we to have from Ireland?—How does the building get on?—when will it be ready?—will the Exhibition be really great, really a fair show of the world's industry? Our Journal will endeavour from week to week to satisfy this growing interest."]

Extract from the Times, v. Great Exhibition of 1851.

Eyre, John, v. Crystal Labyrinth, a Puzzle.

Farewell Lines to the Great Exhibition, 1851.
' God is ever present, ever felt,
In the wide waste, and in the city full;
And where He vital breathes, there must be joy.'
[London: Reed and Pardon, Printers, Paternoster Row. W. y. Privately circulated. Sm. 4to, two pages. A Poem signed S. S. and dated Chelsea, October, 1851.
" Farewell, thou Crystal Palace! now no more
To bless our eyes with thy surpassing glory;
No longer towards thee flocking myriads pour;
Yet shall we tell our sons thy wondrous story,—"]

Farm Yard and Buildings, Models of Improved, J. Baxter, v. Brief Description of.

Fatal Exhibition of 1851, v. England's Doom.

Fate of the Crystal Palace (The). A Letter to H.R.H. Prince Albert, by Leslie Sutton.
I was
Within a temple ymade of glas,
In which there were mo images
Of gold, standing in sundry stages,
Sette in mo rich tabernacles,
And with peerie mo pinnacles,

And

> And mo curious portraitures,
> And queint manner of figures
> Of gold worke, than I saw ever.
>
> *   *   *   *   *
>
> 'Madame,' sayed they, 'we bee
> Folke that here besechen thee
> That thou graunt us now good fame,
> And let our workes have good name;
> In full recompensacioun
> Of good worke, give us good renoun.'—*Chaucer.*

London: 1851.
[Without Publisher's name, but printed by Davidson, 18, Old Boswell Court, Lincoln's Inn, London. Price 2*d.* Post 8vo., pp. 8. A letter in favour of retaining the Crystal Palace in Hyde Park. "In the midst of the rejoicing which universally prevails, a rumour is spread abroad, which from its being clothed in semi-official garb, fills us with dismay and grief. The Crystal Palace is to be pulled down and removed—after the first of May next—removed to a suburb comparatively difficult and costly to approach—to Battersea Fields, where, if it will not be classed among, and brought into competition with, it will at least succeed to exhibitions of the lowest and most degrading natures—walking matches, pigeon shooting, gambling booths, donkey races, rat killing, dog fighting, and men fighting."]

Fauler, M., on Leather, *v.* Travaux.

Fearnside, William Gray, *v.* Holmes's Great Metropolis.

Felkin, W., *v.* Exhibition in 1851. Its Influence upon Labour and Commerce.

Fête Donnée par la Ville de Paris aux Délégués de l'Exposition Universelle de Londres. Les Nations, Ode Mêlée de Divertissements et de Danses. Chantée sur le Théâtre de l'Académie Nationale de Musique, le Mercredi 6 Août 1851. Poésie de M. Théodore de Banville; Musique de M. Adolphe Adam, de l'Institut; Divertissement de M. Arthur Saint-Léon; Décor de M. Despléchin.
Paris Mme Veuve Jonas, Libraire de l'Opéra, Passage du Grand Cerf, 52. 1851. Prix: 50 centimes.
[8vo, pp. 8.

> " Voici l'heure sainte, ô mère Patrie,
> De chanter la Paix, l'Art et l'Industrie!"]

* Fetes Offertes par la Ville de Paris. Programme.
Rendu, Rue Petit Pont No. 10.
[Advertised in Journal de la Librarie.]

Feuchtwanger, Dr. Lewis, *v.* Catalogue of American Minerals.

Few Words (A) upon Canada, and Her Productions in the Great Exhibition.

> ' Although every foreigner the instant he lands in England is struck with the evidence displayed before him, in every direction, of the wealth and energy of the British people, yet a much more striking exemplification of both is to be seen by any one who will carefully survey a *British Colony*'—*Sir Francis B. Head's* '*Emigrant.*'

Published by Authority.
London: W. & T. Piper, Paternoster Row, 1851. Price one Penny.
[Post 8vo, pp. 12. The preface says "The Reader will find in the few pages which are here offered to him nothing more than a plain and truthful statement of the advantages which the important colony of Canada presents to the British Emigrant."]

Fine Arts, Henry Weekes, *v.* Prize Treatise on.

Fine (The) Crystal Palace The Prince Built, *v.* Aunt Busy-Bees.

Fireside Facts from The Great Exhibition. By the Editor of ' Pleasant Pages.'
The Earth is the Lord's, and all that therein is.
Being an amusing series of Object Lessons on the Food and Clothing of All Nations in the year 1851
London: Houlston & Stoneman, 65, Paternoster Row. And all booksellers. Price 3*s.* 6*d.*
[W. y. 12mo, pp. ix, 246. The Preface is dated, Priory House, Clapton, December, 1851. The book is illustrated by lithographs and woodcuts "In conformity with the principles on which the Object Lessons are written, it has been the aim of the Author, not only to convey in an amusing manner a mass of information, but to cultivate in the reader the powers of observation, comparison, induction, and memory, by the exercise of which the mind is trained to investigate and acquire knowledge for itself. It has also been attempted to observe a far more important principle by applying such knowledge to the cultivation of faith in the providence of God; and for illustrating the motto of the Title-page, ' The Earth is the Lord's, and all that therein is.' A history of the Great Exhibition has been added; and illustrations of some of the 'lions,' which will long be remembered by its numerous visitors."]

First [and Second] Report of the Commissioners for the Exhibition of 1851, to the Right Hon. Spencer Horatio Walpole, &c., &c., one of Her Majesty's Principal Secretaries of State. Presented to both Houses of Parliament by Command of Her Majesty.
London : Printed by W. Clowes and Sons, Stamford Street. For Her Majesty's Stationery Office. 1852.
[Royal 8vo, First Report contains pp. liv., 211, with Plans and Diagram ; Second Report, pp. 76.]
[Another Copy on large paper prepared for, and presented with the large Edition of the Jury Reports and Special Reports to Foreign Governments and Her Majesty's Commissioners. Imp. 4to.]

First of May (The) a new Version of a celebrated Modern Ballad by Anna Harriet Drury Authoress of Friends and Fortune, etc. Sixth Edition
London William Pickering 1851
[Price 6d. 18mo, pp. 16.
"And now she gains the Transept,
And now her royal throne :
Now burst the sweet young voices,
And swells the organ's tone :
Now with her Lord and children,
And smiles of winning grace,
She passes through the joyous crowd,
That all may see her face."]

Fish, Hamilton, v. Letters.

Fléchey, L., Extrait du Rapport au Chambre de Commerce d'Alger, v. Chambre.

Fleming, Rev. Fletcher, v. Parable of the Pearl of Great Price.

Fletcher, Rev. Dr. A., v. Bible The Great Exhibition of All Nations.

Flower, Rev. T., v. Great Exhibition of the Industry of All Nations.

Food, v. Fireside Facts—Lectures, Dr. Lindley on—Substances used as.

Foot-passengers, numbers passing Bow Church and Aldgate, v. Report.

Forbes, Henry, v. Lectures [Worsted Manufacture].

Forbes, Professor E., On the Vegetable World, v. Art Journal.

Foreign Quarterly Review, v. Westminster.

Form and Colour, Owen Jones on, v. Gleanings.

Forrester, J. James, on Portugal, v. Oliveira Prize Essay.

Förster, L., v. Grosse (Das) Industrie-Ausstellungs-Gebäude.

Forty-four Sermons delivered in Exeter Hall, on the occasion of the opening of the Great Exhibition, during the Sabbath days, from May to September, 1851, to which are added, Four delivered on Tuesday Evenings, before the Young Men's Christian Association. Together with the Thanksgiving Service, on Nov. 6, 1851. Selected from the Penny Pulpit.
London : James Paul, 1, Chapter House Court, North side St. Paul's Church-yard, and Paternoster Row.
[Price 6s. W. y. 8vo. The Sermons are by the following Authors :—The Rev. W. Brock, T. Aveling, Dr. Hamilton, J. C. Harrison, Dr. Archer, J. Weir, R. Hamilton, C. Stovel, H. Allon, Dr. Beaumont, J. Stoughton, J H. Hinton, Dr. Cox, T. Binney, W. Chalmers, T. E. Thoresby, B. W. Noel, L. Tyerman, J. B. Brown, J. Burnet, G. Smith, G. Clayton, J. Kennedy, J. Aldis, S. Martin, J. C. Miller, Dr. Dixon, Dr. Cooke.]

Fowler, Charles, v. Crystal Palace—Grosse.

Fox, Sir C., v. Crystal Palace that Fox Built—Illustrated London Almanack.

Fragments from the Crystal Palace. By E. Leathes.
London : Hope & Co., Publishers, 16, Great Marlborough Street.
[W. y. Price 6d. 18mo, pp. 18. A Poem.
"Look adown the wondrous structure,
Where the chequer'd shadows play ;
See the scatter'd groups increasing,
Wending up the domèd way."]

Franklin, Robert, *v.* Wanderings in Crystal Palace.

Fraser's Magazine for Town and Country. N°· 260. August, 1851. N°· 265. January, 1852. N°· 275. November, 1852. N°· 279. March, 1853. N°· 282. June, 1853.

London : John W. Parker and Son, West Strand. Sold by T. Bosworth (late Fraser), 215, Regent Street, and all Booksellers and Newsmen in Town and Country. Half-a-crown. Savill and Edwards, Printers, 4, Chandos-street, Covent-garden.

[8vo. No. 260 contains an article (pp. 119–132) on the "Memorabilia of the Exhibition Season." No. 265, an article (pp. 17–32) entitled "Eighteen Hundred and Fifty-one." No. 275, an article (pp. 491–502) on "The Exhibition Jury Reports." No. 279, an article (pp. 341–353) on "The proposed New National Galleries and Museums." No. 282, an article (pp. 686–698) on "National Galleries, Museums, Public Parks, and Gardens." The general tone of these articles was in favour of the undertaking. The following is an extract from the article in No. 265 :—" No circumstance connected with the 'getting up,' and 'management of the affair' is more remarkable than the conduct of the people. It is not to be disguised, that a feeling of alarm existed to a considerable extent while the preparations for the Exhibition were in progress. No man could clearly see his way out of the difficulties that surrounded the undertaking, and that seemed to increase the more he examined it. Regarded in the most favourable aspect, it was at best a leap in the dark. Many persons—artists, manufacturers, and men of science—whose judgment was entitled to respect, predicted that it would turn out a humiliating failure. * * * Then, again, was it quite sure that the Exhibition would open? Up to the last hour there was nothing but an uproar of hammers and saws, and wagons loading and unloading at every entrance, and the litter and confusion filled the most sanguine friends of the project with dismay. It was apprehended, too, that as a variety of contingencies might be expected to arise, for which no human foresight could make provision, the arrangements and regulations must, unavoidably, undergo frequent modifications, which would be productive of serious derangement and disorder. * * * Never were fears or prophecies more satisfactorily set at rest by the event. The Exhibition opened, without a solitary *contretemps,* at the exact hour appointed. The rules and regulations laid down for its control, in the first instance, were never altered or deviated from. Had the Commissioners been occupied all their lives in the management of colossal *fêtes,* they could not have provided more sagaciously for all possible emergencies."]

Fremdenführer durch London. Vollständige Sammlung aller auf die Haupstadt Gross-Brittanniens bezüglichen Documente, Materialien und Nachweisungen. Ein unentbehrliches Handbuch für jeden Reisenden oder Fremden, welcher London in allen seinen Theilen, seine Localitäten, Monumente, Formalitäten, seine Vergnügungen und Hülfsmittel kennen zu lernen wünscht, vor und während seines Aufenthaltes in London, bei Gelegenheit der grossen Ausstellung von 1851, begleitet von: "Der Sonntag in London," oder Ausflüge in die Umgegend. Mit einer Karte. Englische und Französische Ausgaben.

London : Verlag von James Gilbert, Paternoster Row, No. 49. Preis brosch., 2 shilling—geb., 2 shilling 6 pence.

[W. y. 18mo, pp. 268, with a View of the Crystal Palace. Editions will be found in English and French under Gilbert's Visitor's Guide, and Guide.]

French Exposition, 1849, *v.* Report on—Plan-Guide.

Frenchman's Visit to England (A), and the Chrystal Palace. All he saw there, with his remarks upon England and the English People in General, and London in Particular, Translated into English by a Belgian, Revised and Corrected by an American, Printed by a Prussian, Published Everywhere, and Dedicated to Everybody.

London : W. N. Wright, 60, Pall Mall. 1851.

[Price 6*d.* Post 8vo, pp. 24. Concludes with the following words :—" And Monsieur Bull, *permettez-moi,* you must not be angry at what is said of you by the foreigner, *parce que* if you invite the Esquimaux from the North, and the Chinaman from the East, unless you can treat the one to whale-blubber, and the other to chopped worms and bird-nests, properly cooked, *certainement* you must expect that they will be discontented and abuse you. We must all have our hobby-horse to ride. The German his pipe, the Italian his fiddle, the Frenchman his revolution, and the Englishman his umbrella. *A présent, adieu! Au revoir !"*]

Freund, Dr. J. C. H., *v.* Small Contribution.

Friendly Observations, addressed in a spirit of kindness and candour to The Sculptors and Artists of Great Britain. and also to our Foreign Contributors, on some of their Works in the Great Exhibition of the Productions of Art and Industry of All Nations; Viewed in the Light of Artistic Taste and Analogy. By a Lover of Painting and Sculpture.

—'Every Parent who is desirous to preserve a wholesome moral feeling in his family,—and especially every Christian Parent, from the Queen to the humblest visitor of the Crystal Palace—has a deep interest in urging the successful adoption of the *Remedy* suggested in these pages.'

London: John Farquhar Shaw, 27, Southampton Row, Russell Square, and Paternoster Row. Johnstone & Hunter, *Edinburgh.* J. Robertson, *Dublin.* 1851.

[Price 6*d.* 16mo, pp. vi. and 30. The following extract will show the spirit and object of this Tract. "1. For what purpose did you send any one of those works to the Palace of Industry? You answer, 'To be examined, admired, and commended.' Then let me inform you, that by exhibiting a naked statue, you entirely defeat your own intention."]

Frolic & Fun or what was seen and done in London in 1851.

Frolic and Fun,
Or all that was done
By those that would run
To the Great Exhibition
Of 'Fifty-One.'
Vivent Les Souvenirs de L'Exposition.
One Shilling, Plain, 2*s.* 6*d.* Coloured.
Dean & Son, Printers, Threadneedle Street, *London.*

[W. y. A long Sheet of Engravings, bound in a square form.]

Fry, E. H., *v.* Memorials of the Great Exhibition. [A Poem.]

Fuller, Francis, *v.* Illustrated London Almanack—Memoranda—Report—Shall we spend 100,000*l.* on a Winter Garden.

Ful, (O) Tru, un Pertikler Okeawnt o bwoth wat aw seed un wat aw yerd, we gooin too the Greyt Eggshibishun, e Lundun, an o greyt deyle o Hinfurmashun besoide, wele kalkilatud fur to giv thoose foke o gradely hinseet hinto things, us hassent ad nothur toime nur brass fur to goo un see fur thersels; kontaining loikewoise o Dikshunayre, manefakturt fare o purpus fur thoose us ur noan fur larn't. Be o Felley fro Rachde. O fur Sixpunze. Sekund Edishun wele Fettelt, pertikler ith Dikshunayre lyne.

'Englun expekts evuri mon fur to doo is duti.'

Sevent Theawsun.

Rachde: Printud be H. M. Crosskill; un sowd be S. Y. Collins, Fleet-Street, Lundun; A. un J. Heywood, Manchesstur; un o Bukesellurs.

[W. y. 12mo, pp. 60. A story connected with the Great Exhibition in the Lancashire dialect, published at Rochdale.]

°**Furbers Almanac,** 1851 and list of Prices of Wines, Spirits, and Malt Liquors. View of the Crystal Palace for the Great Exhibition.

Hop Pole, William Street, Blackfriars Road, and at Westminster.

[Small folio.]

Furs, J. A. Nicholay, *v.* Historical Account of Skins and.

Fusinata, Maria, *v.* Comical People.

Future Uses (The) of the Crystal Palace. Extracted, by permission of the Proprietors of 'The Art-Journal,' from an unpublished Prize Essay on Art, Science, and Manufacture as an Unity. In Four Chapters. What we have been doing. What we are doing. What we ought to do. What we can do. By George Wallis, Head Master of the Birmingham School of Design; Principal Superintendant of British Textile Manufactures, and Deputy in Charge of Group C of Juries, in the Great Exhibition of 1851; formerly Head Master of the Manchester School of Design.

'Nil actum reputans, dum quod superesset agendum.'

London: Printed by George Barclay, Castle Street, Leicester Square. 1851.

[Privately circulated 8vo, pp. 24. In addition to Future Uses there is a short article entitled "A Hint as to a Closing Ceremonial."]

Fuzzelton Family, *v.* Koh-i-Noor.

Gallery of Arts. From the Great Exhibition of All Nations, 1851.

Published for the Proprietors, by Read & Co. 10, Johnson's Ct. Fleet St.

[W. y.

[W. y. Price 21s. Fcap 4to, pp. vi. 154. The first thirty-six pages contain a History of the Exhibition, the remainder of the volume is devoted to the contents. The work is very fully illustrated, and contains a portrait of Mr. Paxton. The engravings of sculpture appeared also in 'Gems of Art,' and the views of the Building in 'Beautes Architecturales.']

Gambardella, Spiridione, v. What shall we do with the Crystal Palace.

Gaspey, William, v. Tallis's Illustrated London.

Gathering for Peace (The). New Stories for Young Children, By the Author of ' Chickseed without Chickweed,' ' The Favourite Story Book,' Etc. Etc. Price Twopence.
London : Darton & Co., Holborn Hill.
    [W. y. Square 12mo, pp. 16. Child's book, with an emblematical illustration.]

Gathering of the Nations, v. Royal Game of.

Gathering of the Nations, Mrs. Brewer, v. On the.

Gathering of the People, v. Palace of Glass.

Gaussen, M. Maxime, on Mixed Fabrics, v. Travaux.

Geary, Stephen, v. Exhibition Tracts. How to Reward all the Exhibitors—The words to the music of Perry's Sacred Banner were also by Mr. Geary

Gelatine, v. Engravings on.

G., E. M., v. Crystal Palace. The London Season.

Gems of Art, from the Great Exhibition. Being a Series of Drawings of the most interesting Statuary, including a brief account of each subject, by E. Concanen, Esq.
London :—Read & Co., 10, Johnson's Court, Fleet Street.
    [W. y. Price 10s. plain, 16s. cold. Oblong 4to. Contains 28 prints in lithography of groups of Statuary. These Engravings also appeared in another work, v. Gallery of Arts.]

Gems of the Great Exhibition, v. Baxter.

General Outline (A) of a Proposed Plan for the Retention and Occupation of the Crystal Palace, by a London Merchant.
London : Pelham Richardson, 23, Cornhill. 1852. Price Sixpence.
    [8vo, pp. 23. Dated, April 8th, 1852. Contains, in addition to the particular subject in the letter, a proposal for the establishment of a Royal Order of Merit.]

Geographical and Industrial View of the Great Exhibition 1851 From the Official Descriptive and Illustrated Catalogue.
Spicer brothers, and Wm. Clowes & Sons. Standidge & Co. Litho. Old Jewry.
    [W. y. Price 2s. 6d. The large map drawn by Mr. A. Petermann, showing countries exhibiting, published separately.]

Geräthe, v. Landwirthschaftlichen Geräthe (die).

Ghillany, Dr. F. W., v. Tour (Eine).

Giant- and Fairy- Land (The) of Our own Times.
London : George Bell, Fleet Street. 1851.
    [Price 1s. Post 8vo, pp. 16. A few thoughts for young people in reference to the machinery in motion.]

Gibbs, W., on Architectural Ornament, v. Handbook.

Giglio (Il) e l'Ape nel Palazzo di Cristallo di Samuel Warren. Traduzione de Girolamo Volpe.
Londra, Presso Williams e Norgate. 1852.
    [Price 3s. 6d. 12mo, pp. xiii. 196. A Translation of the Lily and the Bee.]

Gilbart Prize Essay (The) on the adaptation of recent discoveries and inventions in Science and Art to the purposes of Practical Banking, by Granville Sharp. Third English Edition, with diagrams and illustrations.
London, Groombridge and Sons ;
Norwich, Fletcher and Alexander. 1854.
    [Price 18s. Royal 8vo, pp. viii., 356 and appendix. Mr. J. W. Gilbart offered a prize of " ONE HUNDRED pounds to the author of the best Essay which shall be written in reply to the
following

following question: *In what way can any of the articles collected at the Industrial Exhibition of 1851 be rendered especially serviceable to the interests of 'Practical Banking?'"* This volume contains portraits of Mr. Gilbart and Mr. Granville Sharp, and a considerable number of engraved specimens of Bankers' notes and draughts, prospectuses of articles applicable to Banking purposes, such as locks, safes, ink, paper, seals, &c., *v.* also another Edition under the title of Prize Essay.]

Gilbert, John, *v.* Crystal Palace that Fox Built.

* Gilbert's Crystal Palace Almanac.
    London James Gilbert 49 Paternoster Row.
        [Price 1*s.* A very large sheet illustrated with Engravings, and published Nov. 1, 1851.]

Gilbert's New Map of London, *v.* Guide (A) for Visitors.

Gilbert's Visitor's Guide to London; containing the completest information connected with the Localities, Customs, Public Buildings, Amusements, and Resources of the Capital of Great Britain : an indispensable Handbook for Travellers and Foreigners desirous of possessing an accurate knowledge of the British Metropolis previous, and during their visit to the Great Exhibition of 1851 : to which is appended 'Sunday in London;' or, Excursions to the Vicinity. With a Map.
    London, 1851. James Gilbert, 49, Paternoster Row. Price 1*s.* 6*d.*, sewed ; or 2*s.* in cloth. Editions also in French and German.
        [18mo, pp. iv., 234. Contains a view of the Exterior of the Building, and a short account of the Exhibition (pp. 61–64). A French edition will be found under Guide, and a German one under Fremdenführer.]

Gladstone, Right Hon. W. G., *v.* Illustrated London Almanack.

Glaisher, James, *v.* Lectures [Philosophical Instruments.]—Reports by the Juries.

Glances at Europe : in a Series of Letters from Great Britain, France, Italy, Switzerland, &c. during the Summer of 1851. Including notices of the Great Exhibition, or World's Fair. By Horace Greeley. Third Edition.
    New York : Dewitt & Davenport, Publishers. 1852.
        [Post 8vo, pp. viii., 350. These letters, it is believed, originally appeared in the "Tribune" New York daily paper, of which Mr. Greeley is the editor. Mr. Greeley was Chairman of the Jurors in Class 22. "There can be no serious doubt that the Fair has good points; I think it is a good thing for London first, for England next, and will ultimately benefit mankind. And yet it would not be difficult so to depict it (and truly), that its contrivers and managers would never dream of thinking the picture complimentary."]

Glaspalast (Der) für die Industrie-Ausstellung aller Nationen von J. Paxton. Mit einer Ansicht und 13 in den Text gedruckten Abbildungen.
    Leipzig, Verlag von J. J. Weber. 1851.
        [Price 5 sgr. 16mo, pp. 48, with Illustrations. A brief description of the Exhibition building, with woodcuts interspersed throughout the text.]

Glass, Apsley Pellatt on, *v.* Explanatory Catalogue.

Glass-Berg (The) A Poem.
    London Saunders and Otley, Conduit Street. 1851.
        [Price 1*s.* 6*d.* 12mo, pp. 21.
            " Now, round the wondering halls the Queen has pass'd,
              She's walk'd her mile of triumph through at last ;
              And when again her foot is to the north,
              She with her noble company goes forth ;
              The barriers fall, the trumpets tell the crowd
                That they are free to go where'er they please,
              So let's obey the call they give so loud,
              And see the Glass-berg's wonders at our ease."]

Gleanings from the Great Exhibition.
    London : published by John Betts, 115, Strand, (nearly opposite Exeter Hall).
        [W. y. Price 3*s.* 6*d.* 12mo, pp. 17. A little book accompanying a puzzle.]

Gleanings from the Great Exhibition of 1851. No. 1. On the Distribution or Form and Colour developed in the Articles exhibited in the Indian, Egyptian, Turkish, and Tunisian Departments of the Great Exhibition. [From the June No. of The 'Journal of Design.']
    [*London :*—Printed by G. Barclay, Castle St. Leicester Sq. W. y. Privately circulated. 8vo, pp. 8. Signed Owen Jones.]

Goggleye's (Mr) visit to the Exhibition of National Industry to be Held in London.
on the 1st of April 1851   With a Catalogue containing Notes & remarks on
the most remarkable works in the Exhibition   1s. Plain 2s. 6d. Col.
London Pubd by Timy Takem'in. Hyde Park.
[W. y. An oblong sheet of colored facetious engravings.]

Goldenberg, M., on Iron, v Travaux.

*Goode, D, What have they seen in thy House? or Reflections on the opening of
the Great Exhibition Preached April 27.
[Price 1s. 8vo. Advertised, but doubtful if it was not a mistake for Dr. Moore's Sermon.]

Gordon, Professor L. D. B., on Machinery of Exhibition, v. Art Journal.

Graham, Professor Thomas. v. Report by the Juries.

Grand Banquet to His Royal Highness the Prince Albert, at the Mansion House,
London, in Honour of the Exhibition of 1851.
London : Printed by W. Clowes and Sons, Stamford Street.
[W. y. Circulated gratuitously. 8vo, pp. 16. Account of the Dinner and Speeches.]

Grand Exhibition of All Nations (The)
C. Paul, Printer, 18, Great Saint Andrew-street, Broad-street, Bloomsbury.
[W. y. Price 2d. A large sheet, containing a colored woodcut of the Building and a
description in French and English.]

Grandiose Exposition Nationale. 1851. Guide de l'Etranger à Londres, par
Crouch. Traduit de l'Anglais en Français par L. A. Cosson (de Nogaret),
Professeur de Langue et de Littérature Françaises à Londres, &c.: Enrichi
d'une magnifique Carte Géographique de la Métropole, disposée suivant un
Système entièrement nouveau. Ce Livre contient la Liste de tous les
principaux Hôtels Garnis, Auberges, Restaurans, Pensions Bourgeoises et
Tables d'hôtes, lieux d'Agrément, Etablissemens et Edifices Publics. Une
Description complète du Palais de Cristal, avec l'Indication des diverses
Directions par les Chemins de Fer et les Bateaux à Vapeur; le Tarif du Prix
des Courses en Cabriolets et Omnibus, en tous sens dans la Métropole, et dans
un Rayon de Quatre Milles de la Banque; les Résidences des Banquiers et
Changeurs à Londres, le Siège des Cours de Justice et d'Equité, des Bureaux
de Police, &c.
à Londres: Chez W. A. Crouch, Tudor Street, Blackfriars; W. & T. Piper, Paternoster Row; et
chez tous les Libraires de Londres et de Paris.
[W. y. Price 1s. 12mo, pp. xii., 210, with a View of the Crystal Palace; and a few pages,
104-112, descriptive of the Building and arrangements.]

Grand Mistake (The), v. Working Man's Papers.

Grand Exhibition of the Products and Manufactures, Arts and Sciences, of all
Nations
[Without Publisher's or Printer's name, or date. Folio, pp. 2. A Prospectus of "the
Visitor's Aid, Accommodation and Protection Society." A society which proposed to assist
"Foreigners and Provincialists" in finding lodgings. It is believed the undertaking never
went further than issuing its Prospectus.]

Grand National Exhibition (The). From the 'Derby Reporter' of May 31, 1850.
W. & W. Pike, Printers, Corn Market, Derby.
[W. y. Privately circulated. Folio, p. 1. Report of a Meeting held at Derby.]

Grand (The) Exhibition of 1851. (Suggested by a Speech at the Mansion-
House, March 21st, 1850.)
Andrews, Printer, Guildford.
[W. y. Circulated gratuitously. Small folio, p. 1. The verses are signed Martin F.
Tupper, Albury: Guildford, March 23rd.
"Hurrah! for honest Industry, hurrah! for handy Skill,
Hurrah! for all the wondrous works achieved by Wit and Will!
The triumph of the Artizan has come about at length,
And Kings and Princes flock to praise his comeliness and strength."]

Grand Procession of Her Majesty to Guildhall.
Paul, Printer, 18, Gt, St. Andrew-Street, Seven Dials.
[A long sheet of engravings relating to Her Majesty's Visit to the Guildhall Ball.]

⁰ Grand Procession of Her Majesty to the Exhibition.
D. Paul, Printer, 18 Great St. Andrew Street, Seven Dials.
[W. y. A long sheet of colored engravings.]

Grandville, J. J.; v. Comical People.

Grangé, E., v. English Exhibition Comédie-Vaudeville.

Granville, Earl, International Postage Association, v. Association.

Graphic Art, v. Brief Survey.

Graydon's Crusader Chess-men, and Table.
London: Reynell & Weight, Printers, Little Pulteney Street, Haymarket. 1851.
[Small 4to, pp. 32. Description of a new set of chess-men, with (pp. 20–32) an " Historical illustration of the Friezes of Ludwig Schwanthaler, in the panels of the Table." An Engraving of the Table is given.]

Gray, Hugh, C., v. Strangers' Guide to London.

Gray, J., v. Musings on the Exhibition. A Poem.

' Great Exhibition' Essay, dedicated by Permission to the Rt. Hon. The Earl of Shaftesbury, (till lately, Lord Ashley, M.P., for Bath) &c., &c., &c. *Reciprocity*, for 1851; or an 'Exhibition' of Humanity and Fraternity and Divinity. By the Rev. D. P. M. Hulbert, M.A., Cantab. Author of Treatises on Ordination, Education, Vectigalia, Emigration, Matrimony, Supremacy, Extreme Unction, &c., &c.
Quicquid agis, Cautio est adhibenda.
The Third issue, corrected.
Canterbury : Printed by Henry Chivers, Palace Street.
Published by Wertheim & Macintosh, Crockford, and Hatchards, *London :*
Simms, and Binns and Co., *Bath :* And may be had of the Author, or through any Bookseller, Price one shilling. One Shilling and six-pence free per Post.
[W. y. Post 8vo, pp. xii., 84.]

Great Exhibition of Doings in London for 1851. B. Clayton Inv, del et sculpsit.
London, Ackermann & Co. Strand, Dean & Son, Printers, 35, Threadneedle Street. Price 2s. 6d. plain, 5s. 6d. cold.
[W. y. An oblong sheet of facetious Engravings.]

Great Exhibition of Industry of All Nations, 1851. [Correspondence between Colonel Phipps and Mr. Drew.]
London: Printed by G. Barclay, Castle St Leicester Sq.
[W. y., but circulated gratuitously in 1849. 8vo, pp. 3.]

Great Exhibition of the Idleness of all Nations, v. Now open.

Great Exhibition of the Industry of All Nations (The), viewed in relation to Christianity. A Sermon preached to the Congregationalists of Wimborne Minster, on Sunday Evening, October 5th.; and in the Independent Chapel, at Bournemouth, on Tuesday Evening, October 21st., 1851, by the Rev. T. Flower. Second Edition. Published by Special Request.
London : Longman, Brown, Green, and Longmans, Paternoster Row.
Wimborne : A. Purkis, Printer, Bookseller, &c. 1851. Price Fourpence.
[8vo, pp. 17. Printed by Mr. Purkis, at Wimborne.]

Great Exhibition of the Works of Industry of All Nations, to be opened in Hyde Park, London, 1st May, 1851. [Extracts from Speeches made at Meeting at the Mansion House, London, on 25th Jan. 1850.]
[Without Publisher's or Printer's name, or date. Circulated gratuitously. 8vo, pp. 4.]

Great Exhibition of 1851 (The): A Poem. By William St. Clair.
London : Partridge and Oakey, Paternoster Row ; and 70, Edgware Road, (Hanbury and Co., Agents). 1850
[Price 6d. Post 8vo, pp. 10. Mr. St. Clair was for some time working upon the Building in the employment of Messrs. Fox and Henderson.
" The careful, tender, unassuming bard,
   Whose honest heart with conscious virtue burns,
   Sends not, with this, his fashionable card—
   (In this strange world sure we must take our turns,
   And want of cards the music never mourns.)
   But, noble Albert, you're a *Man* I ween,
   Such as would please my *sampler*, poet Burns,—
   With whom, in converse, I have ever been,
   Since first his matchless muse gave lustre to my e'en ! "]

Great Exhibition of 1851 (The). [Observations from a London Manufacturer.] Extracted from the Times of Friday, May 24th 1850.
[John Wilson, Printer, 18, Charles-street, Middlesex-hospital. W. y. Privately circulated. 8vo, pp. 4. The Writer gives it as his opinion that "It must be of incalculable advantage to our designers and manufacturers to have the opportunity of studying for four months, at their convenience, the best productions of other countries, without having to incur the loss of time and expenses of travelling and sojourning in the capitals of various European nations. Surely this is an advantage difficult to estimate too highly."]

Great Exhibition of 1851 (The); or, The Wealth of the World in its workshops. Comparing the relative skill of the Manufacturers, Designers, and Artizans of England with that of France, Belgium, Prussia, and other Continental States. By Philoponos.
London: Edward Churton, 26, Holles Street. 1850. Price 2s. 6d.
[8vo, pp. v. 139. "In the following pages, we shall endeavour to illustrate the importance of art as applied to manufacturing industry, and to show the extent to which it has already been applied, by comparing the skilled productions of England with those of the continent, in order that the aim of the *Exposition* may be clearly understood by every intelligent class of the community." Another edition, with the Author's name, will be found under World.]

⁰ Great Exhibition, 1851.
'Praise the Lord all ye nations.'—*Psalm* cxvii. 1.
Entered at Stationers' Hall, July 3, 1851.
Billing and Son, Bermondsey St.
[W. y. Large broadside. A hymn, signed "William Burgess."
"Thou great Exhibiter of pow'r,
By whom the world's huge structure bore;
Here may our eyes with wonder scan
The knowledge thou hast giv'n to man."]

⁰ Great Exhibition, 1851 (The).
London: Published by H. Beal, 3 Shoe Lane, Fleet Street.
[W. y. A Broadside.]

Great Exhibition Prize Essay (The), by the Rev. J. C. Whish, M.A., Incumbent of Trinity Church, East Peckham, Kent. Adjudicators. The Rev. Richard Michell, B.D., *Public Orator of the University of Oxford.* The Rev. Robert Walker, M.A. F.R.S., *Reader of Experimental Philosophy, Oxford.* Donor. The Rev. J. A. Emerton, D.D., *Hanwell College, Middlesex.*
London: Longman, Brown, Green and Longmans. 1851.
[Price 2s. 6d. Post 8vo, pp. xx, 87. "This effort to show in what respect the union of All Nations is calculated to promote the moral and religious welfare of mankind; and thus conduce to the Glory of God," is dedicated to Prince Albert and the Royal Commissioners.]

'Great Exhibition' Spiritualized (The). By the Rev. Henry Birch.
'Love God, love truth, love virtue, & be happy.'—*Pollock.*
Fourteenth Edition. London: John Snow, 35, Paternoster Row. 1853.
[Price 6d. 18mo, pp. 72. "The 'Crystal Palace' itself is a monument of human ingenuity without a parallel!"]

⁰ Great Exhibition, Suggestive and Anticipative (The). By the Rev. John Cumming, D.D., Minister of the National Scotch Church, Crown Court, Covent Garden; Author of 'Voices of the Day,' 'Voices of the Night,' 'Christ receiving Sinners,' etc., etc.
London: John Farquhar Shaw, 27, Southampton Row, Russell Square, and Paternoster Row. 1851.
[Price 1s. Small 8vo, pp. 67. "I hail the occurrence as an augury of good. I hail it as a means under God of helping onward the victory, the triumph, and the reign of peace."]

Great Exhibition (The); Analogies and Suggestions: A Sermon, preached in the Congregational Chapel, Esher-street, Kennington, on Sunday Evening, the 23d of March, 1851. By William Leask.
London: Benjamin L. Green, 62, Paternoster-Row. 1851.
[Price 6d. 18mo, pp. 34. "But for all this, probabilities are in favour of the idea that this Great Exhibition will, upon the whole, realise the expectation of its projectors."]

Great Exhibition (The), and London in 1851. Reviewed by Dr. Lardner, &c.
London: Longman, Brown, Green, and Longmans. 1852.
[Price 14s. Post 8vo, pp. xxviii, 630. Annexed to the reviews and essays of Dr. Lardner, which first appeared in "The Times," are translations of a Lecture (443–476) on the "Comparison of the Industry of Paris and London," addressed by the Baron C. Dupin to his class, at the Conservatoire des Arts et Metiers; and "a selection of Reviews published in the 'Journal des Débats,' by MM. Michel Chevalier, John Lemoinne, and Hector Berlioz." Dr. Lardner's work treats of scientific subjects in connection with the Exhibition.]

Great Exhibition (The). A New Song: to an old Tune.
[Without Publisher's or Printer's name, or date. Royal 8vo, pp. 4.
" With the whitest of chalk mark the beam for to-day,
To bear ever in mind—till with time brush'd away:
We've now not lived in vain; for, this day, by permission,
We have seen The World's Wonder—THE GREAT EXHIBITION."]

Great Exhibition (The), An Opportunity to promote the Glory of God: A Sermon,
preached at the Parish Church of St. Nicholas, Rochester, on Sunday, May 4,
1851. By the Rev. W. Conway, M.A., Curate. Published by Request.
London: Wertheim and Macintosh, 24, Paternoster Row. *Rochester:* W. Shadbolt. 1851.
[Price 3*d.* 12mo, pp. 22. " It was indeed a blessed contrast to the impiety of Belshazzar,
surrounded by the splendour of an eastern court, 'lifting up himself against the God of
heaven,' 'and praising the gods of gold, of silver, of brass, and of iron, of wood, and of stone,'
when our beloved and honoured Queen stood in the midst of that silent multitude, and our
venerable Archbishop, * * * implored the benediction of our common LORD upon this nation,
and on all the kindreds of the human family."]

°Great Exhibition (The): A Poetical Rhapsody. In six parts:—1. The Spirit of the
Age. 2. The Palace of Glass. 3. Industrial Art. 4. The Gathering of the
Nations. 5. The Trees in the Transept. 6. Anticipated Good. By a Visitor.
'It will be obvious, even on a cursory glance at the large collection of
articles exhibited by the Manufacturers of Sheffield, that the reputation of a
place which has acquired a world-wide renown for the excellency of its Cut-
ting Instruments, is admirably sustained.'—*Hunt's Hand Book to the Official
Catalogues.*
Sheffield: Printed by J. Pearce, Jun., 24, High-Street. 1851. Price One Shilling.
[8vo, pp. 45. Dedicated to the Master Cutlers of Sheffield; the Merchants, Manufac-
turers, Artizans, the ' Local Commissioners,' and other inhabitants of Hallamshire, and
printed by " J. Pearce, Jun., Printer, High Street, Sheffield."
" The men of Truth, who here have met,
As friends, from Lands afar,
Their brotherhood can ne'er forget,
In Commerce, Peace, or War—"]

Great Exhibition (The). A Sermon, preached on Sunday, May 4th, 1851. By H.
W. Burrows, B.D. Perpetual Curate of Christ Church, St. Pancras. Pub-
lished by Request. Second Edition.
London. Skeffington and Southwell, 192 Piccadilly, 1851.
[Price 6*d.* 12mo, pp. 22.]

Great Exhibition (The), Here and Hereafter. Second Edition, Price One penny.
Wertheim and Macintosh, 24, Paternoster-Row, *London.*
[W. y. 16mo, pp. 16. A religious Tract.]

Great Exhibition (The): Its Dangers and Duties. Two Sermons, Preached in
York Street Chapel, Walworth, on Sabbath Day, April 27th, 1851. By the
Rev. George Clayton.
London: Benjamin L. Green, 62, Paternoster Row; Burrowes, Penton Row, Walworth Road; and
the Booksellers.
[W. y. Price 6*d.* 12mo, pp. 36, including a third sermon "On the ENCOURAGEMENTS
and ADVANTAGES connected with the Great Exhibition," and paged continuously.]

Great Exhibition (The); Its Palace, and its Principal Contents. With Notices of
the Public Buildings of the Metropolis, Places of Amusements, etc. By
Roberts Stephenson. With Illustrations.
London: George Routledge and Co., Soho Square. 1851
[Price 1*s.* 12mo, pp. iv. and 220. Gives an account of Industrial Exhibitions and Con-
tents of the Crystal Palace (pp. 1–171). The author's name is presumed to be fictitious.]

Great Exhibition (The) of the Works of Industry of All Nations, to be opened in
Hyde Park, London, on the 1st day of May, 1851. President: H. R. H. The
Prince Albert, K.G., &c., &c., &c. [Report of a meeting at Marylebone.]
London: printed by Harrison and Son, St. Martin's Lane.
[W. y. Circulated gratuitously. 8vo, pp. 8.]

Great Exhibition (The). The Times Reprint of the Plan and Description published
on the 1st and 2d of May. Price 3*d.*
[Printed and published at the offices in Printing-house-square and Glass-house-yard, near Apothe-
caries hall, Blackfriars, London, by John Joseph Lawson, printer, of Tottenham Cottage,
Downshire-hill, Hampstead, in the County of Middlesex.—Monday, May 5, 1851. Folio, 2 sides.]

Great Exhibition, *v.* Reminiscences of the, or Annales Facetiarum.

Great Exhibition 'Wot is to Be' (The) or Probable Results of the Industry of All Nations in the year '51. Showing what is to be exhibited; Who is to exhibit it in short, How its all going to be done. By Vates Secundus (who can see thro' a stone wall as well as his neighbours.)

Oh ! my prophetic soul—my uncle !—(Shakspeare).

Pledged to do it.   George Aug: Sala inv. et sculpt.
London. – Published by the Committee of the Society for keeping things in their places, 1850.
[Price 2s. 6d. An oblong sheet of facetious engravings.]

⁰Great Foreign Bazaar (No. 2.) for the Sham Free-Trade Festival, in 1851.
[Printed by Arthur Wallis, Brighton; and sold by Fellowes, No. 55, Fleet Street, London, and by Grant, Castle Square, Brighton, News Agents W. y. Price One Half-penny. 8vo, pp. 4. Signed Thalaba. "If these be valid arguments, which I maintain them to be, against the 'utility' of such 'shows' as the National Repository, with how much greater cogency may they be urged against the preposterous scheme of a national subscription (free-will offerings obtained by an organized system of intimidation) for the purpose of raising a huge bazaar for foreign ' laborious trifles or useless novelties,' in the most fashionable quarter of London."]

Great Glass House, v. Stone the First at.

Great Glass House Opened (The); or the Exhibition Wot is ! ! With a good deal of what isn't—but what ought to have been.—The Front and The Back The Outside and The Inside The Beginning, the Middle, and The End   The whole forming a complete facetious Guide to the Fair by G. A. Sala.
' Peace and goodwill with all the world.'
London, Published by the Compy. of Painters & Glaziers. 1851.
[Price 5s. 6d. An oblong sheet.]

Great Go (The)—A Broad Farce in many acts which will be performed by Her Majesty's Servants, on the 1st of May, 1851.
[Without Publisher's or Printer's name, or date. Folio, pp. 4. A lithograph, personally attacking the principal officers of the Exhibition.]

Great Humbug (The) of 1851.
[Without Publisher's or Printer's name, year, or price. Royal 8vo, pp. 3. "Bull! you are a great fool: but if you allow yourself to be bamfoozled by this barefaced imposition, this impudent job, this conspiracy of art-manufacturers—who can't sell their trumpery wares, then I say, and I say it with the highest respect for your many virtues, that you are a greater fool than I took you for." It is signed Thalaba Academicus, and dated May 1st, 1850. There appear to have been two issues, as copies differ in the language.]

Great Industrial Exhibition of 1851 (The) : Its Importance to the Working Classes. Reprinted from John Cassell's Weekly Publication 'The Working Man's Friend:' Established for the instruction and Elevation of the Working Classes of Great Britain.
London: John Cassell, 335, Strand.
[W. y. Price 2d. 8vo, pp. 24. "The Exhibition will be a kind of universal school. Every one that goes there will come away wiser. * * * The temple rises by the addition of fresh materials; the body grows from new supplies of nutriment, and the mind enlarges itself by appropriating enlightened and instructive thoughts."]

Great Industrial Exhibition of 1851 (The). To the Mayor of Bradford.
Printed from the Bradford Observer, by Wm. Byles, Kirkgate.
[W. y. Royal 8vo, p. 1. A letter signed John Horsfall, and dated Bradford, Yorkshire, July 16, 1850. "I cannot but express my opinion that the tradesmen and shopkeepers, and householders in London, will be great gainers by the immense sums which of necessity will be spent there, solely by reason of the Exhibition, and which sums I cannot estimate at less than several millions sterling, and which should induce them, I think, to give up the odd 20 acres of Hyde Park for twenty-two months, not for the Prince, but for the use of the artists, producers, manufacturers, merchants, and seamen of Great Britain and of the World, at the Prince's powerful request, and not to forget they are granting this boon, not of their own property, but of the property of the Woods and Forests—of the nation at large."]

Great International Exhibition, appointed to take place in London, 1851. An accurate view of the Great Pavilion, as now in course of Erection, from the Plan of Mr. Paxton. Description of the Building, with all the necessary information for the Exhibitor and Spectator ; together with the Speech of H. R. H. Prince Albert.   Contents. View of the ' Crystal Palace.'   1. Prefatory Remarks. 2. The Great Exhibition of 1851. 3. Prince Albert's Speech. 4. The Local Committees. 5. Description of the Building. 6. Mr. Paxton's History of the Building.

Building. 7. The Dignity of Labour. 8. The Sections. 9. The Mineral Produce. 10. The Vegetable Kingdom. 11. Animal Productions. 12. Inventions in Machinery and Models. 13. Manufactures. 14. The Fine Arts. 15. Accommodation of Visitors. 16. Public Amusements.

Glasgow: Thomas Murray & Son, 8, Argyle Street. *London*: J. Clayton, Jr., 265, Strand.—*Edinburgh*: Oliver & Boyd. And sold by all Booksellers. 1851.
[Price Twopence. 24mo, pp. 24. With a song entitled "The Glorious Exhibition," by Andrew Park, author of 'The Rocky Deep,' 'Home of my Fathers,' etc.]

° Great Job of 1851 (The). [signed] Thalaba.
Percival, Typ., 62, Piccadilly, corner of Albemarle Street.
[W. y. 4to, p. 1. "Fellow Countrymen!—workers, either with head or hands, who take an interest in securing for honest English industry its just reward—grant me, I pray, a few moments' attention while I inflate this great bubble of 1851, till it burst, and be resolved into its primitive *lixivium* of soap and water."]

Great National Exhibition of 1851 (The): A description of the Building now erecting in Hyde Park by Messrs. Fox and Henderson, from designs by Mr. Paxton.
London: H. G. Clarke, and Co., 4, Exeter Change. Price One Penny.
[W. y. 12mo, pp. 12, with three illustrations and a ground-plan.]

° Great National Exhibition of 1851. Mons. Parent's Cosmopolitan Key, in Six Languages. Entered at Stationers' Hall. Price One Shilling. N.B. This List will be found indispensable to every Coffee House to assist the Foreigner to point out whatever he may require.
London: Printed & Published by John Shorman, English and Foreign Printer, 196, Piccadilly, next St. James's Church.
[W. y., a large sheet with phrases in English, French, German, Italian, Spanish, and Portuguese, in parallel columns.]

Great National Exhibition, *v.* Descriptive Account.

Great Sights: A discourse delivered in Kingsland Chapel, on the Sabbath Evening preceding the opening of the Great Exhibition. By the Rev. Thomas Aveling, Minister of the Place.
London: Snow, Paternoster Row; Gurney, Kingsland; and Turner, Hackney.
[W. y. Price 6d. 16mo, pp. 32.]

Greeley, Horace, *v.* Glances at Europe.

* Greenhorns of the Exhibition.
Macdonald. Clerkenwell.

Green House of 1851, a Sling & a Stone, *v.* John Bull—Mirror of the Time.

Green, Joseph Henry, *v.* Reports by the Juries.

Greville, *v.* Answer to 'What is to become of the Crystal Palace?'

Greyt Eggshibishun, *v.* Ful.

Griffiths, Thomas, *v.* Chemistry of the Crystal Palace.

Groom, R. S., *v.* Philp's Illustrations.

Gropius, C., *v.* Amtlicher Bericht.

Grossbritannien und Deutschland auf der Industrie-Ausstellung zu London, *v.* Zeitschrift für die gesammte Staatswissenschaft.

Grosse (Das) Industrie-Ausstellungs-Gebäude in London. Inhalt: Seite 1-4, Beschreibung. Tafel Nr. I. Perspectivische Ansicht. Tafel Nr. II. Ebenerdiger Grundriss, Quer-Profil und Façaden. Tafel Nr. III. Grundriss der Galerie und Grundriss des mittleren Aufbaues. Tafel Nr. IV-VI. Constructions-Details. Nach den Mittheilungen des Architecten Herrn Ch. Fowler, jun. in London bearbeitet. Separat-Abdruck aus L. Förster's "Allgemeiner Bauzeitung."
Wien. Verlag von L. Förster's artistischer Anstalt. 1851.
[Price R 2. 20 sgr. Folio, pp. 4, besides the engravings.]

Gruner, Ludwig, *v.* Amtlicher Bericht.

Guiana, *v.* British.

Guide (A) for Visitors to the Great Exhibition of 1851. Gilbert's New Map of London, from actual Survey. With References to Public Offices, Inns of Court, Theatres, and Exhibiting the Routes of Omnibuses, Railway Stations, &c. Price Sixpence.
Liverpool: Published by George Philip and Son.
London: J. Gilbert, 49, Paternoster Row. *Edinburgh:* Oliver and Boyd. *Dublin:* Wm. Robertson.
Glasgow: Griffin and Co.
[W. y. 16mo. An exterior view of the Building on the cover.]

° Guide (A) to the Great Exhibition, showing at one view, the principal objects of attraction, with a list of Amusements open free. Price Twopence. Entered at Stationer's Hall.
E. Ward, 54, Paternoster Row, *London.*
[W. y. Sm. square, pp. 20.]

Guide à Londres et dans ses Environs. Itinéraire Officiel des Chemins de Fer Français, Anglais, Belge et Rhenan; Paquebots a Vapeur. Publié sous le Patronage de la Compagnie du Chemin de Fer du Nord. Suivi d'une Notice sur l'Exposition 1851. Prix: un Franc.
Lille, Imprimerie de L Danel, Grand Place, 1851.
[8vo. pp. 141, xvi.]

Guide Book to the Industrial Exhibition; with Facts, Figures, and Observations on the Manufactures and Produce Exhibited.
London: Partridge and Oakey, Paternoster-Row, and 70, Edgeware Road (Hanbury and Co., Agents). 1851
[Price 1s. Post 8vo, pp. 166. Contains a large number of engravings of articles exhibited.]

Guide-Chaix. Nouveau Guide à Londres pour l'Exposition de 1851 avec deux belles Cartes coloriées.
Paris Librairie Centrale des Chemins de Fer de Napoléon Chaix et Cie, Rue Bergère, 20, près du Boulevart Montmartre.
Londres P. A. Delizy et Cie, Libraires et Agents de Publicité, 13, Regent Street. 1851.
[Price 2 francs. 8vo, pp. xii., 372. Contains a large View of the Exterior of the Building, with a ground-plan of the division of space, a Map of London, and an account, pp. 1–33, of the Exhibition.]

Guide de l'Etranger à Londres comprenant: une Notice Sommaire sur le Palais de Cristal: sa Construction, sa Distribution, ses Divisions Principales, sa Physionomie Générale.—Itinéraire du Voyageur a Londres: les Monumens Anciens et Modernes, les Spectacles, les Établissemens Publics, les Exhibitions. —Conseils et Indications a l'usage des Etrangers. Avec un Plan de Londres gravé sur acier.
Havre Imprimerie de H. Brindeau et Ce. 1851.
[Price 1 franc. 12mo, pp. 96. The first twenty-four pages are devoted to an account of the Exhibition.]

Guide de l'Etranger a Londres, Crouch, *v.* Grandiose Exposition Nationale.

Guide de l'Exposition Universelle. Par E. Heine, Professeur d'Allemand, etc., 43 King Street, Soho, Londres.
Londres: Imprimerie de Reynell et Weight, 16 Little Pulteney Street, Haymarket.
[W. y. Price 8d. A large sheet, on which is printed the names of a number of articles exhibited. They are placed so as to form a sort of ground-plan. There are also editions in English and German; *v.* Key and Schlüssel.]

Guide de Londres, par Kelly. Comprenant une Description Progressive de la Grande Capitale, et de tous les Instituts Nationaux, Édifices Publics, Théâtres, Musées, Panoramas, et autres lieux d'Amusements. En Registré à Stationers' Hall.
à Londres: Chez W. Kent & Cie., Paternoster Row, et chez tous les Libraires.
[W. y. Price 6d. pp. 48, with a Map. This was a French edition of Kelly's Guide. A German translation also appeared. *v.* Kelly.]

Guide du Catalogue Officiel. Synopsis, ou Revue Sommaire des Produits de l'Industrie de l'Exposition Universelle de 1851. Par Robert Hunt, Archiviste des Mines. Traduit par F. Hilaire D'Arcis.
Londres:

Londres: Spicer Frères, & W. Clowes et Fils; Editeurs Privilégiés des Catalogues Officiels, 29, New Bridge Street, Blackfriars, & à Hyde Park. Prix: sixpence.
[W. y., but published in 1851. Small 8vo, pp. vi., 96. A French edition of the Synopsis published by Mr. Hunt, *v.* Companion.]

Guide du Visiteur à Londres, (avec Plan de la Métropole,) Recueil Complet de tous les Documens, Matériaux, Informations, relatifs à la Capitale de la Grande Bretagne, indispensable à tout Voyageur ou Etranger désirant connaître Londres dans tous ses Détails, ses Localités, ses Monumens, ses Formalités, ses Amusemens, et ses Ressources, avant et pendant son Séjour à Londres à l'Occasion de la Grande Exposition de 1851; suivi du "Dimanche à Londres;" ou, Excursions dans les Environs. Par Delepine. Edition Française.
Publiée a Londres: Par James Gilbert, 49 Paternoster Row. Prix, 2s. broché; 2s. 6d. relié. Edition Anglaise et Allemande.
[W. y. 18mo, pp. iv., 258, with a View of the Building. Three pages, 64–66, contain information respecting the Exhibition. English and German Editions appear under Gilbert's Visitor's Guide and Fremdenführer.]

Guide du Voyageur à Londres et dans ses Environs pendant l'Exposition Universelle, comprenant: 1° Une notice détaillée de Londres, ses monuments, ses curiosités, ses institutions, ses amusements, ses théâtres, ses jardins; 2° L'indication des hôtels, maisons garnies, logements, cafés, restaurants, etc., etc.; 3° L'indication des chemins de fer, bateaux à vapeur, diligences, voitures de places, omnibus, avec le tarif; 4° L'indication des frais de séjour. Précédé d'un itinéraire de Paris à Londres par les chemins de fer et les bateaux à vapeur, avec l'indication des prix et la durée du trajet. Nouvelle Edition, ornée d'un Panorama de Londres colorié; d'une vue du Palais de l'Exposition; du Plan intérieur de l'édifice et de jolies gravures sur acier. Par Lake et Richard.
Paris. L. Maison, Editeur des *Guides-Richard*, 3, Rue Christine. 1851.
[Price 2 francs 50 cents. 8vo, pp. xxx., 275. Pages xxiv to xxx are devoted to the Exhibition of 1851.]

Guide du Voyageur a Londres Précédé d'un Itinéraire historique et descriptif des Chemins de fer de Paris à Londres Ouvrage Illustré de 100 Vignettes dessinées d'après nature de cartes et de plans Deuxième Edition.
Paris Librairie de L. Hachette et Cie Rue Pierre-Sarrazin, No. 14.
[W. y. Post 8vo, pp. 239. Pages 215–223 contain an account of the Exhibition with two woodcuts.]

Guide Illustré du Voyageur a Londres et aux Environs précédé d'une Description Historique des Villes, Bourgs, Villages et Sites sur le Parcours des Chemins de Fer de Paris a Londres orné de 100 Vignettes dessinées sur les lieux par MM. Daubigny et Freemann accompagné de Cartes et Plans Gravés par P. Tardieu et Erhard.
Paris Ernest Bourdin, Editeur, 49, Rue de Seine.
Londres W. Thomas et Churchill, 19–21 Catherine Street (Strand). Chez tous les Libraires de la France et de l'Etranger et dans tous les Embarcadères des Chemins de Fer.
[Price 2s. 6d. W. y. 12mo, pp. 240, with two Views of the Building, a Ground-Plan, and a short description, pp. 215–223, of the arrangements and opening ceremony.]

Guide of Guides (The), for Strangers and Foreigners in London during 1851. To which is added, the Royal Albert Hand Map of London, which requires no folding, and by which the Stranger can at once tell what part of London he may be in. Also, besides the usual information, Value of Foreign Money in London, the Squares East and West of Regent-Street,—the Half-way Fares by Omnibus,—Cab Fares, Omnibus and Steam-boat Guide, &c. The French is given at page 53. Entered at Stationers' Hall
London: John Field, 65, Regent's Quadrant, Corner of Air Street. Price One Shilling.
[W. y. 18mo, pp. iv., 74. Has no other relation to the Exhibition than the title shows.]

Guide through London, *v.* Harthill's—Royal Exhibition.

Guide to London, *v.* English.

Guide to the Exhibition, *v.* Popular Guide.

Guide to the Great Exhibition (A); containing a description of every Principal
   Object of Interest.   With a Plan, Pointing out the easiest and most systematic
   way of examining the Contents of the Crystal Palace.   Twentieth Thousand.
   With an Index.
   London : George Routledge and Co., Soho Square.   1851.
      [Price 1*s.* 12mo, pp. viii. and 231.   "Its object is to supply an obvious deficiency in the
      existing Catalogues, namely, the *whereabouts* of some of the most striking and interesting
      articles exhibited."]

Guildhall, *v.* Brief Historical Account of—Grand Procession to.

Gwynne, J. Stuart, *v.* Centrifugal Pumps.

Haghe, Louis, *v.* Dickensons' Comprehensive Pictures.

Hall, Herbert Byng, *v.* West of England.

Hamilton, Rev. Dr., *v.* Forty-four Sermons.

Hamilton, Rev. R., *v.* Forty-four Sermons.

Hammersley, J. A., On the Preparations on the Continent, *v.* Address.

Hammond, W. Parker, *v.* Two Premiums for Essays.

Handbook Guide, *v.* Petters's.

Handbook of Architectural Ornament (The), illustrating and explaining The
   Various Styles of Decoration employed in the Great Exhibition of 1851; and
   intended as a Guide to Designers and Draughtsmen.   By W. Gibbs, Ornamental Engraver, 22, Elizabeth Street South, Pimlico.
   London : Ackermann & Co., 96, Strand.   1851.   Price Half-a-crown.
      [8vo, pp. vi., 56, with numerous illustrations.   "The following pages have been designed
      for the instruction of the *Workman* by appealing to the eye through the media of pictorial
      representations, and at the same time arresting attention by simply-worded descriptions."]

Hand Guide to London, *v.* Registered.

Handkerchiefs, Pocket, *v.* Engravings on Cotton—Engravings on Silk.

Harman, F. M., *v.* Catalogue Officiel.

Harrel, Thomas, *v.* Holmes's Great Metropolis.

Harris, John, *v.* Tit for Tat.

Harrison, Rev. J. C., *v.* Forty-four Sermons.

Harthills' Guide through London, and to the Industrial·Exhibition.   Accompanied
   with a Splendid Map of London, and views of the Interior and Exterior of the
   Crystal Palace.   Price One Shilling.
   London : Effingham Wilson, Royal Exchange;
   Edinburgh : John Harthill & Son; and all Booksellers.
      [W. y. 12mo, pp. viii., 120.   Pages 1–23 contain an account of the Exhibition.   Printed
      at Edinburgh by John Harthill and Son, Anchor Close.]

Hartwich, Ober-Baurath, *v.* Amtlicher Bericht.

Harvey, Daniel Whittle, *v.* Report of the Number of Vehicles.

H., A. W., *v.* Proposal for Erecting a Monument to Shakespeare.

Hawkins, Rev. Ernest, *v.* Jubilee Year—Verses for 1851.

Health of the Metropolis (The) during the year of the Great Exhibition.
   London : Salisbury and Co., Printers, Bouverie-Street and Primrose-Hill, Fleet-Street.
      [W. y. Privately circulated. Imperial 8vo, pp. 11. " By the author of ' The Philosopher's
      Mite.' (Reprinted from the February number of ' Tait's Edinburgh Magazine.') "]

Heeren, Prof. Dr., *v.* Amtlicher Bericht.

Heilige Schrift und der Sabbath, *v.* Anrede.

Heine, E., *v.* Key to the Great Exhibition—Guide de l'Exposition—Schlüssel.

Henning, *v.* House that Albert Built.

Hensman, Henry, *v.* Lectures [Civil Engineering].

Herbert, J. R., *v.* Department of Practical Art.

Here and Hereafter, *v.* Great Exhibition.

Héretique Friere, *v.* Prophecie.

Hermann, Dr. Von, *v.* Amtlicher Bericht.

Herrmann, Professor, *v.* Bericht über die englische Landwirthschaft.

Higginson, Francis, *v.* Koh-i-Noor.

Higginson, Rev. Edward, *v.* World Embracing Truth.

Hinton, Rev. J. H., *v.* Forty-four Sermons.

Historia, *v.* To-morrow.

Historical Account of Skins and Furs. Brief History of Furs & the Fur Trade, their Statistics and Use. Compiled for general information, with a Description of the Collection Exhibited by Messrs. Nicholay & Son, in the Great Industrial Exhibition. Including hints for the Preservation of Furs. By J. A. Nicholay, Chairman for Class XVI. Local Commissioner for the Borough of Marylebone, and Juror for Textile Manufactures Group C.
   London : 82, Oxford Street, nearly facing the Pantheon. 1851.
      [Privately circulated. 8vo, pp. 32. " This little work, compiled by the author, *con, amore,* has been put together, and may, it is hoped, be found useful as a book of reference when the Great Exhibition, which called it into existence, shall have ceased to exist."]

History of the Great Exhibition, *v.* Journal.

Hlubek, Dr. Fr. X., *v.* Bericht über die englische Landwirthschaft.

Hofmann, Professor A. W., *v.* Amtlicher Bericht.

Hofman, Dr. A. W., *v.* Reports by the Juries.

Holland, Joseph, *v.* Reports by the Juries.

Holmes's Great Metropolis: or, Views and History of London in the nineteenth Century. Being a Grand National Exhibition of the British Capital. With historical and typographical notices of each place. Edited by William Gray Fearnside, Esq., and Thomas Harrel. Illustrated with fifty splendid steel engravings.
    [*London :* Published by Thomas Holmes, (Successor to Edward Lacey,) Great Book Establishment, 76, St. Paul's Churchyard. W. y. Price 7s. 6d. Royal 8vo, pp. 211. Contains a view of the Exhibition Building, and nothing else relating to the Exhibition.]

Home Circle (The). A Weekly Family Magazine of Literature, Science, Domestic Economy, Arts, Practical Information, Needlework, Chess, General Knowledge, and Entertainment. No. 82—Vol. 4. Saturday, January 25, 1851. Double Number Twopence. Stamped, 3d.; Montbly Parts, 6d. Containing a Guide to London, in Three Languages—English, French, and German.
   London : Printed and Published by W. S. Johnson, 'Nassau Steam Press,' 60, St. Martin's Lane, where back numbers, volumes, and cases for binding may always be had, and where all communications for the Editor, Pierce Egan, are to be addressed.
    [Royal 8vo. The "Guide is numbered separately, pp. 1–16, and contains a view of the Building, with a short account of the Exhibition. The French title will be found under Bref.]

Honour to Labour, a Lay of 1851. By the Lady Emmeline Stuart Wortley.
   London : W. N. Wright, Bookseller to the Queen, 60, Pall Mall.
    [W. y. Price 5s. 8vo, pp. 78.
       " Hail! All Salutations, Labour,—Health and wealth and Praise to thee,
        Oh! how rightly art thou glorified, 'midst the Gallant and the Free,
        But *thou* in thy mid-triumph join, in another mightier strain,
        Hush—hush! and hearken to that sound, like the storm-voice of the main."]

Hooker, Dr. J. D., *v.* Reports by the Juries.

Horeau, Hector, *v.* Crystal Palace, its Architectural History.

Horsfall, John, Letter to Mayor of Bradford, *v.* Great Industrial Exhibition.

Household Words, *v.* Catalogue's Account of Itself.

Household Words.

> '*Familiar in their Mouths as Household Words.*'—*Shakespeare.*

A Weekly Journal.   Conducted by Charles Dickens.   N°. 43 [and] N°. 74. Price 2*d.*

[Published at the Office, No. 16, Wellington Street North, Strand. Printed by Bradbury & Evans, Whitefriars, *London.* 1851. Royal 8vo. No. 43 contains an article entitled " The Private History of the Palace of Glass:" and No. 74 an article entitled "The Catalogue's Account of Itself," which was afterwards separately printed, *v.* Catalogue.]

House that Albert Built (The) illustrated by Henning

Sold by G. Vickers, Strand, and all Booksellers. [Price Sixpence.]

[W. y. 4to, pp. 16, with woodcuts. Series of verses, illustrated by facetious cuts, in opposition to the Exhibition.

> *Britannia,* last, her offering presents,
> By king of the forest fitly upborne,
> A machine of sovereign power,
> To weed out all tares from a country's corn :]

House that Paxton Built (The).   A new story on an old model.

London : Darton and Co., Holborn Hill. 1851.

[Price 6*d.* coloured. Royal 8vo, pp. 15, with engravings.

> " Here's Mr. Paxton, remarkable man !
> Who built the bright palace, and thought of the plan "]

House that Paxton Built (The), by G. A. S.   George Sala.

London : Ironbrace, Woodenhead, & Co. Glasshouse Street. 1851.

[Published by Messrs. Ackermann. W. y. Price 2*s.* 6*d.* A long folded sheet of colored facetious engravings and explanations.]

Howarth, Rev. Henry, *v.* Sermon.

How to see the Exhibition.   In Four Visits.   By William Blanchard Jerrold.

London : Bradbury and Evans, 11, Bouverie Street. 1851.

[Price 2*s.*, square 16mo. 1st visit, pp. 58; 2nd visit, pp. 52; 3rd visit, pp. 51; 4th visit, pp. 52.]

Hughes, Julio Henry, *v.* World's Fair.

Hulbert, Rev. D. P. M., *v.* Great Exhibition Essay.

Hülsse, Prof. Dr., *v.* Amtlicher Bericht.

Humphreys, Henry Noel, *v.* Ten Centuries of Art.

Humphreys, William, *v.* Clarke's Critical Catalogue.

Hundred Languages, *v.* Memorial.

Hunt, Robert, *v.* Art-Journal Illustrated Catalogue [Science and the Exhibition]— Companion to Official Catalogue—' Guide '—Hunt's Handbook.

Hunt's Hand-Book to the Official Catalogues : an Explanatory Guide to the Natural Productions and Manufactures of the Great Exhibition of the Industry of All Nations, 1851.   Edited by Robert Hunt, Keeper of Mining Records, Author of ' Researches on Light,' ' The Poetry of Science,' ' Synopsis,' &c. &c.   Vol. 1. [Vol. 2.]

London : Spicer Brothers, and W. Clowes & Sons, Contractors to the Royal Commission, 29, New Bridge-Street, Blackfriars, and at Hyde Park.

[W. y. Price 6*s.* 18mo, Vol. 1, pp. viii., 1 to 476. Vol. 2, viii , 477 to 948.]

* Hussard, Hippolyte sur l'Exposition de Londres.

Guillamenin 14 Rue Richelieu.

[8vo, pp. 12. Advertised in Journal de la Librarie.]

Hyde Park, *v.* A l'Etranger dans—To a Stranger in.

Hymn (A) for All Nations.   1851.   By M. F. Tupper, D.C.L., F.R.S., Author of ' Proverbial Philosophy.'   Translated into Thirty Languages. [nearly Fifty versions.]   The Music Composed expressly by S. Sebastian Wesley, Mus. Doc.

London : Printed by Thomas Brettell, Rupert Street, Haymarket; and sold by Thomas Hatchard, 187, Piccadilly; and all Booksellers.

[W. y. Price 3*s.* 8vo, pp. 70. The various versions are all by different authors. " On the whole, I trust that this Polyglot Hymn may prove indeed to be an ' Essay to do good.' Few and simple as the results may seem, they have been gained by no small pains and per-

severance.

severance. At the lowest, they constitute a philological curiosity; so many minds, with such diversity in similitude, rendering literally into thirty languages one plain Psalm: at the highest, this plain Psalm, so multiplied and varied, is a world-wide Call to Man to render thanks to GOD."

> " Glorious God ! on Thee we call,
> Father, Friend, and Judge of all ;
> Holy Saviour, heavenly King,
> Homage to Thy throne we bring !"]

Hymn for the Great Exhibition of Industry of all Nations. By Edward West.
London: Partridge and Oakey, Paternoster Row; and 70, Edgware Road, (Hanbury and Co., Agents). Price one Penny.
[W. y. 24mo. Printed on a Card.
> " Teach us that here no strife should burn,
> No angry thoughts of envy dwell !
> Let each from Thee *this* lesson learn ;
> And then let each, through each, excel—
> Till the whole realm of man shall be
> Working *for all*, yet *most for Thee !*"]

Hymn, *v.* Sovereign of All.

Idleness of All Nations, Great Exhibition of, *v.* Now open the—This is the.

*Illustrated Exhibitors Almanack.
John Cassell [Price 6*d.*]

°Illustrated Exhibition Chronicle (The). No. 1. Price 2*d.*
London : W. Strange, 21 Paternoster Row; Hewitt and Co., 300 Strand; and of all Booksellers
[W. y. 4to, pp. 12. A Periodical.]

Illustrated Exhibitor (The), A Tribute to the World's Industrial Jubilee ; comprising Sketches, by Pen and Pencil, of the Principal objects in the Great Exhibition of The Industry of all Nations. 1851.
> ' The Earth is the Lord's, and the fulness thereof :
> The Compass of the World and they that dwell therein.'

London: Printed and Published by John Cassell, 335, Strand ; and sold by all Booksellers.
[W. y. Price 7*s. 6d.* Royal 8vo, pp. xliv, 556. A weekly periodical, commencing June 7, 1851, ending Dec. 27, 1851. Very fully illustrated.]

Illustrated London Almanack (The) 1852.
London : Published at the Offices of the Illustrated London News, 198 and 227, Strand.
[Price 1*s.* Imperial 8vo, pp. 72. Contains an account (pp. 63-72) of the Exhibition, with portraits of the following gentlemen connected with the undertaking : the Earl of Rosse, the Right Hon. W. E. Gladstone ; Mr. Cobden, M.P. ; Sir Stafford Northcote, Bart. ; Sir William Reid ; Mr. Cole ; Mr. C. Wentworth Dilke, Mr. Fuller ; Mr. M. D. Wyatt, Dr. Playfair ; Lieut.-Col. Lloyd, Dr. Royle, Sir Joseph Paxton ; Mr. Owen Jones ; Sir C. Fox.]

Illustrated London News Grand Panorama (The) of the Great Exhibition of All Nations 1851. Office 198 Strand.
[Price 6*s.* A sheet, twenty feet long, of continuous Engravings in double rows, reprinted from the Illustrated News. Underneath each department are the names of the principal objects exhibited. The " Panorama" is preceded by a Diagram showing the fluctuations in the number of visitors, as affected by different days of the week, different scale of payment, rain, and heat of the Building.]

Illustrated London News (The).
[Printed at the Office, 198, Strand, by William Little. Price 6*d.* and 1*s.* each number. Folio.]
[Ditto in French.] 28 Numbers. Price 6*d.* each.
[Ditto in German.] 8 Numbers. Price 6*d.* each.

Illustrated Plan of London and its Environs, in commemoration of the Great Exhibition of Industry of All Nations, 1851.
Printed and Published by the London Printing and Publishing Company.
[W. y. Price 5*s.* With a view of the Exterior of the Crystal Palace and other engravings.]

Illustrated Pocket Guide (The) to the Exhibition 1851.
Vincent Brooks, Lithographer. 421 Oxford Str. *London.*
[W. y. Price 2*s.* Square 32mo, opening out into five cards, in form of a cross, containing on both sides small maps, colored views of the Exhibition, and information for visitors.]

Illustrations of London, *v.* Philp.

Illustrations of the Great Exhibition of the Industry of All Nations: presented
to the Library of the London Institution, by Thomas Baring, Esq., M.P.
President.
[Without Publisher or Printer's name, or date. Royal 8vo, pp. 8. Simply a catalogue of
the publications and engravings presented by Mr. Baring.]

Illustrirter London-Führer. Ein vollständiges Gemälde der Britischen Metropolis
und ein Reisehandbuch für die Besucher der Industrie-Ausstellung aller
Nationen. Mit Abbildungen der vorzüglichsten Sehenswürdigkeiten, einer
Eisenbahnkarte von Mitteleuropa und einem Orientirungsplan von London.
Leipzig, Verlagsbuchhandlung von J. J. Weber. 1851.
[Price R 1. 20 sgr. 8vo, pp. xii, 449. A guide to London for the visitors to the Exhibition,
compiled before the opening. One chapter (pp. 312–319) is devoted to the building, its
history, and construction. The work is illustrated with numerous woodcuts.]

Important to Intending Visitors.
Charles Woodhall, Printer and Bookbinder, Audus-Street, Selby.
[W. y. Circulated gratuitously. Resolutions, signed George Lowther, Charles Woodhall,
Hon. Secs., relating to visits of Working Classes.]

Imprimerie (L') la Librairie et la Papeterie a l'Exposition Universelle de 1851
Rapport du XVIIᵉ Jury Présenté par M. Ambroise Firmin Didot Membre du
Jury Central de France   Seconde Édition, avec quelques Additions.
Paris Imprimerie Impériale. 1854.
[Price 3s. 8vo, pp. 142.]

Imprimeurs, a MM. les, v. Exposition de Londres.

Indian Archipelago. Articles collected by the Local Committee of Singapore for
the Exhibition of Arts and Industry of All Nations. President the Hon.
Lieut.-Col. Butterworth, C.B., Governor. Secretary T. Oxley, Esq. Members
—the Hon. T. Church. Captain H. Man. G. G. Nicol, Esq. G. W.
Earl, Esq. W. W. Ker, Esq. H. C. Caldwell, Esq. Tan Kim Seng, Esq.
Syed Omar, Esq. Corresponding Members—the Hon. E. A. Blundell, Esq.,
Resident Councillor, Pinang; the Hon. Captain I. Ferrier, Resident Councillor,
Malacca. Sub-Committee for arranging and Packing T. Oxley, Esq. Captain
H. Man. G. W. Earl, Esq.
[Without Publisher's or Printer's name, or date. 8vo, pp. 23, with an outline map of the
Indian Archipelago. Contains a list of 652 articles forwarded, with the prices in British
currency, the place of production, and remarks as to their respective uses.]

Indian Sale at close of Exhibition, v. Catalogue of.

Indicateur Général des Produits Belges admis a l'Exposition Universelle de Londres,
avec Mention des Prix de Vente.
Bruxelles, M. Hayez, Imprimeur de l'Académie Royale, 1851. Prix: 50 centimes.
[18mo, pp. 142. In addition to the prices it contains more details of the articles exhibited
by Belgium than is afforded by the English catalogues.]

Indications addressées a MM. les Producteurs, v. Commission Française.

Industrial Arts (The) of the Nineteenth Century. A Series of Illustrations of the
Choicest Specimens produced by every Nation at the Great Exhibition of
Works of Industry, 1851. Dedicated, by permission, to His Royal Highness
the Prince Albert. By M. Digby Wyatt, Architect.
London: published by Day and Son, Lithographers to the Queen. 1851.
[Price 17 guineas half-bound. 2 vols. Folio, pp. xii., 236, and 158 colored lithographed
drawings.]

Industrial, College, v. British Quarterly—Notes on—Papers.

°Industrial Exhibition for 1851 (The). Illustrated News Paper
London: Published by Henry Beal, 3 Shoe-Lane, Fleet Street, Price Twopence.
[Folio.]

°Industrial Exhibition of All Nations Almanac, 1851.
London: Published by W. M. Clark, 17 Warwick-Lane, Paternoster-Row; and sold by all Booksellers. Price One Penny.
[Has an exterior view of the Building, a portrait of Prince Albert, and four of the medals
to which prizes were awarded.]

Industrial Exhibition of 1851 (The). Being a few observations upon the general advantages which may be expected to arise from it. By Louis Alexis Chamerovzow.

London: T. C. Newby, 30 Welbeck Street, Cavendish Square; and of all Booksellers.
[8vo, pp. 16. "It is palpably an embodiment of pacific principles and tendencies; and it is no detraction to say, that its chief merit consists in its being a practical assertion of their truth and political soundness; whilst the advantages which may be expected to arise from it are exclusively of a character calculated to render those principles permanent." Dated London, 1st May, 1851.]

°Industrial Exhibition Remembrancer The Building was erected in Hyde Park and opened Publicly May 1st. 1851.

[Without Publisher's or Printer's name, or date. 18mo. A card containing a Diary for Memoranda. On the back a small view, and ground-plan, of the Crystal Palace. The same as Moniteur and Errinnerer.]

Industrial Instruction, v. British Quarterly Review.

Industrial Instruction in England, being A Report made to the Belgian Government. By the Chevalier de Cocquiel, Doctor of Laws. Translated into English, by Peter Berlyn, Author of 'A Popular Narrative of the Great Exhibition,' etc., etc., etc.

London: Chapman and Hall, 192, Piccadilly. 1853.
[Price 1s. 6d. 8vo, pp. iv., 83. v. 'De L'Enseignement.']

Industrial Movement in Ireland (The), as illustrated by the National Exhibition of 1852; By John Francis Maguire, M.P., Mayor of Cork.

Cork: John O'Brien, 45, Patrick-Street;
London:—Simpkin, Marshall and Co.; Dublin:—J. M'Glashan. 1853.
[Price 7s. 6d. Large paper 12s. 6d. 8vo, pp. vii., vi., 476. Touches incidentally on the Great Exhibition.]

°Industrieausstellung in London (Die). Von C. Sartorius, Verfasser der 'Bilder aus Mexiko,' in der A. A. Ztg.

Darmstadt, Druck und Verlag von C. Schäffer. 1851.
[Small 4to, pp. 80.]

Industrie-Ausstellungs-Gebäude, v. Grosse (das) Industrie-Ausstellungs-Gebäude.

Industrie de Toutes les Nations, v. Publication Officielle.

Industries Comparées de Paris et de Londres, Tableau Présenté, le 4 Janvier 1852, par le Baron Charles Dupin; dans le Séance d'ouverture du Cours de Géométrie appliquée a l'Industrie et aux Beaux-Arts, au Conservatoire National des Arts et Métiers.

Paris, Librairie de Firmin Didot Frères, Imprimeurs de l'Institut, Rue Jacob, 56. 1852.
[Price 2 francs 50 c., pp. 80. "Soyez-en sûrs, les Anglais continueront à nous demander nos dessins et nos dessinateurs pour toutes les élégances, et nos artisans et nos artistes dans les genres les plus français; puis, comme ils l'ont fait en 1851, ils combattront sans la moindre honte, en ajoutant nos combattants et nos armes aux leurs. Ils finiront par nous emprunter jusqu'à l'art d'avoir du goût!"]

Industry of All Nations. Be Just before you are Generous.

[Without Publisher's or Printer's name, date, or price. 8vo. Printed on a fly-leaf. "Many of the most important inventions are irretrievably lost to the community through the withering influence of the Patent law."]

Industry of Nations (The), as exemplified in the Great Exhibition of 1851. The Materials of Industry. Published under the direction of the Committee of General Literature and Education, appointed by the Society for Promoting Christian Knowledge.

London: Printed for the Society for Promoting Christian Knowledge; sold at the Depository, Great Queen Street, Lincoln's Inn Fields; 4, Royal Exchange; and 16, Hanover Street, Hanover Square; and by all Booksellers. 1852.
[Price 6s. Post 8vo, pp. 411. Illustrated with a ground-plan and numerous engravings. "The result of the combination of philosophy with industry has been to enlarge and ennoble the latter; and it has also directly tended to the advancement of the former. It is consequently found that a vast store of instruction, and that of a high description and of great interest, is to be found in connection with the occupations of the mechanic and artizan of every department of labour. To this and to the intrinsic importance of the subject may be attributed much of the growing interest taken in it. But it is also probable that the exhibitions of works of industry of various kinds, which have been held at various times and in different places, have largely assisted to create and sustain the interest thus felt in the

I
labours

labours of the humbler classes. It may therefore be considered advisable to append to this work some account of the exhibitions to which the events of our day have communicated a sort of historical value."]

Industry on Christian Principles.   By H. C. Barlow, M.D. Author of the 'Moral Tendency of Disease,' etc. etc.
'Whatsoever ye do, do all to the glory of God.' — 1 *Cor.* x. 31.
Seeleys. Fleet Street, and Hanover Street, London. 1851.
[Price 6*d.* 12mo, pp. 36. Dedicated to the President and members of the Society for Promoting Universal Peace, and printed by L. Seeley, Thames Ditton.]

Ingram's Exhibition Knitting and Crochet Book.   Containing a choice variety of Elegant and Useful Patterns.   Price One Penny.
London: Published by G. Ingram. 3, Britannia Street, City Road.
[Not otherwise relating to the Exhibition than the title shows.]

Institutions of Science and Art, *v.* Observations on.

Intercepted Letters, *v.* Crystal Palace.

Interior (The) of the Crystal Palace in London.   A view into the Life and Doings of London during the Great Industrial Exhibition.
[Without Publisher's or Printer's name, date, or price. An expanding view for children. There seem to have been two editions, one perhaps published abroad, as the spelling in one case is incorrect. The title was also set out in German, French, and Italian.]

°International Club (The), 2, Albert Gate, Hyde Park.
Printed by W. Clowes and Sons, Stamford Street.
[W. y.. Folio, pp. 3. A prospectus of a proposed new Club, "Originated at the suggestion of several English, French, and German gentlemen * * * deeply interested in the Industrial Exhibition of 1851."]

International Postage, *v.* Association.

Inventors—On the Principles of Jurisprudence which should regulate the Recognition of the Rights of Inventors.
[Without Publisher's or Printer's name, date, or price, but issued by the Society of Arts. Folio, pp. 19, *v.* Rights of Inventors—Voices from the Workshop.]

Janin, Jules, *v.* Mois de Mai à Londres.

Jerrold, W. Blanchard, *v.* How to see the Exhibition.

Job of 1851, *v.* Great Job.

John Bull's Green House of 1851.   A Sling and a Stone for the Great Exhibition. From the 4th Number of the Mirror of the Time.
[Petter, Duff, and Co. [Printers.] Crane Court, Fleet Street. W. y. Folio, pp. 2. Another form of the article in the Mirror of the Time, with slight variations, *v.* Mirror.]

John Bull Physicking Popery, *v.* Doubly Great Exhibition.

Johnson, Benj. P., *v.* Report of.

°Jolige Reis naar de Tentoonstelling te Londen, in het Jaar 1851.   Van twee Amsterdammers, die voor pleizier van huis gingen.
Zierickzee, P. D. J. Quanjer. 1851.
[Pp. 43.]

Jones, Edwin Owen, *v.* Palace of Universal Labour.

Jones, Owen, on Decorative Art, *v.* Attempt to Define.   Gleanings from the Exhibition—Illustrated London Almanack—Lectures [Colour in Decorative Arts].

Jones, W., *v.* Account of Kenilworth Buffet—Description of.

*Journal des Intérêts Industriels, 1851.
Bruxelles.
[Price 4 francs.]

Journal Illustré de l'Exposition de 1851, *v.* Palais de Cristal.

Journal of Design, *v.* Gleanings.

Journal of Industrial Progress (The).   Edited by William K. Sullivan, Chemist to
the Museum of Irish Industry.   No. 1.   January, 1854.   Price One Shilling.
Dublin: W. B. Kelly, 8, Grafton-Street;
London, Simpkin and Marshall; *Edinburgh*, Oliver and Boyd; *Cork*, J. O'Brien, Patrick-St.; and all
Booksellers.
[8vo.   Contains an article (pp. 1–6) " On the uses of Industrial Exhibitions; — The
Great Industrial Exhibition of 1853, and its influence upon the Development of Industry in
Ireland.   By Sir Robert Kane, F.R.S., M.R.I.A."   "Thus the Great Exhibitions, by showing
to the public, in a palpable and unmistakeable form, the grandeur and the complexity of
industry, and by illustrating the amount of talent and knowledge necessary for its successful
exercise, has paved the way for the organization of the means necessary for maintaining
Great Britain in her proper place at the head of the World of Industry, and for even extending and perfecting, in every direction, the industrial forces which we now possess."]

Journal (The) of the Exhibition of 1851.   Its Origin, History, and Progress.
London: John Crockford,—The Critic, London Literary Journal Office, 29, Essex Street, Strand.
1851.
[Price 6s.   4to, pp. iv., 324.   A Periodical, published in fortnightly Nos., price 6d.,
stamped, 6½d. each.]

Journet, M. V., sur l'Industrie du Papier Blanc, v. Rapport.

Jubilee Year (The): Comprising ' Verses for 1851,' and several Additional Poems,
in commemoration of The Third Jubilee of the Society for the Propagation of
the Gospel.
London: George Bell, 186, Fleet Street; Hatchard and Son, Piccadilly.   1852.
[Price 3s. 6d.   12mo, pp. viii., 228.   This is the second Edition of a work which will be
found under " Verses for 1851."   The preface to this Edition is signed Ernest Hawkins, and
dated 79, Pall Mall, May 1852.]

Junius, v. England's Doom—Working Man's Papers.

Jury Reports, v. Reports—Fraser's Magazine.

Juvenile Missionary Record (The) and Sabbath Scholar's Magazine in connexion
with the Church of Scotland.   Vol. 12, No. 9.   Vol. 12, No. 10.
Edinburgh: Paton and Ritchie, 3 South Hanover Street;
Thomas Murray and D. Bryce, *Glasgow*; L. Smith & G. King, *Aberdeen*; F. Shaw, *Dundee*; Smith
and Co., *Montrose*; R. A. Baird, *Greenock*.   Price One Halfpenny, or 3s. 6d. per Hundred.
[W. y.   12mo.   Contains articles (pp. 98–101 and 110–113) on the Koh-i-Noor and the
Crystal Fountain, with two illustrations.]

Kane, Sir Robt., v. Journal of Industrial Progress.

Karmarsch, Director, v. Amtlicher Bericht.

Kelly's Ausstellungs-Führer durch London.   1851.   Enthaltend eine progressive
Beschreibung der Welt-Stadt und deren Öffentlichen Gebäude, National-
Anstalten, Theater, Ausstellungen, Museen, etc. etc.   Registrirt.
London: W. Kent und Co., Paternoster Row und in allen Buchhandlungen.
[W. y.   Price 6d.   Pp. 48, with a Map.   This was a German edition of Kelly's Exhibition
Guide.   A French translation also appeared, v. Guide de Londres.]

* Kelly's Exhibition Guide through London for 1851.
Kent & Co.
[Price 6d.   Translations will be found under Guide de Londres and Kelly.]

Kenilworth Buffet, v. Account of the—Description of.

Kennedy, Rev. J., v. Forty-four Sermons.

Kensington, v. Proceedings at a Public Meeting—Observations.

Key to the Great Exhibition.   1851.   By E. Heine.   Price Eight Pence.   Entered
at Stationers' Hall.
London: Published by Ackermann and Co., 96 Strand.   By Appointment, to H. M. the Queen,
H.R.H. Prince Albert, H.R.H. the Duchess of Kent, and the Royal Family.   To be had of all
the Booksellers and Stationers.   Printed by Reynell and Weight, Little Pulteney Street,
London.
[W. y.   A large sheet, folded in an 8vo form, on which is printed the names of a number
of articles exhibited.   They are placed so as to form a sort of ground-plan.   There are also
editions in French and German, v. Guide and Schlüssel.]

Khypoor, Articles from, v. Tabular and Descriptive Lists of.

Kirchhofer, Paul, *v.* Bericht über die Abtheilung.

Kladderadatsch in London. Humoristische Schilderungen der Industrie-Ausstellung. Verantwortlicher Redacteur E. Dohm.

> Verlag Von A. Hofman & Comp. in Berlin, Unterwasserstr. 1. Druck von A. Bahn & Comp. in Berlin, Schleuse 4.
>
> [W. y. Price 20 sgr. Royal 4to, pp. 64, with Illustrations. Supplements to "Kladderadatsch," the Berlin kinsman of "Punch," published during the time of the Exhibition, with numerous woodcuts.]

Kleyle, Karl Ritter von, *v.* Kurze Beschreibung der 1851 vom k. k. Ministerium für Landeskultur und Bergwesen in England angekauften Acker-Geräthe.

Knight's Cyclopædia of the Industry of All Nations. 1851.

> *London:* Charles Knight, Fleet Street.
>
> [Price 8*s.* 8vo, pp. xxiv. and 1810. The introduction (pp. i.–xxiv.) is devoted to an Historical Account of Industrial Exhibitions at home and abroad. The Cyclopædia is illustrated by numerous engravings.]

Knitting and Crochet Book, *v.* Ingram.

°Koh-i-Noor; or the Great Exhibition, and its Opening. The Adventures of the Fuzzelton Family. By Francis Higginson, R.N.

> *London:* Pretyman and Nixon, 29, Poultry.
>
> [Price 5*s.* 8vo.]

Königliche Börse (Die) und der Gewerbe-Pallast oder die mögliche Zukunft Europas und der Welt. In drei Theilen. Aus dem Englischen.

> Gedruckt auf Kosten der religiösen Tractat-Gesellschaft, Paternoster Row, London. 1851.
>
> [Price 2*s.* 12mo, pp. 154. A Translation from the English, *v.* Royal Exchange. A French Translation was also published, *v.* Bourse.]

Kramsta, Gustav, *v.* Amtlicher Bericht.

Krystall-Palast (Der) in Hyde-Park. Merkwürdige Aufschlüsse über die Entstehung und Einrichtung des grossen Glasgebäudes für die Industrieausstellung in London. (Mit einer Abbildung) 1851. (Nach dem Englischen.)

> *Basel,* Offizin von Felix Schneider. (Leonhard Geering.)
>
> [Price 6 sgr. 8vo, pp. ii, 20; with Illustrations. Written for a charitable purpose, and giving an epitome of the various stages of the Crystal Palace during its erection, and a short description of its interior arrangements.]

Krystall-Palatset, eller den Stora Byggnaden för Industri-Expositionen i London år 1851; jemte nagra inledande ord om London, passande till handledning för Resande, som ämna besöka den stora Expositionen. Med en Planche.

> *Stockholm.* Alb. Bonniers Förlag.
>
> [Price, with Engraving, 32 sk.; without the Engraving, 8 sk. banko. 8vo, pp. 16. A pamphlet, the latter half of which only is devoted to the Crystal Palace.]

Kulturhistorische Skizzen aus der Industrieausstellung aller Völker. Von L. Bucher.

> *Frankfurt a. M.,* C. B. Lizius Verlag. 1851.
>
> [Price R 1. 15 sgr. 8vo. pp. vii, 272. A Reprint of letters written by Mr. Bucher, an ex-member of the Prussian Parliament, to the Berlin journal, the 'National Zeitung.' The headings of Mr. Bucher's chapters are characteristic; e. g, § 6. Savage Nations (Bushmen, New-Hollanders, New-Zealanders, Tscherkessians, Bedouins). § 7. Tame Nations (Chinese, Japanese, Hindoos, Russians). § 8. Nations, which are neither savage nor tame (Turks, Persians, Greeks). § 9. Free Nations (Americans, Swiss, Scandinavians). § 10. The Nations which are neither tame nor free (Italians, Spaniards, Portugueze, Germans). § 12. The Nations which would not be free (English, French, Belgians).]

Kunheim, Dr., *v.* Amtlicher Bericht.

Kurze Beschreibung der 1851 vom k. k. Ministerium für Landeskultur und Bergwesen in England angekauften Acker-Geräthe sammt den Berichten des Herrn Ministerialrathes Karl Ritter von Kleyle über: a) englische Acker-geräthe und b) Drainage. Mit einer lithographirten Beilage.

> *Wien,* 1852. Druck von Carl Gerold und Sohn.
>
> [Price 15 sgr. 8vo, pp. 58. Contains also a short description by Prof. Dr. Arenstein of the agricultural implements bought at the Exhibition by order of the Imperial Austrian government, and exhibited in the Polytechnic Institution at Vienna, with a priced list of the same.]

Labahn, Th., *v.* Bericht über landwirthschaftliche Maschinen.

Labour and Commerce, Felkin, W., *v.* Exhibition in 1851.

Labour, *v.* On the Dignity of.

Labourier, Theodore, *v.* Marque de Fabrique.

Ladies' Carpet (The).
> [4to, p. 1. Without Publisher's or Printer's name, or year. A circular signed by Mr. Wyatt Papworth, respecting the presentation of the carpet to Her Majesty. There is also an engraving of the carpet.]

Lake et Richard, *v.* Guide du Voyageur.

Lancashire Dialect, Account of Visit to Exhibition in the, *v.* Ful.

Landwirthschaftlichen (Die) Geräthe der Londoner Ausstellung im Jahre 1851, Amtlicher Bericht mit Zusätzen und Abbildungen von Dr. Karl Heinrich Rau. Grossh. Bad. Geh. Rath und Prof. zu Heidelberg.
> *Berlin,* 1853. Verlag der Deckerschen Geheimen Ober-Hofbuchdruckerei.
> [Price R 1. 6 sgr. Royal 8vo, pp. iv, 164, with Illustrations. A reprint of the 9th class from the 'Amtlicher Bericht . . . ,' with numerous additions, illustrated by woodcuts. The report on beehives is by Dr. Dünkelberg.]

° Lane's Telescopic View, of the Ceremony of Her Majesty Opening the Great Exhibition, of all Nations Designed by Rawlins 1851.
> Printed & Published by C. A. Lane, 46, Stanhope St Hampstead Rd. Entered at Stationer's Hall, 15th August, 1851.
> [Price 5s. 6d. An expanding view.]

Lane's Telescopic View of the Interior of the Great Industrial Exhibition, Lithographed & Printed at C. Moody's Lithographic Establishment, 257, High Holborn.
> Published by C. Lane. 46, Stanhope St, Hampstead Rd. Entd at Stationer's Hall, June 3rd. 1851.
> [Price 7s. 6d. Square. An expanding view.]

Languages, A Sentence from Holy Writ in One hundred, *v.* Memorial.

Lankester, Dr. Edwin, *v.* Reports by the Juries.

Lanner, Mons., *v.* Palais de Cristal ou les Parisiens a Londres.

Lansdowne Association (The), held at the Marquis of Lansdowne, Thomas Street, Hackney Road, for promoting the Great Exhibition of All Nations, 1851. Address.
> [Without Publisher's or Printer's name, or year. Folio, p. 1. "The efforts of the middle and humble classes must ever prove the mainstay of the nation! Upon these efforts Great Britain now throws herself. It is for them to sustain her glory and renown. Never more apt than now those heart-stirring words, 'England expects that every man this day will do his duty.' The Nation will be honoured, and the Royal Commissioners gratified, more by the long lists of *small* subscriptions than the princely donations of wealthy individuals:" *v.* also Dedicated to the Artisans of All Nations.]

Lardner, Dr., *v.* Great Exhibition and London in 1851.

La Sagra, Don Ramon de, *v.* Memoria sobre los objetos estudiados — Notes.

Last Call at the Palace of Glass (A).
> G. J. Palmer, Savoy Street, Strand.
> [W. y. Privately circulated. 8vo, p. 1. A Poem signed Martin F. Tupper.
> "Like an Aloe, late in time,
> With its fairy flags unfurl'd
> Stands in beauty half-sublime
> This last wonder of the world :"]

Last Great Exhibition (The); or, 'The end of all Things.' Fifth Edition of Ten Thousand.
> Trenchard & Whitby, *Yeovil;* Nisbet, Berners Street, *London;* Hance, King's Road West, Chelsea. Price 2s. per Hundred.
> [W. y. 32mo, pp. 8. A religious tract printed by Trenchard and Whitby, of Yeovil.]

Laughing Library, *v.* Little Folks.

Lawson, Peter, *v.* Synopsis of Vegetable Products of Scotland.

Lay of the Palace (The). By Mrs. Napier.
> *London:* John Ollivier, 59 Pall Mall. 1852.
> [Price

[Price 1s. 8vo, pp. 19.
" And now a prayer sincere
For him whose genius brought such wonders here.
God kindly grant to Albert health and peace,
Whilst public and domestic good increase.
May he behold his children rise in mind
To wisdom turned ! their little hearts as kind
As is his own! an honour to his name,
Which to remotest time this Palace shall proclaim ! "]

Leader Newspaper, *v*, Workmen.

Leask, Rev. Wm., *v*. Great Exhibition, Analogies and Suggestions.

Leathes, E., a Poem, *v*. Fragments from Crystal Palace.

Lecture (A) upon Cotton as an Element of Industry, delivered at the rooms of the
Society of Arts, London, in connexion with the Exhibition of 1851. His Royal
Highness Prince Albert, K.T. G.C.B. &c. President, in the Chair. By
Thomas Bazley, Esq., President of the Chamber of Commerce and Manufactures
at Manchester; and Member of the Royal Commission for the Exhibition of
1851, &c.
London : Longman, Brown, and Co.
Manchester : Simms and Dinham; J. and J. Thomson. 1852.
[Price 1s. Post 8vo, pp. vi., 70. "If the labouring classes of the United Kingdom were
well educated, their superior attainments would be alike more profitable to their employers
by increased skill, and a nearer approximation to perfection; and to themselves, not only in
augmented rewards, but in the knowledge that would promote their general comfort and
each other's welfare; for could every worker be well clothed, dwell in abodes furnished with
manufactured products, and all requisites for rendering the home fireside attractive, there
would arise a universal demand for the results of labour beyond all precedent. If there be
then no higher motive for removing the lamentable ignorance which pervades many of the
labouring classes amongst us, why does not even the censurable cupidity of the age remove
the stigma?" The work was printed by Ireland and Co., Pall Mall, Manchester.]

Lectures on the Results of the Great Exhibition of 1851, delivered before the
Society of Arts, Manufactures, and Commerce, at the suggestion of H. R. H.
Prince Albert, President of the Society.
London : David Bogue, 86 Fleet Street. 1852.
[Price 15s. Post 8vo, two volumes, pp. viii , 634 ; vi., 466. Contains the following lectures :
Rev. W. Whewell, On the general bearing of the Great Exhibition on Art and Science—Sir
H. T. de la Beche, Mining—Prof. Owen, The Raw Materials from the Animal Kingdom
— Jacob Bell, Chemical Processes and Products— Prof. Playfair, Chemical Principles
involved in Manufactures — Prof. Lindley, Substances used as Food — Prof. Solly, The
Vegetable Substances used in Arts and Manufactures,—Rev. R. Willis, Machines and Tools
—J. Glaisher, Philosophical Instruments and Processes—H. Hensman, Civil Engineering
and Machinery—Prof. Royle, Arts and Manufactures of India—Capt. Washington, Naval
Architecture—Prof. J. Wilson, Agricultural Products and Implements—J. Macadam, Flax—
J. Bazley, Cotton—S. H. Blackwell, Iron-making in the United Kingdom—G. Shaw, Glass
Manufacture—Prof. Tennant on Precious Stones—D.Wyatt, Principles of Form in Decorative
Arts—O. Jones, Employment of Colour in Decorative Arts—H. Forbes, Worsted Manufac-
tures—Prof. Ansted, Non-metallic, Mineral Manufactures—L. Arnoux, Ceramic Manufac-
tures—H. Cole, International Results of Exhibition.]

Leeds District: West Riding Agency for Railway Conveyance & Lodgings for
the Working Classes.
C. Kemplay, Printer, 'Intelligencer' Office, *Leeds.*
[Large Folio.]

Lefevre, Grenier; *v*. Reports by the Juries.

Lefroy, Edward, Address to the Mechanics' Institute at Basingstoke, *v*. Card.

Legentil, M., on Flax and Hemp, *v*. Travaux.

Le Maout, A., *v*. Exhibition de Londres.

Lemoinne, John, *v*. Great Exhibition and London in 1851.

Le Play, M. F., on Cutlery, *v*. Travaux.

Lerouge, E., *v*. Palais de Cristal ou les Parisiens a Londres.

Les Nations, Ode Mêlée de Divertissements, *v*. Fête.

[Letters from Hamilton Fish, Governor of the State of New York, from Mr. C. S.
Woodhead,

Woodhead, Mayor of the City of New York and John M. Clayton, introducing Mr. John Jay Smith; and a Letter from Mr. J. J. Smith, relating to proposed Transfer of Exhibition to America, v. Proposal.]
[Without Publisher's or Printer's name, or year. Circulated gratuitously. 4to, pp. 3.]

[Letter from Mr. Harry Chester to the Society of Arts, dated Highgate, Nov. 28, 1851.]
[Without Publisher's or Printer's name. Circulated gratuitously. 8vo, pp. 3. This letter, consequent on the Exhibition, led to the union of above three hundred Mechanics' Institutes and Literary Institutions with the Society of Arts.]

Letter (A) to Lord John Russell, on the Future Location of the National Gallery and Royal Academy.
London: John W. Parker, West Strand. 1850.
[Price 1s. 8vo, pp. 32. This letter is signed John Doyle, and dated 17, Cambridge Terrace, Hyde Park, June 20, 1850. Mr. Doyle advocates the removal of the National Gallery to Kensington.]

Letter (A) to one of the Commissioners for the Exhibition of 1851 : Being remarks on that part of the second Report of the Commissioners which recommends the teaching of Practical Design as applied to Calico Printing by the State, by Edmund Potter, Reporter to the Jury on Printed Fabrics, Class 18, in the Exhibition.
London: John Chapman, 142, Strand.
Manchester: Johnson, Rawson, and Co., Corporation Street. 1853.
[Price 1s. 8vo, pp. 34. "A careful examination of every specimen of printed fabric in the Exhibition certainly led the Jury to no such timid conclusion as that promulgated by the Commissioners,—'that this country (or the Print trade, particularly selected by the offer of aid,) will run serious risk of losing that position which is now its strength and pride.' For myself (I believe my opinions will be those of a large majority of the trade when consulted,) I really have no fears of any retrograde movement—or even pause. Remembering how our position has been gained without any State petting or aid, and how consolidated by the recent Free Trade measures, I know not how to account for such an expression of opinion." The letter is dated Dinting Lodge, Glossop, Feb. 1, 1853, and is printed at Manchester by Johnson, Rawson, and Co.]

Letter (A) to the Board of Visitors of the Greenwich Royal Observatory in reply to the Calumnies of Mr. Babbage at their Meeting in June 1853, and in his Book entitled *The Exposition of* 1851. By the Rev. R. Sheepshanks, M.A. one of the visitors.

Lædere gaudes
Inquis ; et hoc studio pravus facis. Unde petitum
Hoc in me jacis? est auctor quis denique eorum
Vixi cum quibus?

London: printed by G. Barclay, Castle St. Leicester Sq. 1854.
[Price 1s. 8vo, pp. iv. and 92.]

Lettis, J. W., *v.* Post Office Guide.

Lettres sur l'Angleterre (Souvenirs de l'Exposition Universelle) par Edmond Texier.
Paris Garnier Frères, Libraires 215, Palais-National, 10, Rue de Richelieu 1851.
[Price 2 francs. Post 8vo, pp. 269.]

Lettres sur l'Exposition Universelle de Londres, Précédées d'un Préambule et suivies du Rapport Présenté a l'Institut National de France, par M. Blanqui, Membre de l'Institut, Professeur au Conservatoire des Arts et Métiers, Directeur de l'Ecole supérieure du Commerce.
Paris, Capelle, Libraire-Editeur, Rue Soufflot, 16, près le Panthéon. 1851.
[Price 3 fr. 50 cents. 12mo, pp. viii., 325. These letters, which originally appeared in 'La Presse' newspaper, give an account of the Exhibition and of the doings in connexion. M. Blanqui's views in relation to commerce and trade will be judged of from the following extract from his preface: "N'oubliez jamais, ami lecteur, que la pensée de l'Exposition universelle est née en France, la contrée mère des expositions, et qu'elle y a été étouffée à sa naissance par une école d'hommes qui soutiennent qu'un grand pays comme le nôtre, où le peuple change de gouvernement tous les quinze ans et se met en république, quand il est de mauvaise humeur, n'a pas le droit d'acheter un canif en Angleterre, une carafe en Bohême et un rideau de fenêtre en Suisse. Notez cela, et voyez combien nous sommes inconséquents. Nous renversons aux dépens de notre fortune et de notre repos nos vieilles institutions les meilleures, les plus éprouvées; et nous gardons fidèlement nos octrois, nos douanes, nos tarifs et nos prohibitions. Nous chassons nos vieux rois comme des laquais, sans pitié pour l'âge, sans respect pour les services, et nous n'entrons pas une fois dans cette bonne ville de Paris, où se passent les belles choses qui nous rendent si fiers, sans qu'on
ouvre

ouvre nos malles, si nous en avons les clefs, et sans qu'on les enfonce, si nous ne les avons pas." M. Blanqui, in the Preface, p. vii, says, thanks to his translator, M. Berlyn, that his Letters have obtained a large sale in England. This translation was published in the ' Illustrated Exhibitor.']

° Lettre sur l'Exposition de Londres, adressée a Lord John Russell, Premier Ministre de S. M. La Reine d'Angleterre, Par M. Cros-Mayrevieille, President de la Société des Arts et·des Sciences de Carrassonne, Membre de Plusieurs Sociétés Savantes Françaises, et Etrangères.
Carcassone, Imprimerie de la L. *Pomiér.*
[8vo, pp. 14. Dated *Londres,* Juillet 1851.]

Librairie (La) et la Papeterie, Rapport du XVIIe Jury A. F. Didot, *v.* Imprimerie.

Librarie, Fonderie, Imprimerie, Plon freres, *v.* Paris.

Libraries, *v.* Museums.

Lily and the Bee (The) an Apologue of the Crystal Palace by Samuel Warren F.R.S.
> Hunc circum innumeræ gentes populique volabant.
> Ac veluti in pratis, ubi apes æstate serena
> Floribus insidunt variis, et candida circum
> Lilia funduntur: strepit omnis murmure campus.—*Æneid.* vi. 706-710.

William Blackwood and Sons *Edinburgh* and *London* 1851.
[Price 5*s.* 12mo, pp. xii., 224.
> " —Go then, Thou grand One of the Present,
> grandly into the Past.
> And for the Future,
> Leave no trace behind, but in the Mind,
> Enriched, expanded, and sublimed.
> Only a noble Memory."

A translation will be found under Giglio.]

Limbird's Hand Book Guide to London: or What to Observe and Remember of the Public Buildings, Cathedrals, Churches, Halls, Parks, Theatres, and Exhibitions: including a list of the Scientific Societies, Museums, Libraries, and Schools for the cultivation of the allied Sciences; with the names of their Presidents and Secretaries. And a descriptive Panorama of the Thames from Gravesend to Hampton Court. Embellished with views of Public Buildings, a Map, and an Engraving on Steel of the Great Exhibition Building.
London: John Limbird, 143 Strand. 1851.
[Price 1*s.* 6*d.* 18mo, pp. x., 198. Contains a short account of the Building.]

Limner, Luke, *v.* Rejected Contributions to the Great Exhibition.

Lindley, John, *v.* Lectures [Substances used as Food].—Report of the Commissioners.

Liste Complete des Jurés Anglais, *v.* Commission Française.

* Liste des Exposants Français.
Place de la Bourse No. 12.
[Advertised in Journal de la Librarie.]

* Liste des Medailles.
Panckoucke 1851.
[8vo, pp. 38. Advertised in Journal de la Librarie.]

° List of Articles contributed from Bengal to the Exhibition of Works of Industry and Art of All Nations of 1851, Drawn up in accordance with the decisions of H. M. Commissioners, February, 1851.
[Without Publisher's name, year, or price; but "Printed by J. F. Bellamy, Englishman Office." 8vo, pp. 60. Short details are given of 2699 articles. *v.* also Catalogue of East Indian Productions.]

List of Drugs, &c. &c. proposed to be Shewn at the Exhibition of Industry, 1851.
[Without Publisher's or Printer's name, or date. Privately circulated. 8vo, pp. 14.]

Little Folks' Laughing Library (The). The Exhibition. By F. W. N. Bayley, Author of the ' New Tale of a Tub,' Etc.
London: Published for the Author, by Darton and Co., Holborn Hill. 1851.
[Price 1*s.* 8vo, pp. 32. A poem, with eight illustrations.
> " All the things that all men look for,
> There appear without omission—
> We get up this little book for
> Glory to the Exhibition."]

Little Henry's Holiday at the Great Exhibition. By the Editor of Pleasant Pages.'

London: Houlston & Stoneman, and all Booksellers. Price 2*s.* 6*d.*

[W. y. Sq. 24mo, pp. 168. Illustrated with four lithographs and several woodcuts. Dialogues upon the Great Exhibition for the instruction of young people. "Contents. Part I.—GOING THERE. Chap. 1. How the idea arose. 2. How the money was raised. 3. How the idea of the palace arose. 4. How the Crystal Palace arose. 5. How the idea was realised. 6. How it brought forth fruit. Part II.—WALKING THROUGH. Chap. 1. The plan of the Exhibition. 2. The 'lions' of the Exhibition. 3. The goods from England. 4. The goods from the colonies. 5. The goods from Europe. 6. The goods from Asia. 7. The goods from Africa. 8. The goods from America. Part III.—GOING HOME. Chap. 1. Thoughts about the Exhibition. 2. Thoughts about *Peace* and Brotherhood."]

Little Henry's Records of His Life-Time. By the Author of 'Pleasant Pages.' Old Eighteen-Fifty-One; A Tale for Any Day in 1852. In which the Good Old Fellow gives a true account of himself, and makes up a remarkable Year-Book.

'We spend our years as a tale that is told.'—*Psalm* xc. 9.

London: Houlston and Stoneman; and all Booksellers.

[W. y. Price 1*s.* Sq. 24mo, pp. vi., 114, with engravings. A chapter relates to the Exhibition of 1851, with woodcuts.]

Lloyd, J. A., *v.* Papers, Colleges of Arts and Manufactures—Illustrated London Almanack.

Londensche (Het) Nieuws Gedurende de Tentoonstelling van 1851. Door C. M. Mensing. Met Twee Honderd Houtgravuren.

Te 's Gravenhage, Bij K. Fuhri. 1851.

[Price 19*s.* Folio, pp. 200. A daily journal written during the time of the Exhibition, giving a description of the most interesting incidents at, and of the most remarkable objects in, the Crystal Palace.]

London and the Exhibition, *v.* Stranger in London.

London as it is To-Day: Where to go, and What to see, during the Great Exhibition. Illustrated with a Map of London, and upwards of two hundred Engravings on Wood, by Prior, Shepherd, Delamotte, Gilks, Bissagar, and other Eminent Artists.

London: H. G. Clarke & Co., 4, Exeter Change. 1851.

[Price 4*s.* 6*d.* Post 8vo, pp. iii., 437, vi. Contains nothing, except a view, relating to the Exhibition.]

London, Ball of Corporation of, at Guildhall, *v.* Brief Historical Account.

London Companion, *v.* Beasland.

London Conductor (The); being a Guide for Visitors to the Great Industrial Exhibition, through the Principal Portions of the Metropolis; including a brief history and description of the Palaces, Parks, Churches; Government, Legal, and Commercial Buildings; Bridges, Statues Museums, Hospitals, Club-Houses, Theatres, and Streets of London; and the Remarkable Places in its Vicinity.

London: John Cassell, 335, Strand, and all Booksellers. 1851.

[Price 9*d.* 12mo, pp. 92.]

The Same. Fourth Illustrated Edition, embellished with Views of the principal Buildings in the Metropolis, in addition to the superb map of London and its Environs.

[Price 1*s.* 12mo, pp. 92. Contains Map of London and View of the Building; but nothing else relating to the Exhibition.]

Londoner Briefe über die Weltausstellung von H. Scherer.

Leipzig. Verlag von Hermann Schultze. 1851.

[Price R 1. Post 8vo, pp. x, 244. Series of 24 letters, which (I believe) were originally published in the Cologne Gazette, giving a description of the Industrial Exhibition, and of the contents of the Crystal Palace. The author thinks to have witnessed therein the dawn of American Art, and speaks with high praise of the Swiss contributions. He concludes his work with these words: "The idea of an international exhibition of all the five parts of the globe begins a new era in the history of civilisation of mankind."]

London Exhibited in 1851; Elucidating its Natural and Physical Characteristics its Antiquity and Architecture; its Arts, Manufactures, Trade, and Organiza-

K   tion;

tion; its Social, Literary, and Scientific Institutions; and its numerous Galleries of Fine Art. With 205 Illustrations, executed by Mr. Robert Branston, Mr. O. Jewitt, Mr. J. R. Jobbins, and others; including a newly-constructed Map, engraved by Mr. Wilson Lowry.
Edited and Published by John Weale. *London*.
[W. y. Price 9s. Post 8vo, pp. 910. Contains very little relating to the Exhibition.]

Londonführer, *v.* Illustrirter Londonführer.

London Gazette (The). Published by Authority. Friday, January 4, 1850, Numb. 21056. Tuesday, February 26, 1850, Numb. 21071. Friday. October 17, 1851. Numb. 21254.
Published by Francis Watts, Editor, Manager, and Publisher, of No. 1 Warwick Square, Pimlico, in the Parish of St. George, Hanover Square, at 45, St. Martin's Lane, in the Parish of St. Martin-in-the-Fields, both in the County of Middlesex. Printed by Thomas Richard Harrison, and Thomas Harrison, Printers, at their Office, No. 45, St. Martin's Lane, in the Parish and County aforesaid. Price Two shillings and eight pence.
[Folio, pp. 23-56, and 534-543, and 2587-2723. No. 21,056 contains the Queen's Warrant appointing the Commission; No. 21,071, the Classified List; and No. 21,254, the Award of Prizes.]

London Illustrations, *v.* Philp.

London im Jahre 1851. Ein praktisches Handbuch für Reisende nach England.
Leipzig, Verlag von Carl B. Lorck. 1851.
[Price R 1. 20 sgr. 12mo, pp. viii, 144. A guide to London, with a few remarks only on the Exhibition building and its history.]

London in all its Glory; or, how to enjoy London during the Great Exhibition.
London: H. G. Clarke & Co., 4, Exeter Change. 1851.
[Price 1s. 6d. 24mo, pp. 208, with woodcuts. Contains a very short account of the Exhibition. A translation will be found under Londres dans toute sa Gloire.]

London Institution, *v.* Illustrations presented to, by Mr. Baring.

London in 1851: embracing A Week's Ramble through the Great Metropolis, with its Description and History, Sports and Pastimes; Accounts of its National Establishments, Public Buildings, Exhibitions, Theatres, Operas, Concerts; Show Houses of the Aristocracy; Picture Galleries; Museums; Scientific Institutions; Bazaars; Divans; Casinos; and Refectories of every Class. With all that can delight the Eye or improve the Mind & Heart. In three Parts. Illustrated with a New Map of London constructed expressly for the Use of Strangers of all Nations; combining, with References to Two Hundred and Seventy-one Localities, and Objects of Interest, a simple method of finding them, and ascertaining Cab Fares, Distances, etc.
London: Cradock & Co. 48, Paternoster Row
[W. y. 18mo, Part 1, pp. vi., 64. Part 2, iv., 64. Part 3, iv., 64. Contains a short account of the Crystal Palace, and a View of the Transept.]

London Made easy, being a Compendium of 'The British Metropolis:' containing six maps, arranged upon an entirely new principle, shewing at once the exact and relative positions of the various objects of interest in the Metropolis. One Shilling.
London: Arthur Hall, Virtue, and Co. 25, Paternoster Row. 1851.
[12mo, pp. xv., 84, with Maps. Contains an account of the Exhibition (v.-xiv.).]

London Manufacturer, Extract from the Times, *v.* Great Exhibition of 1851.

London, Map of, *v.* Reynolds.

London Merchant, *v.* General Outline.

London Season, *v.* Crystal Palace.

London, seine Bewohner und Umgebungen von Dr. Woldemar Seyffarth, Verfasser der Federstriche aus England, Briefe aus London u. a. Zweiter Abdruck.
Stuttgart, J. B. Müller's Verlagshandlung. 1851.
[Price R 1. Pp. viii., 320. A guide-book to London, has nothing relating to the Exhibition.]

London: What to see, and How to see it. With numerous Illustrations.
London: H. G. Clarke & Co., 4, Exeter Change. 1851.
[Price 1s. 24mo, pp. 208. Contains a short account of the Great Exhibition.]

Londres, dans toute sa Gloire! Manière d'y Employer ses Moments de Loisirs, en Visitant tout ce qui s'y Trouve de Curieux pendant la Grande Exposition. Avec de Nombreuses Illustrations.

Edité par H. G. Clarke & Co., 4, Exeter Change, et Publié et Vendu par l'Office du Conseiller de l'Étranger à Londres, 3, Oxendon Street (Coventry Street). 1851.
[Price 1s. 6d. 18mo, pp. viii., 264. A translation, v. London in all its Glory. Pages 258–260 are devoted to the Exhibition, with a View of the Exterior.]

Londres en 1851: ou, Vue Complete de la Métropole de l'Empire Britannique, avec tous ses Etablissemens Nationaux; ses Institutions Littéraires et Scientifiques; ses Ecoles d'Art; ses Théâtres; ses Galeries de Tableaux; ses Eglises et Chapelles, etc.; ses Hôtels; ses Restaurans; ses Divans; ses Bazars, etc. Ouvrage précéde d'une Introduction Historique et Descriptive de la Capitale, depuis sa Fondation jusqu'à l'Année 1851. Illustre d'une Carte des Rues de Londres, specialement faite pour l'Usage des étrangers de toutes les Nations; et complété par une description du Palais de Cristal, ou du Temple de l'Industrie et des Arts, dans Hyde Park; avec le Classement des Articles de la Grande Exposition.

Londres: Cradock and Co., 48, Paternoster Row. Prix, 2s. 6d Relié.
[Small 8vo, pp. vi., 122. Pages 106–116 are devoted to the Exhibition.]

Londres et la Grande Exposition. Dédié à Joseph Paxton, l'Architecte du Palais de Cristal. Le Pilote de Londres, Guide et Conseiller de l'Excursioniste à Londres et à l'Exposition Universelle; comprenant une Description éxacte des Ressources, des Curiosités, des Plaisirs, etc., de la Métropole Anglaise; precede de Conseils aux Etrangers sur le Choix du Logement, Orné d'un bon Plan de Londres, et suivi d'une Instruction pour connaître Londres en huit Promenades; d'un Aperçu des Environs de Londres; d'une liste des Banquiers de Londres; des adresses des Ambassadeurs et des Consuls étrangers; d'un Tarif des Voitures de place; du Cours des monnaies étrangères; &c.

Londres: Thomas Richardson & Son, Imprimeurs Editeurs, Fleet Street, No. 172, City.
[Price 1s. W. y. 18mo, pp. 232. An account of the Exhibition is contained in pages 179–185.]

⁰ Londres et l'Exposition ou Guide du Voyageur. Plan de l'Exposition indiquant le classement des Produits exposés et autres details speciaux. Plan de Londres avec details sur ses Monuments. Prix: 1 franc et 1 franc 50 centimes avec plans coloriés.

Se vend chez MM. Durr et Cie, A Paris, Rue Tronchet 18, et a Londres, King William Street. A Cologne, a la Librairie d'Eisen, Rue Frederic-Guillaume.
A Bruxelles, Chez Kiessling et Cie, 26, Montagne de la Cour, A Anvers et Ostende, chez Corneker Libraire.
[W. y. 12mo, pp. 38.]

Lord Stanley on the Exhibition of Industry of All Nations In 1851. Extract from the Speech at the Grand Dinner given by the Lord Mayor to Prince Albert, March 21st, 1850.

Bradbury & Evans, Printers, Whitefriars.
[W. y. Circulated gratuitously. Folio, p. 1. Lord Stanley, now Lord Derby, said: " I look with satisfaction on the encouragement that will be given to the industry of all nations, and as much as any to the industry of this country, by the Great Exhibition of 1851."]

Love and Loyalty. By the Author of Irrelagh.

London William Pickering 1851.
[Without year or price. 18mo, pp. 46. A series of poems, bound in a green and gold cover, bearing this title, preceded by an "Argument," in which it is said, "Superstition subversive of Loyalty and Royalty; that Love wedded to Loyalty produces Industry and a desire for universal love and brotherhood, proved by the invitation of all Nations to the Crystal Palace; the opening scene; the cause of Erin advocated; her sufferings and unmurmuring resignation; her triumphant struggles against a dark creed; Britain cautioned against the wiliness of Popery; for, to the Protestant Religion is she indebted for her prosperity."

" Behold as guards, her children smiling round,
Her safety in her confidence is found;
Despots may seek a shield from rebel darts,
But our Queen's citadel is loyal hearts!"]

Love versus War, v. Placards.

Lowther, George, Selby, *v.* Important.

Loyal Stanza (A) On the Merits of Prince Albert and The Grand Exhibition. By James Prior.
[Without Publisher's or Printer's name, or year of publication. Dated Bath, April 19, 1851. Folio.

> " We cannot wish him happiness more,
> Than we trust he does possess ;
> With more domestic happiness,
> No prince was ever blest."]

Luke Limner, *v.* Rejected Contributions to the Great Exhibition.

Luntley, John, *v.* Air Navigation by means of a Rotatory Balloon.

Macadam, James, *v.* Lectures [Flax].

Machinery and Models sent by Maudslay, Sons, & Field, of Lambeth, to the Great Exhibition of 1851. Exhibited in Class 6. No. 228.
London : Printed by W. Clowes and Sons, Stamford Street and Charing Cross.
[W. y. Imperial 8vo. Illustrated by numerous engravings.]

Machinery of the Nineteenth Century (The) ; illustrated from original drawings, and including the best examples shown at the Exhibition of the Works of Industry of All Nations. Description of Plates. By G. D. Dempsey, C. E. [Parts 1 to 5.]
London : Atchley & Co., 106, Great Russell Street, Bedford Square ; C. Muquardt, *Brussels ;* and to be had of all Booksellers.
[January to May, 1852. Price 5*s.* each part, including plates, or with additional French Text 6*s.* 4to, pp. 60. Only 5 numbers were published ; each monthly part was accompanied by 5 large folio plates of diagrams in a separate wrapper. A prospectus of this work states that the objects aimed at " are to preserve a worthy record of the admirable Machinery by which the manufacturing arts are now facilitated in this country, and to embody a correct description of the splendid specimens shown at the Exhibition of the Works of Industry of all Nations."]

Machines, *v.* Metropolitan District.

McNevin, J., *v.* Souvenir.

Madras Central Committee, *v.* Proceedings of.

Maguire, John Francis, *v.* Industrial Movement in Ireland.

Malwa, Articles from, *v.* Tabular and Descriptive Lists of.

Mann's Country Visitors' Guide, *v.* Country.

Mansion House, *v.* Grand Banquet—Great Exhibition of the Works, Extracts from Speeches at a Meeting at the,—Report of a Meeting.

Map of London, *v.* Penny Map.

Marie, Auguste, *v.* Palais de Cristal ou les Parisiens a Londres.

* Marque (La) de Fabrique, signe Theodore Labourier.
Imprimerie de Briere, Rue St. Anne 55.
[8vo. Advertised in Journal de la Librarie.]

Marshall, T. L., *v.* Moral Aspects.

Martin, John Horatio, *v.* Ode in Commemoration.

Martin, M., *v.* Notes sur le Section 5.

Martin, Samuel, *v.* Useful Arts—Forty-four Sermons.

Marylebone, *v.* Speech of R. Cobden—Great Exhibition.

Materials of Industry, *v.* Industry of Nations.

Maudslay & Field, *v.* Machinery.

Mayhew, Henry, *v.* 1851.

Mechanics' Home for 1851, *v.* Ranelagh Club.

Mechanics' Magazine (The), Museum, Register, Journal, and Gazette. [Numbers 1379, 1380, 1382, 1383, 1386, 1389, 1390, 1392, 1396, 1409, 1410, 1425, 1440, 1447, 1449, 1472, 1483, 1484, 1485.]
> [*London :* Edited, Printed, and Published by Joseph Clinton Robertson, of No. 166, Fleet-street, in the city of London, and 99 B, New-street, *Birmingham.* — Sold by A. and W. Galignani, Rue Vivienne, *Paris ;* Machin and Co., *Dublin ;* W. C. Campbell and Co., *Hamburgh.* 1850–1852. Price 2*d.* each. 8vo. Contains a series of attacks upon the originators of the Exhibition, and upon the principles on which it was proposed to be carried out.]

Medical Man's Plea (A) for a Winter Garden in the Crystal Palace.
> *London :* John Van Voorst, 1 Paternoster Row. 1851.
> [Price 6*d.* 8vo, pp. 16. "Were the Crystal Palace, however, at our disposal, together with the surplus thousands in the hands of the Royal Commissioners, we would go much further than either Denarius or Mr. Paxton. We would have, in addition to the shrubs and fountains —both of great utility as agitators and renovators of the air—Springs of living water for personal use. We would sink wells in the Crystal Palace, and establish a system of Baths, which should combine all that is desirable in the Spas of Germany with all that is decent in the Roman Thermæ. We would have a copious and well-arranged Library and Reading-rooms, Retiring and Reclining-rooms, Couches for Repose disposed about the building, Hand-carriages of every description, and a scale of Refreshments so liberal and complete, as to furnish those who would spend the whole day in the place with the most ample and convenient means of doing so."]

M., E. G., *v.* New Order of Merit.

Meister Tolpatsch auf der Londoner Welt-Industrie-Ausstellung im Sommer 1851.
> *Leipzig,* C. W. B. Naumburg. 1852.
> [Price 10 sgr. 8vo, pp. 45, with Illustrations. "No," exclaimed Master Tolpatsch, the smith, "those fellows must be mad, to build a palace of glass. Surely the whole is meant for a hoax, to attract people." In spite of his unfavourable opinions, however, he sets out, accompanied by a friend, to view the Exhibition ; their adventures in the metropolis are told in a humorous style.]

Melzer, Dr. E. Friedr., *v.* Nach London!

Memento (A) of the Great Exhibition of 1851.
> J. & R. Robinson & Co. 30 Milk St.
> [Two specimens of weaving in silk, accompanied by a card of explanations.]

Memoranda relative to the International Exhibition of 1851, by Francis Fuller, 29, Abingdon Street, Westminster.
> [Privately printed. W. y. 8vo, pp. 186, and Appendix of pp. 18. "Compiled for the purpose of preserving correct information for my Family and Friends."]

Memorandum relative to the Private View previous to Re-opening of the Exhibition of the Products of French Industry, by M. Sallandrouze de Lamornaix, at No. 13, George Street, Hanover Square.
> *London—Private Press.* W. S. Johnson, "Nassau Steam Press," 60 St. Martin's Lane.
> [W. y. 8vo, pp. 8. A brief account of the articles exhibited in 1850 by M. Sallandrouze. Prepared for the opening night, March the 9th, *v.* also Exposition des Produits.]

Memorial (A) of the Great Industrial Exhibition of All Nations in London, 1851. Consisting of a Sentence from Holy Writ in above One Hundred Languages.
> ' God hath made of one blood all nations of men.'
> Have we not all one Father?
> Behold how good & how pleasant it is for brethren to dwell together in unity!
> *London :* Partridge & Oakey, Paternoster Row ; and 70, Edgeware Road (Hanbury & Co. Agents).
> [W. y. Price 2*s.* 6*d.* A sheet with two illustrations.]

Memorial of the Great Exhibition, 1851. Statistics of the Exhibition.
> *London.* Published 1st Novr., 1851, By Ackermann & Co. 96, Strand, and W. P. Metchim, 20, Parliament St. Westminster.
> [W. y. Price 1*s.* A sheet, giving a daily return of the largest number of persons in the Building. Signed James Wade. With a view of the exterior of the Building. See also Illustrated London News Grand Panorama—Statistical Chart.]

Memorials of the Great Exhibition, and other Poems. By Edward H. Fry.
> *London :* John King, 120, Fleet Street. 1852. Price 2*s.* 6*d.*
> [12mo, pp. vi., 68. Many of the poems bear the names of statues in the Exhibition.
> " Hampden and Falkland here are side by side,
> Together in immortal glory crowned ;
> And that unrighteous War which did divide
> The holy ties wherewith our lives are bound,
> Hath given place to one consent of Peace,
> And here the fruit in this the world's increase."]

Memoria Presentada al Excmo. Señor Ministro de Comercio, Instruccion y Obras Públicas Por la Junta Calificadora de los Productos de la Industria Españloa, reunidos en la Exposicion Pública de 1850.
Madrid. Establecimiento Tipografico de D. Santiago Saunaque, Calle de la Colegiata, núm. 11. 1851.
> [4to, pp. 638. Report on the Spanish Industrial Exhibition of 1850, compiled by Señor José Caveda, Director General of Agriculture, Industry, and Commerce, by order of the Committee of Examination. The book alludes slightly to the anticipated Exhibition in London.]

Memoria sobre los objetos estudiados en la Exposicion Universal de Lóndres y Fuera de Ella bajo el punto de vista del adelanto futuro de la Agricultura é Industria Españolas. Presentada al Excmo. Señor Ministro de Fomento por Don Ramon de la Sagra Comisionado por S. M. y Miembro del Jurado. Primera Parte. Materias Primeras resultantes de la Agricultura, la Economia Rural y la Mineria.
Madrid. Imprenta del Ministerio de Fomento, a Cargo de D. S. Compagni, calle de la Luna, núm. 29. 1853.
> [Imperial 8vo, pp. lxxix., 440. This first portion of a work descriptive of the Exhibition, projected on a large scale but interrupted by the illness of the Author, contains, besides, a general Introduction of some length, a detailed account of the Raw Produce Section exhibited at the Crystal Palace. The Appendix contains various references to the sources from which the work has been compiled,—a summary of the Collection of Samples placed at the disposal of the Writer during the Exhibition, and subsequently deposited with the Spanish Government,—a List of the Books obtained by the Author from the English, French, and Belgian Governments,—and, finally, a List of the Exhibitors who transmitted to him catalogues, prices, statements, and specimens. "If we consider what is going on in the most active and civilized countries, we easily gain the conviction that, with the exception of those things upon which only the sense of the beautiful can impress the characteristic stamp, inanimate power, assisted by machinery, may not only replace human strength and skill, but almost supersede them; the machines offering, besides their precision, the advantage of unlimited supply and the constant uniformity of the productions, advantages which human power alone can obtain. * * * This circumstance cannot but bring about an entire revolution in the social condition of future nations, as the production and transformation of raw materials into articles of consumption will require of man only a small part of his intelligence. Henceforward work will cease to be painful, incessant, and trying, and the exertions for the support of life not requiring the sacrifice of the whole time of the producer, will allow his mind to devote itself to those sublime ideas which constitute our moral existence."]

°Memories of the Great Metropolis: or, London, from the Tower to the Crystal Palace. By F. Saunders.
> ' I pray you let us satisfy our eyes
> With the memorials and the things of fame
> That do renown this city.'

New York: G. G. P. Putnam, 155 Broadway. 1852.
> [8vo, pp. xii., 311. With engravings. Pages 34-44 contain an account of the Exhibition.]

Mensing, C. M., *v.* Londensche Nieuws (Het).

Merrifield, Mrs., On Harmony of Colours, *v.* Art Journal.

Merryweather, Dr. George, *v.* Essay on Tempest Prognosticator.

Merveilles de Londres (Les). Par MM. Day et Bush, Auteurs de ' Trois Jours à Paris.'
a Londres : Chez T. Bosworth, 215 Regent Street. Prix, 60 cent.
> [12mo, pp. 24, with an outline Map of London on the cover. A Guide to the Public Sights of London.]

*Merveilles (Les) de l'Industrie Francaise a l'Exposition de Londres.
Devoyé.
> [5 centimes. Advertised in Journal de la Librairie.]

Metropolitan District. Class IV. Machines for Direct Use, &c. A classified list of articles for which space has been granted, alphabetically arranged, together with an alphabetical list of the names and addresses of Exhibitors, also an alphabetical list of Withdrawn Vouchers. Duplicate Vouchers. Cancelled Vouchers. and Miscellaneous Vouchers.
Miller and Field, Printers, 6, Bridge Road, Lambeth.
> [W. y. Circulated gratuitously. Post 8vo. Special Remarks are appended to some few articles.]

Miller, Rev. J. C., *v.* Forty-four Sermons.

Milner, the Rev. J. W., *v.* Design of God.

Mimerel, M., on Cotton Goods, *v.* Travaux.

Mining Journal Report, *v.* Origin of the Great Exhibition.

° Ministère de l'Agriculture et du Commerce, Division du Commerce extérieur. Bureau du Mouvement général du commerce et de la navigation. Exposition Universelle de Londres en 1851. Liste des Médailles et Mentions honorables décernées aux Exposants français. 1°. Médailles de Conseil (council medals); 2°. Médailles de prix (prize medals); 3°. Médailles de mention honorable. *Paris* Typographie Panckoucke Rue des Poitevins, 8. 1851.
[8vo, pp. 38.]

Minutes of the Proceedings of Her Majesty's Commissioners for the Exhibition of 1851. [Private and Confidential.] 11th January 1850, to 24th April 1852. *London:* Printed by William Clowes and Sons, Stamford Street, for Her Majesty's Stationery Office, 1852.
[4to, pp. 24, 453; with an Index.]

Mirror of the Time a Weekly Magazine and Journal. No. 4. Saturday, August 24, 1850. Price 1½*d.* [Contains article] The Green House of 1851. A Sling and a Stone for the Giant Exhibition.
[Printed and Published for the Proprietor by R. Russell, at the office of the 'Mirror of the Time,' 11 A Wellington-street North, Strand, *London.* Imperial 8vo, pp. 16. Contains an attack upon the originators of the Exhibition and the principles upon which it was proposed to be carried out. It was also printed in another shape, which will be found described under John Bull's Greenhouse.]

Missionary Record, *v.* Juvenile.

Mittheilungen über die Industrie-Ausstellung aller Völker zu London im Jahre 1851. Aus den Berichten der von der österreichischen Regierung delegirten Sachverständigen. Erste Lieferung: Einleitung.—Berg- und Hüttenproducte mit Ausnahme der Gusswaaren. Zweite Lieferung: Chemicalische und pharmaceutische Processe und Erzeugnisse.—Chemicalien und Rohstoffe des Pflanzen- und Thierreiches als Genussgegenstände.—Thierische und vegetabilische Substanzen zu gewerblichen Zwecken.—Maschinen zum directen Gebrauche (mit Einschluss von Wagen), auch Eisenbahn- und Schiffs-Mechanismen.—Gewerbliche Maschinen und Instrumente.—Civil-Ingenieur-, Architectur- und Bauwesen.—Schiffbau und Kriegsmaschinen.—Ackerbau-Maschinen und Geräthe. Dritte Lieferung: Mathematische, physikalische, musikalische, horologische und chirurgische Instrumente.—Baumwollwaaren.—Schafwollwaaren.— Seidenwaaren.— Stoffe aus Flachs und Hanf.—Gemischte Gewebe, Shawls. — Leder und Lederwaaren; Sattler-, Riemer-, Taschner-, Kürschner-Arbeiten; Federn und Haare.—Papier, Buchdruckerei, Buchbinderei.—Färberei und Farbendruck auf Gespinnste und Gewebe.—Teppiche, Spitzen, Stickereien.—Bekleidungs-Gegenstände.—Messerschmid-Waaren und Schneidwerkzeuge.— Metallwaaren, Gussarbeiten.—Arbeiten aus edlen Metallen, Juwelen und deren Nachahmungen. — Glaswaaren. — Porzellan-, Steingut-, Töpferwaaren. — Möbel, Decorations-, und lackirte Waaren.— Arbeiten aus mineralischen Stoffen für bauliche Zwecke und Ornamente.— Arbeiten aus Thier- und Pflanzenstoffen.—Verschiedene Manufacte und Kurze Waaren.—Schöne Kunst.
Wien. Aus der kaiserlich-königlichen Hof- und Staatsdruckerei. 1852-3-4.
[3 Lieferungen. Price R. 2 15 sgr. 8vo, pp. 560. A detailed description of the contents of the Crystal Palace, based upon the official reports of the Austrian delegates, with additional matter. One of the principal objects of the compilers was to throw light upon the industrial condition of the Austrian dominions. Sections two and three contain engravings.]

M., J. M., *v.* Palais de Cristal, ou le Géant de Hyde-Park.

Model Houses for Families (The), built in connexion with the Great Exhibition of 1851, By Command of His Royal Highness the Prince Albert, K.G. President of the Society for Improving the Condition of the Labouring Classes. By Henry Roberts,

Roberts, F.S.A. Fellow of the Royal Institute of British Architects, Honorary Architect to the Society for Improving the Condition of the Labouring Classes. Published by Request, and Sold for the Benefit of the Society for Improving the Condition of the Labouring Classes, at No. 21, Exeter Hall, Strand, *London; also* by Seeleys, Fleet Street, and Hanover Street; Nisbet & Co., Berners Street; J. W. Parker and Son, West Strand; and Hatchard, Piccadilly.

[W. y. Price 4s. Imperial 8vo, pp. 32, with plates and estimates of prices.]

° Mois a Londres (Un) par Emile Bouchaud.

Paris Perrotin, Libraire-Éditeur 41, Rue Fontaine-Molière 1851.

[8vo. pp. 224. The author in his preface says, " To sketch with rapid strokes the great image of London, to serve as a guide to travelling friends, to take them up at their exit from the grand industrial concourse sheltered beneath the Crystal Palace in order to conduct them through the immense city, and to bring by turns before their eyes or into their minds, monuments, landscapes, institutions, naval pictures, or pictures of interiors, such has been my humble object."]

Mois de Mai à Londres (Le) et l'Exposition de 1851. Par Jules Janin.

'In quodam apparatu vidi totas opes Urbis, cælatas et auro et argento, et his quæ pretium auri argentique vicerunt; exquisitos colores, et vestes, ultra non tantum nostrum, sed ultra finem hostium advectas . . . et alia, quæ, res suas recognoscens, summi imperii fortuna protulerat.'—*Sénèque, Lettre CX.*

'J'assistais, l'autre jour, à l'une des expositions solennelles des richesses de Rome; là je vis des merveilles, des chefs-d'œuvre d'or et d'argent, et d'une forme plus précieuse que l'or ou l'argent; il y avait aussi des etoffes et des teintures exquises, des costumes venus de plus loin même que les frontières romaines . . . Je vis, en un mot, d'un œil ébloui, toutes les magnificences qu'etalait, dans sa fastueuse revue, la fortune éclatante du peuple-roi.'

Londres: Chez J. Mitchell, 33, Old Bond Street; et W. Sams, 1, St. James's Street.

Paris: Michel Lévy Frères, Libraires-Editeurs, Rue Vivienne, 2 Bis. 1851.

[Price 7s. 8vo, pp. 172, with a Portrait of the Author. A reprint of M. Janin's letters to the 'Journal des Débats.']

°Moniteur de l'Exhibition de L'Industrie. L'Edifice fut bati a Hyde Park, et ouvri au Public Mai 1st 1851.

[18mo, a card. The same as Industrial Exhibition Remembrancer, and Errinnerer.]

Montémont, Albert, Ode, *v.* Palais de Cristal.

Moore, Rev. D., *v* " What have they seen in thine House ?"

Moral (A) and Religious Guide to the Great Exhibition, by the Rev. J. A. Emerton, D.D.

'I believe it to be the duty of every Educated person to watch and study the time in which he lives, and as far as in him lies to add his humble mite of individual exertion to the accomplishment of what he believes Providence to have ordained.'—*His Royal Highness Prince Albert.*

'On this great occasion, the character of the English nation, as a Christian people should be upheld. The opportunity afforded by an unprecedented concourse of strangers from every quarter should be diligently, and at *any cost* improved, not merely for the encouragement of mechanical industry, but, under the Divine blessing, for the diffusion of sound Christian principle among all nations.'—*Bishop of London.*

London: Longman, Brown, Green, and Longmans. 1851.

[Price 1s. 8vo, pp. vi., 47.]

Moral Aspects of the Great Exhibition of 1851. A Sermon, preached in the High Street Chapel, Warwick, on Sunday, May 4th, 1851, by Thomas L. Marshall, Minister of the Chapel.

'Much remains to conquer still;
Peace hath her victories,
No less renowned than War.'—*Milton.*

Warwick: H. Sharpe, Advertiser-Office, High Street. *Leamington:* J. Glover. *London:* Simpkin, Marshall, and Co., Stationers' Hall Court; and E. T. Whitfield, Essex Street, Strand. 1851.

[Price 6d. 8vo, pp. 23. Printed by H. Sharpe, Printer, Advertiser-Office, Warwick. " By what instrument can the noblest of revolutions be accomplished, and war and national contention be known no more upon earth? *Commerce, liberalized and emancipated commerce,* spreading, as it everywhere does, the conviction more widely every day, that it is not only more *profitable,* but, in every sense, more *Christian* and *benevolent,* to be engaged in the interchange of friendly communication than to live isolated from each other, directing every energy of the mind, and all the resources of the nation to works of natural hostility: *Commerce, free* and *unrestricted,* and conducted in the spirit of equal justice; Commerce, the great agent of peace, the source of national plenty, the creator and stimulus of honourable industry."]

Moriarty, Edward A., *v.* Amtlicher Catalog.

Morison, Rev. Dr. John, *v.* Unity of the Race.

Morning Stars (The); a Treatise (En Permanence) as suggested by the Grand Exhibition of the Works of Industry of All Nations. By the Rev. W. Pashley, M.A., Curate of Sedgeberrow.

London: T. Hatchard, 187, Piccadilly. 1851.

> [Price 6*s.* 6*d.* Post 8vo, pp. iv., 251. "And we must view all the handy-works of human industry in connexion with the works of God, to which, under his divine blessing, they are all subordinate, and upon whom they are entirely and wholly dependent."]

Moseley, Rev. Henry, *v.* Reports by the Juries.

Mr. & Mrs John Brown's. Visit to London to see the Grand Exposition of All Nations. How They were astonished at its Wonders ! ! . Inconvenienced by the Crowds, & frightened out of their Wits, by the Foreigners. Designed & Etched by T. Onwhyn　Price 1*s.* 6*d.* plain 3*s.* 6*d.* col^{d.}

London. Pub by Ackermann & Co.

> [W. y. An oblong sheet of facetious engravings.]

Mulhouse, *v.* Rapport.

Munday, Contract between the Society of Arts & Mess Munday, *v.* Copies.

Murray, Rev. T. B., *v.* Day in the Crystal Palace.

Murraie, J. P. C., *v.* Nouveau Guide de l'Etranger.

Museums, Libraries, and Picture Galleries, Public and Private; Their Establishment, Formation, Arrangement, and Architectural Construction. To which is appended The Public Libraries Act, 1850, and remarks on its adoption by Mechanics and other Scientific Institutions; with illustrations. By John W. Papworth, Fellow of the Royal Institute of British Architects; etc. etc. and Wyatt Papworth, Architect; Hon. Sec. of the Architectural Publication Society; and Hon. Member of the Yorkshire Architectural Society.

> 'It is impossible to disguise from ourselves the paramount importance that— public opinion should be rightly informed, rightly instructed, and rightly directed.'—*Bishop of Manchester.*

The Authors reserve to themselves the right of Translation in Foreign Countries.

London: Chapman and Hall, 193, Piccadilly. 1853.

> [Price 12*s.* Imperial 8vo, pp. iv., 80. With sections and ground-plans. Bears on the arrangement proposed to be carried into effect at Kensington Gore.]

Music.

> Anelli,—National Quadrille—L'Enfant Quadrille.
> Barker, George—The Temple of Peace.
> Bernard, Francois—Hyde Park, Promenade Polka.
> Blockley, P. A.—Crystal Garden Polka—Crystal Garden Quadrilles.
> Bonner, H. E. W.—Grand Exhibition Schottisch.
> Boosé, Charles—Fairy Palace Waltzes.
> Buller, Karl—Amazon Gallop.
> Callcott, J. G.—Prize Medal Quadrille.
> Callcott, William Hutchins—The Mourners.
> Cooper, J.—Great Polka of all Nations.
> Coote, Charles—London in 1851.
> D'Albert, Charles—Crystal Palace Waltzes—Grand Exposition Quadrille.
> Etherington, James William—Grand March of All Nations.
> Fischer, Henri—Amazon Polka.
> Fowle, Thomas Lloyd—Hymn of Praise for All Nations.
> Glorious Exhibition.
> Hardwick, F. A.—National Exhibition—Exhibition Prizes—'Authorized Comic Catalogue.'
> Höchst, Carl—Quadrilles of All Nations.
> Jullien,—Crystal Fountain Polka—Great Exhibition Quadrille—Greek Slave Waltz.
> Kirkham, Miss Ellen—New Crystal Polka.

*Knox Ompax.—The Crystal Brunnen, a Song.
Labitzky,—Great Quadrille of All Nations.
Lavenu, L. H.—Sovereign of All.
Ling, J. R.—Crystal Palace Polka—Crystal Palace Quadrille—Crystal Palace Waltzes.
Linley, G.—Country Girl's Account of the Exhibition.
Linter, Ricardo—Polkas of All Nations.
Magnus, D.—La Perle de L'Exposition.
Major John Stenson—Crystal Palace Grand Exhibition Waltzes.
Matthey, Alphonso—State Polka.
Mengis, Herr—The Gathering of the Nations.
Musical Bouquet, Nᵒˢ· 19 and 20—284—285—289 and 290—297—305—308 —416 and 417.
Napoli, Henri—Royal Polkas of All Nations.
New Palace of Aladdin.
New, S. W.—Greek Slave.
Patey, C. A.—Broken Drum Polka—Crystal Waltzes.
Perry, George—British Sacred Banner.
Pianista, No. 127—Crystal Palace Polka.
Price, Elizabeth—Crystal Palace Quadrilles.
Quinton, F. T.—Two Polkas.
Russell, Henry—England's Welcome to All Nations.
Smith, Lydia B.—Hymn of the Crystal Palace.
Tussaud, Frank B.—Great Exhibition Polka—Great Exhibition Quadrilles —Great Exhibition Waltzes.
Wade, James—Crystal Palace Fantasia.
West, W.—Carpenter's Original Comic Songs.
Wickes, C. A.—Koh-i-Noor Waltzes.
Wilson, Haydn—Crystal Palace Second Set of Waltzes.
Wilson, W.—Dream of the Chrystal Palace—Exhibition Lodging House—Humours of a Parliamentary Visit.
Wood, W. Thorold—Meeting of the Nations.
Wybrow, Annie—England's Merry Polka.

Musical Department, Rev. W. W. Cazalet, *v.* On the.

Musical Instruments in the Great Industrial Exhibition of 1851. By William Pole, F.R.A.S., Organist of St. Mark's, Grosvenor Square. Reprinted, with additions, from Newton's London Journal of Arts. (For Private Circulation.) *London.* 1851.
   [8vo, pp. 99. Printed by R. Folkard, Devonshire Street.]

ᵒMusings on the Exhibition of All Nations, in London, May, 1851. By J. Gray, Islay.
Glasgow: Printed by Wm. Gilchrist, 145 Argyle Street. 1851.
   [Demy 8vo, pp. 8. A poem in praise.]

Mynegiad o Cyfansoddiad A Dybenion Arddangosfa Diwydrwydd y Byd, A Fwriedir Gynnal yn Llundain yn 1851; ynghyd a Phenderfyniadau dirprwywyr ei Mhawrhydi ar y mater.
John Thomas, Argraffydd, *Llanelli*
   [W. y. 8vo, pp. 8. A Welsh account of the proposed Exhibition.]

Nach London! Zur unterhaltenden und nützlichen Vorbereitung auf die Reise zur Welt-Ausstellung. Unter Benutzung der amtlich verfassten Uebersichten der Preuss. Commission für die Londoner Industrie-Ausstellung herausgegeben von Dr. E. Friedr. Melzer. Mit einem Plane von London—einer Karte der Eisenbahnen und Dampfschifffahrtsverbindungen Englands—einer Uebersichts-Karte der Eisenbahnen Mittel-Europa's und einem Panorama der Themse von London bis zur Mündung.
Breslau, Verlag von Trewendt & Granier. 1851.

                                                                   [Price

[Price 15 sgr. 24mo, pp. ii. 114. A guide-book for German visitors, written before the opening of the Exhibition. The author discusses the unsocial manners of the English.]

Napier, Mrs., *v.* Lay of the Palace [a Poem].

Nash, Mr., *v.* Dickensons' Comprehensive Pictures.

National Exhibitions, *v.* To-morrow.

National Galleries *v.* Art Education—Fraser's Magazine—Letter [Doyle].

National Gallery (The), as it is, and as it might be. A Lecture delivered at the Northampton and Northamptonshire Mechanics' Institute, 22 March 1853.—1853.
[*London:* Printed by Henry Hansard, near Lincoln's Inn-Fields. 8vo, pp. 26. Affects the question of the removal of the National Gallery to Kensington.]

National Gallery (The) its Formation and Management considered in a letter addressed, by permission, to H.R.H. The Prince Albert, K.G. &c. &c. &c. by William Dyce, Esq. R.A. Professor of the Theory of the Fine Arts in King's College, London.
' ——Si quid novisti rectius istis
Candidus imperti ; si non, his utere mecum.'
London: Chapman and Hall, 193 Piccadilly. 1853.
[Price 1*s.* 8vo, pp. 84. Bears on the question of the Kensington-Gore Proposal.]

Neuer Plan von London.
Published by James Wyld Geographer to the Queen and H.R.H. Prince Albert Charing Cross East (opposite Northumberland Street) London.
[Price 1*s.* A large sheet, the same work as Wyld's Map.]

New Exhibition (A).
Three Songs of never a' one,
Suited for every one ;
I ask, is't cleverly done
In good mix't sense?
No State exempt, nor Season,
True tale, *with* rhyme and reason,
As falsest tongue agrees on ;
Price but Sixpence.
London: Walter Cooper, 24 New Quebec Street. 1851. Entered at Stationers' Hall.
[12mo, pp. 23. A poem, dated " August 20th, 1851.
"Historic proverb crystallized, its wars inhuman cease,
Mercy and good-will flourishes with fair Industrial Peace."]

*New Map of London; also a full description & the authorized arrangements of the Crystal Palace, its Origin, Construction Dimensions &c. [Price 1*s.*]

New ' Order of Merit ' (The), as propounded in The Athenæum Of November 1st. 1851, discussed by E. G. M.
' What shall be done unto the man whom the King delighteth to honour ?'—*Book of Esther*, Chap. vi.
'Thy wish was, Father to that thought.'—*King Henry IV., Shakspere.*
[Without Publisher's or Printer's name, or date. 8vo, pp. 4.]

New Song to an Old Tune, *v.* Great Exhibition.

New York, Report to State of, Benj. P. Johnson, *v.* Report.

Nicholay, J. A., *v.* Historical account of Skins and Furs—Reports by the Juries.

Nijverheid's Paleis te Londen, *v.* Wereld.

° Nobleman's (The) Own Book of the Great Exhibition of 1851 ; or the Battle of the Cranes and The Frogs.
How fares the poor industrious working man ?
As well as any one on seven shillings a week can !
By getting up at four, and perhaps toiling till evening's eight,
Thus losing all his strength, reducing too, his weight ;
By slaving hard for little, or next kin to nothing—seven shillings per week.
Behold, Englishmen ! your labourer's fare—they are your countrymen.— *The Author.*
Read all; all read, read, and think, think, think and consider ; what you
think of, say out the thoughts; forming the best plans, scrutinize the plans,
and analyze them well, then draw deductions; make such deductions bear;
oft range them to proper order, next be set, then when made perfect let them
be

be sent forth into the world for the best and momentous wise discovery can
find for the sole use of man ; and man without distinction.—*The Author.*

> The end is not yet; oh no, not yet,
> Although 'tis slave and slave driving it used to be ;
> But 'fore Old England's sons, its golden sun will set,
> The slave will well do, as well as the driver, will be free.

London: James Thomas, 35, Bedfordbury, Covent Garden; and Sold by Appleyard, Farringdon
Street, and all booksellers. 1851.

[8vo, pp. 42. Pieces in verse and prose on the condition of the agricultural laborers in
England.]

Noel, Rev. B. W., *v.* Forty-four Sermons.

Nördlinger, Dr. H., *v.* Querschnitte von hundert Holzarten.

Northampton, *v.* National Gallery, A Lecture at— Rules of Provident Society.

Northcote, Sir Stafford, *v.* Illustrated London Almanack.

Notes and Sketches of Lessons on subjects connected with The Great Exhibition,
  Published under the Direction of the Committee of General Literature and
  Education, appointed by the Society For Promoting Christian Knowledge.
  London : Printed for the Society For Promoting Christian Knowledge; Sold at the Depository,
  Great Queen Street, Lincoln's Inn Fields ; 4, Royal Exchange ; 16, Hanover Street, Hanover
  Square; and by all Booksellers. 1852.
  [Price 1*s.* 4*d.* 12mo, pp. viii., 183. Prepared for the use of teachers.]

Notes on the Organization of an Industrial College for Artizans. By T. Twining,
  Jun. For Private circulation.
  [*London :*—Printed by G. Barclay, Castle St. Leicester Sq. W. y. 8vo, pp. 31. Has
  reference to a College of Trades. "But the Great Exhibition has altered the face of things.
  People's notions have expanded with the rapidity of a mushroom growth, and the nervous
  cautiousness which did things piecemeal, and spoiled them, has given place to a just
  appreciation of the scale on which affairs of national importance must be done; to a
  consciousness of the advantages of embracing at once all the bearings of a scheme in a
  single-minded arrangement, and to a sense of the paramount value for institutions of this
  kind of a centralised administration."]

Notes on the Woollen Manufactures of Belgium, Prussia, and France, made in the
  year 1850. By the late Samuel Walker, Esq. of Millshaw, Leeds. Printed
  for the Members of the Leeds Chamber of Commerce.
  Leeds : Printed by J. Swallow, Corn-Exchange. 1851.
  [Privately circulated. 8vo, pp. iv., 25, with a preface by Mr. Martin Cawood.]

* Notes sur le Section 5 par M. Martin.
  Lange Levy. [8vo. Advertised in Journal de la Librarie.]

Notes sur Les Produits Espagnols envoyés à L'Exposition de Londres suivies de
  quelques considérations sur L'Etat Présent et L'Avenir de L'Industrie Espa-
  gnole et d'un Exposé Méthodique des Mêmes Produits. Par M. Ramon de La
  Sagra, Commissaire Espagnol, Membre du Jury Mixte.
  Londres : Hippolyte Baillière, 219, Regent Street, 1851.
  [Price 1*s.* 8vo, pp. 88. A detailed and classified list of articles exhibited.]

Notice concernant l'Etablissement Typographique de M. Paul Dupont de Paris.
  Paris Imprimerie de Paul Dupont, Rue de Grenelle-St.-Honoré, 45. 1851.
  [Privately printed. Royal 8vo, pp. 56. Two editions, one French, one French and English.]

Nottingham, *v.* Address by J. A. Hammersley on the Preparations on the Continent.

Nouveau Guide à Londres, *v.* Guide-Chaix.

Nouveau Guide de l'Etranger à Londres, pour l'Année 1851 ; divisé en 12 Journées
  et Soirées : précèdé de deux Vignettes, en Taille-douce, représentant l'Extérieur
  et l'Intérieur du Palais-Vitre, où a lieu l'Exposition Industrielle de toutes les
  Nations du Globe ; et du Nom des Hôtels et des Parties de la Ville où il doit
  établir son Domicile : suivi d'un Plan de la Métropole, coloré de manière à
  indiquer ; les endroits, les rues, les bâtimens publics, les institutions, &c. &c.,
  qu'il a à visiter dans chaque journée ou soirée ; Guide explicatif à tous les
  Panoramas, Dioramas, Exhibitions, Institutions de Londres, &c., approprié aux
  personnes qui ne comprennent pas l'Anglais, sans être obligé d'avoir recours à
  aucun autre Guide que le Plan. Par J. P. C. Murraie.

Londres :

Londres: Chez Dulau et Cⁱᵉ·, 37, Soho Square. 1851. (Entered at Stationers' Hall.)
> [Price 2*s.* 6*d.* 8vo, pp. viii., 77. Contains a very short account of the Exhibition. The name of the writer is an assumed name.]

Nouveau Plan de Londres.
> Published by James Wyld Geographer to the Queen and H.R.H. Prince Albert Charing Cross East (opposite Northumberland Street) London.
> [Price 1*s.* colored, 6*d.* plain. A large sheet, *v.* Wyld and Neuer.]

Nouveau Tableau de Londres, comprenant un aperçu rétrospectif de l'histoire de cette Metropole, et une notice détaillée de ses Monuments, ses Curiosités, ses Institutions, etc. avec une description complète du Chateau de Windsor, de Hampton Court, Woolwich, Greenwich, Chelsea, et autres lieux ce ses environs. Le tout orné de cinquante neuf vues de ses monuments publics, suivi d'un Plan pour visiter la Capitale en sept jours, et précédé d'une nouvelle Carte de Londres, indiquant les rues principales, les routes des omnibus, les chemins de fer, etc. Dernière Edition.
> *Londres:* G. F. Cruchley, Editeur, 81, Fleet Street.
> [Price 2*s.* W. y. 12mo, pp. vi., xii., 312. The book contains an account, pp. i-vii, of the Exhibition, and "un plan Géométral de l'Edifice de la Grande Exposition de l'Industrie."]

Now Open, the Great Exhibition of The Idleness of All Nations, and may be carried away, for one shilling. Printed by Dean & Son Threadneedle St. 2*s.* if colᵈ.
> 'For Satan finds some mischief still,
> For idle hands to do.'

G. Mann, Cornhill.
> [W. y. A sheet of facetious engravings, folded. A number of the engravings appear to have been used in another work, which will be found under the title This.]

Objections to the Exhibition, *v.* Exhibition of 1851.

Observations on the Expediency of carrying out the Proposals of the Commissioners for the Exhibition of 1851, for the Promotion of Institutions of Science and Art at Kensington, rather by the Public themselves than by Government, Submitted, by permission, to His Royal Highness Prince Albert, President of the Royal Commission, by Henry Cole, C.B.
> *London:* Chapman and Hall, 193 Piccadilly. 1853. Price Sixpence.
> [8vo, pp. 15. "I have attempted to show that the comprehensive proposals made in the Second Report of the Royal Commissioners for aiding the establishment of Institutions to promote Science and Art at Kensington would be most effectively carried out by the Public themselves rather than by Government."]

°Ode in Commemoration of the Great Exhibition, by John Horatio Martin.

Ode on the Great Exhibition, 1851.
> *Ex paucis plurima concipit ingenium.*
> [Kingcombe, Printer, 46, High Street, Camden Town. W. y. Printed for private circulation. 12mo, pp. 7.
> "All distant worlds look down and bless the hour,
> And aiding with *their* power,
> Proclaim as they shine in the purple sky,
> That the first Great Gala of Earth is nigh!"]

Odernheimer, F., *v.* Amtlicher Bericht.

Oechelhäuser, Wilhelm, *v.* Amtlicher Bericht.

Official Catalogue of Articles from the German Zoll-Verein and Northern Germany sent to the London Exhibition of Industry. With the Prices and Classes, an Alphabetical List of the Names of the various Exhibitors, a Table of German Money, Weights, Measures etc. reduced to the English Standard, and a Register of the Sections.
> *Berlin,* 1851. R. Decker, Chief Printer to his Majesty the King of Prussia.
> *London,* 1851. Franz Thimm, German Bookseller 88 New Bond Street Two doors from Oxford Street.
> [Price 1*s.* Post 8vo, pp. viii, 390. A German edition will be found under Amtliches.]

Official Catalogue of the Great Exhibition of the Works of Industry of All Nations, 1851

'The

'The Earth is the Lord's, and all that therein is:
The compass of the World and they that dwell therein.'

London: Spicer Brothers, Wholesale Stationers; W. Clowes & Sons, Printers; Contractors to the Royal Commission, 29 New Bridge Street, Blackfriars, and at the Exhibition Building, Hyde Park.
[Price 1s. Small 4to, pp. 320.]
The Same. " Corrected Edition."
The Same. " First Corrected Edition."
The Same. " Second Corrected and Improved Edition, 1st July, 1851." Has an extra page.
The Same. " Third Corrected and Improved Edition, 1st August, 1851."
The Same. " Fourth Corrected and Improved Edition, 15th September, 1851."

Official Descriptive and Illustrated Catalogue. By Authority of the Royal Commission. In three Volumes. Vol. 1. Index and Introductory. Section 1.—Raw Materials, Classes 1 to 4. Section 2.—Machinery, Classes 5 to 10. Vol. 2. Section 3.—Manufactures, Classes 11 to 29. Section 4.—Fine Arts, Class 30. Colonies. Vol. 3. Foreign States. — Supplementary Volume. United Kingdom.—India.—Foreign States. Index to annotations. First and second Reports of the Royal Commissioners.
London: Spicer Brothers, Wholesale Stationers; W. Clowes and Sons, Printers; Contractors to the Royal Commission, 29 New Bridge Street, Blackfriars, and at the Exhibition Building. 1851.
[Price 4l. 4s. Crown 8vo. Vol. I., pp. cxcii., 1 to 478, 465* to 478* Vol. II., 479 to 1002. Vol. III., 1003 to 1469. Supplementary Vol., xxviii , 1470 to 1532; liv., 211; 76.]
[Another Copy on large paper.]
[Price 20 guineas.]

[Another Copy on large paper, illustrated with photographs and with half titles peculiar to this Edition, prepared for and presented with the large Edition of the Jury Reports and Special Reports to Foreign Governments and Her Majesty's Commissioners. Imperial 4to.]

Old Cornish Woman, *v.* Aunt Mavor.

Old Eighteen-Fifty-one, *v.* Little Henry.

Old Mother Bunch, *v.* Aunt Mavor.

Oliveira, Meeting at Mr. Oliveira's, *v.* Crystal Palace, Report.

Oliveira Prize-Essay (The) on Portugal: with the Evidence regarding that Country taken before a Committee of the House of Commons in May, 1852; and the Author's Surveys of the Wine-Districts of the Alto-Douro, as Adopted and Published by Order of the House of Commons. Together with a Statistical Comparison of the Resources and Commerce of Great-Britain and Portugal. By Jos^h; James Forrester ;. (C∴ R∴ ✠∴) Wine-Grower in the Alto-Douro.
' Je dirai ce que je pense des affaires : je tâcherai autant qu'il est en moi, de donner à la nation conscience de son état: de la relever dans sa propre estime, et aux yeux de l'étranger.'—*La Revolution Sociale.*
' Espero com esta pequena memoria despertar a actividade adormecida, e dirigir com segurança, e economia a industria publica, e particular.'— *Joze Bonifacio d'Andrade.*
London: John Weale, 59, High Holborn. John Menzies, *Edinburgh:* Coutinho, *Oporto.* 1853.
[Price 10s. 6d. 8vo, pp. xxx., 286, and an Appendix, pp. iv. Mr. Oliveira offered " Fifty Guineas for an Essay on Portugal, in connection with the Objects of the Great Exhibition."]

1851, *v.* Year.

1851 : or, the Adventures of M^r and Mrs Sandboys and family, who came up to London to ' enjoy themselves,' and see the Great Exhibition. By Henry Mayhew, and George Cruikshank.
London: David Bogue, 86, Fleet Street.
[W. y. Price 2s. 6d. 8vo, pp. 248. With illustrations. The contents of this book may be judged of by the List of Illustrations. " All the world going to the Great Exhibition Looking for Lodgings London crammed and Manchester deserted The Opera Boxes during the time of the Great Exhibition The opening of the Great Bee-hive The first shilling day Some of the drolleries of the Great Exhibition Odds and ends, in, out, and about the Great Exhibition Dispersion of the Works of All Nations".]

One of the Public, *v.* Reasons.

On the approaching Close of the Great Exhibition. And other Poems. By the Lady Emmeline Stuart Wortley.
London: W. N. Wright, Bookseller to the Queen, 60 Pall Mall. 1851.
[Price 2*s.* 6*d.* 8vo, pp. 99. The poem on the Exhibition occupies pages 1–47.
"Praise ye sang at the Commencement,—Sing, Oh! Sing, too, at the Close!—
As bright the star shines of Success, as the star of Promise rose;—
For the atchieved Success,—the onlooking Hopes,—Yea! bring ye prayer and praise,—
And on that grand Anthem's sounding wings, your thoughts and spirits raise."]

On the Closing of the Great Exhibition. Saturday, October 11th, 1851.
[Without Publisher's or Printer's name, or date. 4to, p. 1. A poem signed Robert Snow.
" 'Tis done! Now Art to Nature shall repay
The acres trusted to those CRYSTALL HALLS :
Upon no bankrupt Stage we end the Play,
For to a World's applause the Curtain falls!"]

On the Construction of the Building for the Exhibition of the Works of Industry of All Nations, in 1851. By Matthew Digby Wyatt, Assoc. Inst. C. E. With an abstract of the discussion upon the Paper. Excerpt Minutes of Proceedings, Vol. X. of the Institution of Civil Engineers. By Permission of the Council.
London: Printed by W. Clowes and Sons, Stamford Street. 1851.
[8vo. pp, 67. With a view of the Building and other engravings.]

On the Dignity of Labour. Great Exhibition of the Works of Industry of All Nations in London, 1851. Speech of the Bishop of Oxford at the Westminster Meeting.
Bradbury and Evans, Printers, Whitefriars.
[W. y. 25 copies for 3*d.* 8vo., pp. 2. Published by the Westminster Committee.]

° On the Gathering of the Nations : lines by Mrs. Brewer.

On the Great Exhibition of 1851. Nos. XVII. and XVIII. of Occasional Sermons, Preached in Westminster Abbey, by Chr. Wordsworth, D.D. Canon of Westminster. Price Two Shillings.
[Published by Rivingtons St. Paul's Churchyard, and Waterloo Place, London. W. y. 8vo, pp. 37. Preached Sunday, July 6, 1851.]

On the Musical Department of the late Exhibition. Read before the Society of Arts, May 6th, 1852. By the Rev. W. W. Cazalet, A.M., late Associate Juror of Class XA of the Exhibition.
[Without Publisher's or Printer's name, or date. Price 6*d.* 8vo, pp. 16.]

[On the Origin and details of Construction of the Building for the Exhibition of 1851.]
[Levey, Robson, and Franklyn, Great New Street, Fetter Lane. 8vo., pp. 5, with an engraving. Read before the Society of Arts Nov. 13th, 1850, and printed in their Transactions.]

Onwhyn, T., *v.* Mr. and Mrs. John Brown—What I Saw at the World's Fair.

Opening (The) of the Crystal Palace considered in some of its relations to the Prospects of Art. By John Ruskin, M.A., Author of 'The Stones of Venice,' 'The Seven Lamps of Architecture,' 'Modern Painters,' etc.
London: Smith, Elder, and Co., 65. Cornhill. 1854.
[Price 1*s.* 8vo, pp. 21. Has reference to the Crystal Palace at Sydenham and to the declaration that it is to produce "an entirely novel order of Architecture." Incidentally, Mr. Ruskin speaks of the old Exhibition Building. He goes on to say, "Another interesting fact connected with the history of the Crystal Palace as it bears on that of the art of Europe, namely, that in the year 1851, when all that glittering roof was built, in order to exhibit the petty arts of our fashionable luxury—the carved bedsteads of Vienna, and glued toys of Switzerland—and gay jewellery of France—in that very year, I say, the greatest pictures of Venetian masters were rotting at Venice in the rain, for want of roof to cover them, with holes made by cannon-shot through their canvass."]

Order of Merit, *v.* New Order.

Origin of the Great Exhibition. (From 'The Mining Journal,' Nov. 1, 1851.)
[Without Publisher's or Printer's name, or year. 4to, pp. 4. An article in English and French, printed in parallel columns (pp. 1–3), advocating Mr. Whishaw's claims in reference to the Exhibition. "That the name of the individual from whom the idea emanated, no less than his to whom the public are indebted for the achievement, should be concealed, is not in unison with the English character; yet such would appear to be now attempted—
a veil

a veil having purposely been thrown over the real origin of the great gathering, and all the credit attributed to Prince Albert alone." Page 4 contains an article " From the 'Liverpool Albion' of Nov. 24, 1851," on the same subject.]

Our Heartless Policy.   Dedicated to the High-minded and Reflecting of All Nations, at the approaching Exhibition.   By ' An Etonian.'
London: James Ridgway, Piccadilly.   1851.
[Price 2s.   8vo, pp. 72.   "This work is intended for those of all—though most of Christian—nations, about to visit our shores, who, whether sternly advocating the necessity for, or supinely conniving at, the continuance of the judicial murder of their fellow-creatures, in their several communities, are totally unconscious, it is charitably presumed, how the course they are pursuing is at utter variance with the very first principles of the doctrine which, as Christians, they profess."]

* Ouvriers (Les) de M. Charriere.   Chant par Aristide Bosc.
[Chassaignon, Imprimeur.   Advertised in Journal de la Librarie, but not known to M. Charriere, or to be heard of in his establishment.]

Overend, Wilson, *v.* Address of the Local Commissioners for Sheffield.

Overland Journey (An) to the Great Exhibition   Showing a Few Extra Articles & Visitors.   By Richard Doyle.
London: Chapman and Hall, 193, Piccadilly.   Price 3s. plain; 5s. coloured.
[W. y.   A long sheet of facetious engravings.]

Owen, Richard, *v.* Lectures [Raw Materials, Animal Kingdom]—Reports by Juries.

Oxford, Bishop of, *v.* On the Dignity of Labour.

Παγκοσμιος (H) Εκθεσις Δημοσιευθεῖσα εἰς τὴν Αμαλθειαν, καὶ Αθηναν, τὸ 1851.   Υπο Στεφανου. Θ. Ξενου.   Συγγραφέως τοῦ Διαβόλου ἐν Τουρκίᾳ, τῆς 'Επιθεωρήσεως τοῦ Λονδίνου, Περιηγήσεως εἰς Μάνζεστερ, Μιᾶς ἑσπέρας εἰς τὸ Πάρκον τοῦ 'Αγίου 'Ιακώβου, κ.τ.λ. κ.τ.λ.

" Fortuna vitrea est; tum cum splendet, frangitur."
PUB. SYRUS.
Εν Λονδίνω 'Εκ τῆς Τυπογραφίας τῶν Κ. Κ. Wertheimer καὶ Συντρ., Κατὰ τὴν ὁδὸν London Wall, 1852.
[Price 15s.   4to, pp. 187, with numerous Illustrations.]

*Palace of Glass and the City of Gold.   [Price 1d.   Wertheim.]

Palace of Glass (The) and the Gathering of the People.   A Book for the Exhibition.
Humani generis progressus,
Ex communi omnium labore ortus,
Uniuscujusque industriæ debet esse finis :
Hoc adjuvando,
Dei opt : max : voluntatem exsequimur.
The progress of the human race,
Resulting from the common labour of all men,
Ought to be the final object of the exertion of each individual.
In promoting this end,
We are carrying out the will of the great and blessed God.
London : The Religious Tract Society ; 56, Paternoster Row, and 65, St. Paul's Churchyard.   1851.
[Price 2s.   12mo, pp. vi., 162.   The following are the heads of the various chapters : The Poet's Dream—Contrast between the Past and Present—Voices of Hope and Warning —Associations, Secular and Sacred—Beneficial Results, probable and possible—Lessons, Pertinent and Practical."   An Edition was subsequently published bearing the name of the Rev. J. Stoughton as the Author.]

Palace of Glass.   (From the Leeds Mercury of September 21st, 1850.)
[Edward Baines and Sons, Printers, Leeds.   W. y.   8vo, pp. 4.   A sheet with four engravings of the Exhibition, and a ground-plan, and on the back of the engravings a short description, set up as 4 pages 8vo, of the proposed undertaking.   " Amidst all that is wonderful connected with this Exhibition, we will hope for much that is socially and morally good. It cannot but be that industry will receive an impulse all over the world, and that we shall get our full share; and whilst the opulent are gainers by the refining of taste, the multitude will be still greater gainers by the improvement of those arts which provide the necessaries of life—food, clothing, and furniture."]

Palace of Glass (The) or London in 1851 Designed by Watts Phillips and Percy Cruikshank.   Drawn & Etched by Watts Phillips.   Price 1s. 6d. plain 3s. 6d. col^{d.}

Published

Published by Ackermann & Co 96 Strand
  [W. y. An oblong sheet of facetious engravings.]

Palace of Industry: A Brief History of its Origin and Progress: with A Descriptive
  Account of the most interesting portions of the Machinery employed in its
  construction. Illustrated with numerous Engravings on Wood.
  London: John Ollivier, 59, Pall Mall. 1851.
    [Price 1s. Small 4to, pp. 44.]

Palace of Industry (The). A Comprehensive and Popular Account of The Great
  Exhibition Building, in Hyde Park, erected by Messrs. Fox & Henderson,
  from the designs of Joseph Paxton, Esq. by W. J. B. Saunders.
  London: Effingham Wilson, Royal Exchange. 1851.
    [Price 1s. 12mo, pp. 62. "It will be unnecessary, it is presumed, to offer any apology
    for the minuteness with which the author has applied himself to describe the progress of that
    masterpiece of English art which has already filled the world with its fame, and is now
    delighting every eye with its glittering surfaces of glass, the bold proportions of its elegant
    transept, and the far-retiring perspective of its long and stately avenues of iron." It is
    illustrated with diagrams.]

Palace of Universal Labour (The). Lines suggested by the Industrial Exhibition
  of 1851. By Edwin Owen Jones.
  London: J. O. Clarke, Printer, 121, Fleet Street, and Racquet Court.
    [W. y. Circulated gratuitously. Post 8vo, pp. 8.
          " 'Twas in summer evening's vision,
            When repose, with dreams Elysian,
            Shrouds in sleep the cares of day,
          I a palace saw, in glory
          Far excelling all that story
            Did in prose or verse portray."]

Palacio (El) de Cristal. Esposicion de la Industria Universal en Londres en 1851
  por J. J. Arnoux. Editores Propietarios MM. X. de Lassalle y Mélan.
  Paris en la Administracion General del Correo de Ultramar. Calle del Faubourg Montmartre,
    n. 10. 1851.
    [Price 10 francs. 8vo, pp. 246, with two large engravings. A series of articles on the
    Exhibition, arranged according to countries. The largest account is devoted to France, for
    which country the author, apparently opposed to freedom of trade, claims the honour of the
    first conception of the Exhibition. He also occasionally animadverts upon the supposed
    national selfishness of the English:—"The English having gained the conviction that they
    were about to die of plethora, what remedy did they resort to? To this. They proclaimed
    limited free trade, and opened their ports to foreign commerce. This remedy, due to Sir R.
    Peel, was nothing more than the first step towards the attainment of their object; the second
    was made by Prince Albert, who, acting under the impulse of the English spirit, had proposed
    to himself to impart it to the British nation at large. From underneath this grand manœuvre
    lurks another purpose. 'Open your ports,' says Great Britain to all the other nations of
    the globe, 'as I have opened mine; send me your merchandize, and receive mine instead.'
    But only let the foreign nations lend a ready ear to England and she will inundate the whole
    world with her countless productions, and drown, by her overwhelming competition, every
    great local industry."]

Palais de Cristal (Le). Journal Illustré de l'Exposition de 1851.
  London: Printed by Joseph Thomas, of No. 1, Finch Lane, Cornhill, in the City of London; and
    Published by the said Joseph Thomas, at No. 1, Finch Lane, Cornhill, in the City of London.
    1851, May 7 to October 11.
    [Price 6d. each number of 16 pp. Folio: 231 engravings of the Building and of the
    articles exhibited appear in the 368 pp. An edition is said to have been printed in Italian,
    under the title of Il Palazzo.]

Palais de Cristal (Le). Ode.
        'Is't an edifice built by human hand?'—*A Day Dream, by Eleanor Darby.*

Albert-Montémont, Chevalier de la Légion-d'Honneur, Membre de plusieurs
  Sociétés Scientifiques et Littéraires.—Paris, 16 Septembre 1851.
  Paris.—Imp. Boisseau et Cᵉ, pass. du Caire, 123-124.
    [8vo, pp. 4.
            " Admirez sa voûte de glace,
              Qui, belle de sa nouveaute
              Et d'un long parc tenant la place
              Du chêne abrite la fierté !
              Monarque des bois, que ta cime,
              Sous ce dôme, au faîte sublime,
              Repose son feuillage épais ;
              Vainqueur de l'invincible obstacle,
              Jamais plus étonnant spectacle
              A-t-il frappé l'œil de la Paix ?"]

M

Palais de Cristal (Le) ou les Parisiens a Londres Grande Revue de l'Exposition
Universelle en Cinq Actes et Huit Tableaux.　Par MM. Clairville et Jules
Cordier.　Mise en Scène de M. Daudel.—Musique du Ballet de MM. Adam,
Lanner, Pilati et Adolphe Vaillard.—Ballet composé et arrangé par M. E.
Lerouge.—Costumes dessinés par M. Alfred Albert.—Décors de M. Devoir.—
Machines de M. Auguste Marie.　Représentée pour la première fois, à Paris,
sur le théâtre de la Porte-Saint-Martin, le 26 Mai 1851.
> *Paris* Beck, Libraire Rue des Grands-Augustins, 20. Tresse, successeur de J. N. Barba, Palais-
> National. 1851.　Prix: 60 centimes.
> [8vo, pp. 34.　Scene laid in London.]

* Palais de Cristal, ou l'Union des Peuples par J. B.
> Devoyé.
> [Advertised in Journal de la Librarie.]

Palais (Le) de Cristal, ou le Géant de Hyde-Park, Par M. J. M., Professeur dans
l'un des principaux établissements de la Belgique.
> *Bruxelles.*　C.-J.-A. Greuse, Imp.-Libr.-Editeur, Rue Boughem, 6, Faub. de Schaerbeek.　1851.
> [Price 1s.　18mo, pp. 100.　With Exterior and Interior Views, a ground-plan and plan of
> the Galleries.　The headings of the various chapters are Historical Account of Exhibitions—
> the idea of the Crystal Palace and the birth of the Giant in Hyde Park.]

Palazzo (Il) di Cristallo.
> [Without Publisher's or Printer's name, date, or price.　32mo, 4 pp.　It commences "Che
> immensa folla di popolo," and is a small religious tract.]

*Palazzo di Cristallo.　A Newspaper, *v.* Palais de Cristal.

Panizzi, A., *v.* Reports by the Juries.

Papers referring to the Proposed Contributions from India for the Industrial Exhibition of 1851.　By J. Forbes Royle, M.D.
> *London :* Printed for the Author.　1851.
> [8vo, pp. 21.　The pamphlet treats " on the Exhibition of Raw Products and Manufac-
> tured articles from India," Dr. Royle's " views on the desirableness of India contributing to
> the Great Exhibition," and gives a " List of the Raw Products and Manufactured Articles
> suggested to be sent from India."　In the second division Dr. Royle observes—" The
> proposed Exposition of Raw Materials, Manufactured Articles, and Inventions of All
> Nations, novel in idea and grand in conception, will be an occasion when the latent
> resources of distant provinces and the skill of the least-known artist may compete with the
> produce of the most favoured regions or the works of the most successful genius.　It will
> enjoy the advantage, moreover, of having almost everyone you could wish for as spectators ;
> for few, either of the commercial, manufacturing, literary, scientific, or fashionable worlds,
> will omit to visit what can hardly fail to be one of the most interesting displays the world
> has ever seen.　The only fear is, that it may become overwhelming from its magnitude.
> * * *　Though India might contribute something in all the above departments, as, for
> instance, Sculpture, as practised in the rude representations of the Hindoo Pantheon, and
> Invention, as exemplified in the several machines which they were probably among the first
> to apply to various arts and manufactures, it is only under the head of Raw Materials and
> Manufactured Articles that the products of India will hold a conspicuous place, in the
> present day, among the accumulated products of the world.　A more extensive knowledge
> among European manufacturers of the Raw Products of the Indian soil could hardly fail to
> increase its commerce ; while an exhibition of its manufacturing skill may still extort
> admiration, without, perhaps, increasing the demand for Dacca muslins or for Benares
> brocades, or in making these more fashionable."]

Papers relating to Proposals for Establishing Colleges of Arts and Manufactures for
the Better Instruction of the Industrial Classes.　J. A. Lloyd, F.R.S., F.G.S.
Member of Council of the Royal Geographical Society ; Member of Council of
the Institution of Civil Engineers, etc.　For Private Circulation.
> *London :* Printed by W. Clowes and Sons, Stamford Street.　1851.
> [8vo, pp. 40.　" I have endeavoured to show that the present is the most favourable and
> opportune moment for grafting on the results of the Exhibition a better and more general
> system of scientific education for the rising generation of manufacturers, than can at present
> be attained except in very isolated cases."]

Papeterie (La), la Librarie, Rapport du XVIIe Jury, A. F. Didot, *v.* Imprimerie.

Papier Blanc, MM. Journet et Rieder, *v.* Rapport sur.

Papier pour Tentures par M. Jean Zuber, *v.* Rapport sur.

Papworth, J. W. and W., *v.* Museums.

Parable (The) of the Pearl of Great Price, explained and applied with reference to The Great Industrial Exhibition, by the Rev. Fletcher Fleming, Perpetual Curate of Rydal, Westmorland.

Kendal: Printed by John Hudson.

London: Whitaker and Co., Ave-Maria Lane. *Ambleside:* Mrs. Nicholson, and T. Troughton. *Bowness:* J. Allen. 1851.

> [Price Threepence. 8vo, pp. 16. " I would entreat those of my readers who may yet visit the Crystal Palace, and, when they have duly inspected it, with its sparkling Crystal Fount, and the numberless articles which it contains, of a useful, ornamental, scientific, ingenious, and curious description,—to raise their thoughts to the contemplation of the ' Palace' of the ' Great King,' and of its pure, and holy, and happy inmates."]

Parent's Cosmopolitan Key, *v.* Great National Exhibition.

Paris. Fonderie, Imprimerie, Librarie. Plon Frères. A Messieurs les Membres du Jury. Exposition de Londres 1851.

> [Without Publisher's or Printer's name, or date. Small 8vo, pp. 16. A List of the different products of Messieurs Plon's establishment. The work was printed by Messrs. Plon, " Rue de Vaugirard—36—á Paris."]

Park, Andrew, *v.* Great International Exhibition.

Park (The) and the Crystal Palace Presenting a complete series of exterior Views displaying the beautiful combinations of that magnificent Structure with the surrounding scenery Drawn by Philip Brannon Artist & Author of the picture of Southampton, the Stranger's Guide to Netley Abbey, Geology Simplified & Illustrated, &c. Dedicated by Permission to His Royal Highness Prince Albert.

London Published, June, 9th, 1851, by Ackermann & Co. 96, Strand, by Appointment to the Queen, H.R.H. Prince Albert, and the Royal Family.

> [Price, plain £1 1*s.*; coloured, £1 15*s.* the series. Royal folio, pp. 2. With six views. " Our intention is, as we shall more fully explain in our introductory remarks, to show the actual appearances of the Crystal Palace amidst the scenery in which it is located, by giving a series of accurate Sketches from all the principal points of view, a labour which has not yet been attempted by any Artist."]

Parliamentary Papers, *v.* Copy of a Letter – Copy of Warrant—Report of the Commissioners—Tower of London.

Parlour Magazine (The) of the Literature of All Nations.

London: Houlston & Stoneman.

> [W. y., but printed in the Crystal Palace. Royal 8vo, pp. 426. A periodical. Price 7*s.* 6*d.* The preface to the 2nd volume says : " We had originally intended to have terminated our labours with that Great Idea—the World's Exhibition—which first suggested our project ; but finding at that time that we had not fulfilled our comprehensive title, the ' Literature of All Nations,' we proceeded to its fulfilment."]

Pashley, Rev. W., *v.* Morning Stars.

Patents, *v.* Rights of Inventors.

Patston, Caroline, *v.* Thoughts on the Crystal Palace.

Paxton, [Sir] Joseph, *v.* Account of Mr. Peabody's Dinner (Speech at Derby)— Glaspalast, Der—House that Paxton Built—Illustrated London Almanack. On the origin of the Building—What is to become of the Crystal Palace.

Peabody, George, Dinner given by Mr., *v.* Account of.

Pellatt, Apsley, on Manufacture of Flint Glass, *v.* Explanatory Catalogue.

Peligot, M. E., on Glass, *v.* Travaux.

Penny Map of London (The), or Great Exhibition Guide.

London: Published by George Vickers, Strand ; and W. M. Clark, Warwick Lane.

> [W. y. A sheet. Has nothing, except the title, relating to the Exhibition.]

Penny Plan and Guide to the Great Exhibition of the Works of Industry of All Nations, 1851.

> [*London:*—Spicer brothers, and W. Clowes and Sons, Contractors to the Royal Commission, 29 New Bridge Street, Blackfriars, and at the Exhibition Building. W. y. Post 8vo, pp. 4.]

Perfumed Almanack Great Exhibition of Industry open to all Nations 1851

Eugene Rimmel, Perfumer. 39, Gerrard St. Soho, *London.*

> [Printed on a card.]

Persoz, M., on Printed and Dyed Goods, *v.* Travaux.

Perspective Views, *v.* Spooner—Telescopic.

Petermann, Augustus, *v.* Austrian Section—Geographical.

Petter's Handbook Guide to London: or What to observe and Remember of the
Public Buildings, Cathedrals, Churches, Halls, Parks, Theatres, and Exhibitions:
and a descriptive Panorama of the Thames from Gravesend to Hampton Court.
Embellished with views of public buildings, a map, and an Engraving on Steel
of the Great Exhibition Building.
London: G. E. Petter, 102, Cheapside. 1851.
[18mo, pp. x., 198. Pages 94 and 95 contain an account of the Exposition Building.]

Philanthropos, *v.* Spare the Crystal Palace.

Phillips, W., *v.* Palace of Glass.

Philoponos, *v.* Great Exhibition of 1851, or Wealth of the World in its Workshop.

Philosopher's Mite (The) to the Great Exhibition of 1851.
' Forewarned, Forearmed.'
London: Houlston and Stoneman, 55 Pater Noster Row. Price One Shilling.
[W. y. 8vo, pp. 34. Addressed to Prince Albert. "It would be a mere senseless display
of book-knowledge were we to refer you to the hundreds of instances of pestilence accruing
upon great international meetings. Take up what history you like; choose any quarter of
the globe, any *siècle*, any nation, any metropolis, any great city, and still the fact will
encounter you. You have near you good and truly learned men, who will refer you to the
historic proofs that the most widely-spreading and most exterminating pestilences of Great
Britain followed upon, and were traceable to, sudden and enormous influx of foreigners."]

Philp's Illustrations of London, in 1851. Lithographed from original drawings, by
Robert S. Groom. The Great Exhibition,—Hyde-Park.
London:—Houlston & Stoneman. Entered at Stationers' Hall.
[W. y. Price 2s. 6d. An oblong sheet of engravings. Has nothing relating to the
Exhibition, except an exterior view on the cover.]

Phipps, Colonel, Correspondence with Mr. Drew, *v.* Great Exhibition.

Picken, Thomas, *v.* Souvenir.

Pictorial Key, *v.* Baxter.

* Pieces Lues au Banquet de la Saint Charlemagne. Lycee Bonaparte Annee 1852.
Exposition de Londres par Maurice Reynaud, demeurant 108 Rue St. Lazare.
[Advertised in Journal de la Librarie.]

Pierre Reillor, *v.* Prophecie. [A poem.]

Pilati, Mons, *v.* Palais de Cristal ou les Parisiens a Londres.

Pilote de Londres (Le), *v.* Londres et la Grande Exposition.

*Pilote (Le) de Londres. A Newspaper.

Pipe, Mrs., and Family, *v.* Wanderings of.

Pipes, Pumps, and Conduits of Bristol (The); together with the Sparrows of the
Crystal Cage (an Incident of the Great Exhibition); and the Derby Crisis,
(showing the interior of Osborne House in a public emergency); being original
papers reprinted from The Bristol Times and Felix Farley's Journal.
London: Hamilton, Adams, & Co.
Bristol: John Ridler. Price, One Shilling.
[W. y. 12mo, pp. ii., 41. The article entitled "The Sparrows of the Crystal Cage,"
pp. 30-36, is an imaginary dialogue on the subject of the Crystal Palace. The other
essays have no reference to the Exhibition. Printed by J. Leech, Bristol Times and Felix
Farley's Journal Office, 11, Small Street.]

Placards exhibited in conspicuous places within the Crystal Palace, designed to for-
ward one of the grand objects of the Royal Commission—warmly responded
to by the Queen, and suitably dwelt upon by the Archbishop, viz.;—' The
Strengthening the Bonds of Peace and Friendship among all Nations of the
Earth.'
[Without Publisher's or Printer's name, year, or price. Royal 8vo. Fly leaf. Eleven
short pieces of poetry, including "Crystal Palace," "Arbitrate! Arbitrate!" "Love versus
War," and other poems, variously placed on the different guns.]

Plan and Description of the original Electro-Magnetic Telegraph with Prefatory note to the Royal Commissioners of the Exhibition of the Works of Industry of All Nations, and Relative Documents. By the inventor William Alexander, Esq. writer to Her Majesty's signet in Scotland; Fellow of the Royal Society of Edinburgh; Fellow of the Royal Scottish Society of Arts, etc.
London: Longman, Brown, Green, and Longmans.
Edinburgh: A. & C. Black. 1851.
[Royal 8vo, pp. 31. Illustrated with an engraving. Mr. Alexander claims that his was "the first definite and complete plan ever shown in operation."]

Plan de Londres, *v.* Nouveau.

Plan et Guide de la Grande Exposition.
Londres: Spicer. Prix 2 pence.
[A sheet.]

Plan-Guide Souvenir de l'Exposition Nationale Industrielle et Agricole 1849.
Chez Bouqillard, Editeur, Papetier, Impr. Lithographe, 226, Rue St. Martin, 226, près des Arts et Métiers. Prix: 30 cs.
[A ground-plan of the arrangements in the building, for the Paris Exhibition of 1849, in a cover, on which are printed the names of the Departments of France and the Arrondissements of Paris.]

Plan of London and Environs, *v.* Illustrated.

Plan of the Building in Hyde Park for the Exhibition of 1851.
Published by James Wyld, Geographer to the Queen & H.R.H. Prince Albert, Charing Cross East & 2 Royal Exchange, *London.* November 9th. 1850.
[Price 1*d.* A sheet containing a ground-plan of the arrangements proposed, and the approaches, with an exterior view. It also bore a French and German title—Plan du Bâtiment pour servir à l'Exposition Industrielle—Plan des Gebäudes für die 'Industrie-Ausstellung. It is also described under "Plan."]

Plan of the Great Exhibition Building. 1851.
London: Spicer brothers, Stationers; W. Clowes & Sons, Printers. Contractors to the Royal Commission.
[Price 1*d.* W. y. A folio sheet.]

Playfair, Dr. L., *v.* Chemistry—Illustrated London Almanack—Lectures—Science.

Plon, Freres, Fonderie, Imprimerie, Librarie, *v.* Paris.

Ploucquet's Stuffed Animals, *v.* Aunt Mavor—Comical Creatures.

Pocket Handkerchiefs, *v.* Engravings on Cotton, on Silk.

Poems, *v.* Ballads—Bayley, F. W. N.—" Belgravia "—Brewer, Mrs.—Burgess, W.—Colsey, Thomas—" Commerce "—" Crystal Hive "—" Crystal Palace that Fox Built "—" Crystal Palace, the London Season "—David, J. C.—" Dedicated "—De Verdon, Rev. T. K.—" Dioramic Sketches "—" Doubly Great Exhibition "—Drury, Anna Harriet—Edmond, A.—Edwards, Sutherland—" Elegy "—" Exhibition Lay "—" Exhibition 1851 "—" Farewell Lines " [S. S.]—Franklin, Robert—Fry, E. H.—Gray, J.—" Glass-Berg "—" Great Exhibition, a New Song "—" Great Exhibition, a Poetical Rhapsody "—Hawkins, Rev. Ernest—" House that Albert built "—" House that Paxton built "—Hughes, J. H.—Jones, E. O.—Leathes, E.—" Love and Loyalty "—Maout, A. le—Martin, J. H.—Murray, Rev. T. B.—Napier Mrs.—" New Exhibition "—" Ode on the Great Exhibition "—Patston, Caroline—Polson, T. R. J.—Prior, James — " Prophecie " — " Recollections and Tales " — Reeve, I. — Smythies, Mrs. Y.—Snow, R.—Songs—Soper, R. C.—Stodart, Miss—" Sovereign of All "—Tupper, M. F.—Turner, J.—West, E.—Wortley, Lady E. S.—" Year 1851."

Poetical Rhapsody, A, *v.* Great Exhibition.

Pole, William, *v.* Musical Instruments.

Politique Nouvelle (La) Revue Hebdomadaire, Politique, Sciences, Litterature, Beaux-Arts. 16 Mars.—3e Livraison. [20 Juillet.—21e Livraison.]
Paris Au Bureau de la Politique Nouvelle 141, Rue Montmartre (entrée Rue Brogniart, 1). 1851.
[Price 75 centimes each. Royal 8vo. The Number for the 16th of March contains an article, pp. 140-147, by M. Ad. Blaise (Vosges) on "Exposition de Londres ses Caractères Généraux—ses Conséquences Philosophiques et Economiques." The number for the 20th of July contains an article, pp. 379-387, by M. Arles-Dufour on " L'Exposition Universelle."
M. Arles-Dufour,

M. Arles-Dufour, the Secretary of the French Exhibition in 1855, thus speaks of that of 1851: "Il est impossible que ce grand fait matériel de l'Exposition Universelle ne donne pas naissance à quelque grand fait moral; il est impossible que ces prud'hommes, qui auront étudié et comparé consciencieusement, pendant plusieurs mois, les produits du travail des principaux peuples de la terre, n'aient pas été conduits à examiner les conditions d'existence de leurs travailleurs; il est impossible alors, surtout pour ceux qui viennent des contrées agitées par l'esprit des réformes sociales, qu'un sentiment de tristesse et d'inquiétude ne les ait pas saisis et ne les dispose pas à répondre sympathiquement à l'appel qui leur viendrait d'en haut de concourir à la solution de ces menaçants problèmes."]

Polson, Thomas R. J., *v.* England and her Palace of Peace [a poem].

Popular Guide to the Great Exhibition of the Works of Industry of all Nations. 1851.

> The earth is the Lord's, and all that therein is:
> The compass of the world and they that dwell therein.
>
> Ne nostra, ista quœ invenimus, dixeris—
> Insita sunt nobis omnium artium semina,
> Magisterque ex occulto Deus producit ingenia.
>
> Say not the discoveries we make are our own—
> The germs of every art are implanted within us,
> And God our instructor, from his concealment,
>   Develops the faculties of invention.
>
> Humani generis progressus,
> Ex communi omnium labore ortus,
> Uniuscujusque industriæ debet esse finis:
>   Hoc adjuvando,
> Dei opt: max: voluntatem exsequimur.
>
> The progress of the human race,
> Resulting from the common labour of all men,
> Ought to be the final object of the exertion of each individual.
>   In promoting this end,
> We are carrying out the will of the great and blessed God.

With a Plan of the Building, Rules for Visitors, and Suggestions for the Guidance of Large Parties Visiting the Exhibition.
London: Spicer Brothers, Wholesale Stationers; W. Clowes and Sons, Printers; Contractors to the Royal Commission, 29 New Bridge Street, Blackfriars, and at the Exhibition, Hyde Park, and sold by all Booksellers. Price Twopence.
[W. y. Small 4to, pp. 32. The introduction contains a short history of Exhibitions.]

Popular Narrative (A) of The Origin, History, Progress, and Prospects of the Great Industrial Exhibition, 1851. By Peter Berlyn.
London: James Gilbert, 49, Paternoster Row. 1851.
[Price 2*s.* 6*d.* 18mo, pp. 186. Contains an exterior view, a ground-plan, and also a "View of the Birmingham Exposition Building." "All speculation or mere heresay gossip will be carefully eschewed, and the 'round unvarnished' facts of history dealt with from authentic records, in such a manner as to fairly trace out the progress of this most important movement, big with the most momentous consequences to the future industry and arts of this country, and even of the world at large, which the history of any period has recorded. Previous to entering upon this task, it is desirable to repudiate all bias in favour of any person, class, or party, and to announce a zealous wish to do justice to all who have assisted, either indirectly in preparing the public mind for the reception of this stupendous scheme, or directly in working out the details of the earlier kindred attempts— the acorn from whence has sprung this majestic oak,— or more directly still, endeavouring in the full and complete sense to mature the details of this gigantic undertaking which is about to astonish and enlighten the world by its results."]

Portugal, Wines of, *v.* Oliveira.

Postage, International, *v.* Association.

Post Office Guide (The). Under the Sanction of Her Majesty's Postmaster-General, the Right Honourable Ulick John Marquis of Clanricarde, K.P. by J. W. Lettis, of the General Post Office. Second Edition.
London: Longman, Brown, Green, and Longmans. 1851. [Entered at Stationers' Hall.] Price 2*s.* 6*d.*
[18mo, pp. 130. With a list of the Commissioners and Local Committees of the Exhibition.]

Potonie, D., *v.* Des Diverses Classifications—Programme de l'Agence Jacques Cœur.

Potter, Edmund, *v.* Calico Printing—Letter on Design—Reports by the Juries.

Preis Catalog, *v.* Amtliches Verzeichniss.

Premaray, Jules de, *v.* Promenades Sentimentales.

Preparations for the Exhibition of 1851. (From the Birmingham Journal of September 28th, 1850.)
[Without Publisher's or Printer's name, year, or price. 4to, p. 1. An article reprinted.]

Preservation of the Crystal Palace *v.* Beta—Crystal Palace—Cruikshank, Percy—Denarius—Elegy—Fate of the Crystal Palace—Fuller, F.—General Outline—Greville—Medical Man's Plea—Reasons for—Reasons why—Removal of the Crystal Palace—Removal of the Crystal Palace from Hyde Park—Rendle, W. E.—Report of the Commissioners [Lord Seymour, Sir W. Cubitt, and Dr. Lindley]—Report of the Meeting at Mr. Oliveira's—Spare the—What is to become—What is to be done—What shall we do with.

Preservation of the Crystal Palace. General Committee.
[Bradbury & Evans, Printers, Whitefriars. W. y. Post 8vo, pp. 24. An alphabetical list.]

[Preservation of the Crystal Palace. Letter from Mr. B. Oliveira, M.P. to Sir Joseph Paxton [dated] London, 5th April, 1852. 8, Upper Hyde Park Street.]
[A lithographed foolscap sheet.]

Preservation of the Crystal Palace. Reply of the Sub-Committee to the Report of the Treasury Commission.
Bradbury and Evans, Printers, Whitefriars.
[W. y. Folio, pp. 3. The Report of the Commissioners will be found under Report.]

Preservation of the Crystal Palace.
[Without Publisher's or Printer's name, or date. Folio, pp. 4. Report of final meeting of the General Committee held May 11th 1852, at the King's Arms Hotel, New Palace Yard, Westminster, Rear Admiral Sir George Sartorius in the Chair. With division list of the House of Commons on 29th April 1852, on Mr. Heywood's motion.]

Preservation of the Crystal Palace. Report of the Sub-Committee to the General Committee appointed to secure the preservation of the Crystal Palace, and submitted by the Committee for the consideration of the public.
Bradbury and Evans, Printers, Whitefriars.
[W. y. Folio, pp. 3. Signed ' Joseph Paxton, Chairman.']

President de la Republique, Speech of, *v.* Exposition Universelle.

Prière offerte par l'Archeveque de Canterbury, à l'occasion de l'Ouverture de L'Exposition Universelle.
Foreign Conference and Evangelization Committee for 1851, 47, Leicester Square.
[W. y. 8vo, p. 1.]

Prince Albert, H.R.H., *v.* Bolton, Resolutions respecting a Statue to—Great Exhibition, Correspondence with Mr. Drew—Reports by the Juries—Speech of.

Prince and the People (The). A Poem. In two Cantos. By Mrs. Yorick Smythies, Author of ' Cousin Geoffrey,' ' The Life of a Beauty,' ' The Bride Elect,' etc., etc., etc.
London : William Skeffington, 163, Piccadilly. 1854.
[Price 2s. 6d. Royal 8vo, pp 32. Contains only a few incidental lines on the Exhibition.
" Yes, from that Crystal Palace was unfurled,
A spell that still is working through the world,
And chastened Taste, and sweet Refinement finds
Its way to countless homes, and countless minds!"]

Prinsep, William, *v.* Reports by the Juries.

Prior, James, *v.* Loyal Stanza.

Prize Essay (The) on the Application of Recent Inventions collected at the Great Exhibition of 1851, to the purposes of Practical Banking. By Granville Sharp.
' The Earth is the Lord's, and all that therein is ;
The compass of the World and they that dwell therein.'—*Psalms.*
London : Reprinted from the Bankers' Magazine of January and February, 1852, by Waterlow & Sons, London Wall. 1852.
[8vo, pp. 43. Appeared also in an enlarged form which will be found under Gilbart.]

Prize Essays, *v.* Briggs, Thomas—Emerton, Rev. Dr. J. A.—Forrester, J. J. [Portugal]—Gilbart—Hulbert, Rev. D. P. M.—" Two Premiums "—Wallis, George—Weekes, Henry—Whish, Rev. J. C.—Wornum, Ralph Nicholson.

Prize Treatise (The) on the Fine Arts Section of the Great Exhibition of 1851. Submitted to the Society of Arts in competition for their medal. By Henry Weekes, A.R.A.

'Docti rationem Artis intelligunt, indocti voluptatem.'—*Quintilian.*

London: Vizetelly and Company, 135 Fleet Street.　1852.
[Privately circulated.　Post 8vo, pp. viii., 150.　This treatise obtained the gold medal offered by the Society of Arts.　"If the gathering together of works in Hyde Park is to have any beneficial result, that result has yet to be manifested.　The Arts and Sciences cannot be made to spring up in a moment, nor can good taste become general all at once, even by the high-pressure power thus applied to it; but it may be reasonably hoped that such will gradually appear, now that the year 1851 has opened the field for it.　What is here written will, however, be found applicable to the Fine Arts generally, as well as to the particular collection indicated by the title-page; and this the author trusts will plead his excuse for publishing it."]

Proceedings at a Public Meeting, convened at the King's Arms, Kensington, 20th March, 1850, for the purpose of forming a Local Committee, to collect sub-scriptions and otherwise promote the Exhibition of the Works of Industry, of All Nations.　To be held in the year 1851.　The Right Honourable W. S. Lascelles, M.P., in the chair.

Printed by Samuel Bird, Kensington, and Bedford Street, Strand.　1850.
[8vo, pp. 22.]

Proceedings of the Central Committee of the United States on the Industrial Exhi-bition of 1851, at the Meeting held September 16th 1850.

Washington.　Robert A. Waters, Printer.　1850.
[8vo, pp. 40.　Contains copies of the documents, issued by Her Majesty's Commission, bearing on the Foreign portion of the Exhibition, and the steps proposed to be taken in reference to American contributions.]

Proceedings of the Madras Central Committee, for the Exhibition of the Industry and Art of all Nations, held in London in the Year 1851.

Madras: Printed at the Fort St. George Gazette Press, 1853.
[Folio, pp. lxxxii. 373.　Contains full details of the articles collected by the various com-mittees corresponding with the Madras Central Committee, with the uses to which they are applicable—the quantity in which they are procurable—nearest seaport for shipment—cost of carriage to seaport, and prices at which the articles may be obtained—and other remarks—with plates worked from several varieties of lithographic stones.　There is also bound up with this volume a report, in 25 pp., by Dr. Wight, on the "Forest Trees of Southern India," with their distinctive characters and the uses they might be turned to.]

Procession of the Queen to open the Chrystal Palace in Hyde Park.

Printed and Published by M. Elliot, 14, Holywell Street, Strand.
[A long sheet of colored engravings, *v.* also Grand.]

°Procession to open the Great Exhibition.
[A long sheet of engravings, without Publisher's or Printer's name, year, or price.]

Productions (The) of All Nations!!　About to appear at the Great Exhibition of 1851.

London:—Printed and Published by H. Elliot, 475, New Oxford Street; Winn, Holywell Street; Collins, Fleet Street; and Sold by all Booksellers in Town and Country.—Price one penny.
[W. y.　A broad sheet of facetious engravings.]

Programme de l'Agence Jacques Cœur.　Signed D. Potonié, 5, Rue Neuve-Saint-François (Marais).

Paris.—Imprimerie de Mᵐᵉ Ve Dondey-Dupré, Rue Saint-Louis, 46, au Marais.
[W. y.　4to, pp. 4.　A circular announcing an agency for the Exhibition.]

Projects and Prospects of the Day.

London: Effingham Wilson, Royal Exchange.　1850.　Price One Shilling.
[8vo, pp. 60.　The subjects treated of are "The Projects of the Day"—the Exhibition—"Universal Language League"—"Our prospects under the new Regime"—and "Female Emigration."]

Promenades Sentimentales dans Londres et Le Palais de Cristal par Jules de Premaray.

'Toutes ces choses errantes et ce bourdonnement d'une si grande cité me produisaient l'effect d'un songe.'—*J. Janin.*

Paris D. Giraud et J. Dagneau, Libraires-Editeurs de la Bibliothéque Théatrale 18 Rue Guénégaud 1851.
[Price 3 francs 50 c. Post 8vo. pp. x., 343.]

Prophecie (Ye) of Pierre Reillor, an Heretique Friere of ye Abbey of Holie Crosse by Waltham. In ye whiche is dimlie foreshadowedde ye Greate Exhibitionne of Eighteene Hundrede and Fiftie-One.

'This Prophecie, when that I am dede and gone,
Shall come to passe in Eighteene-Fiftie-and-One.'

London: Published from ye Elde, by Houlston & Stoneman, 65, Paternoster Row. 1851. Price Sixpence.
[8vo, pp. 15.

" When house of strength and house of blether
By house of glass is held together;
When house of strength and house of brawling,
By house of glass is kept from falling ;
*   *   *
Look out ! look out ! for the coming danger !"]

Proposal for Erecting a Monument to Shakespeare. Read before a Meeting of the Society of Arts, February 5, 1851, H. T. Hope, Esq. M.P. in the chair.
London : Cundall & Addey, 21 Old Bond Street. 1851.
[Price 6d. 8vo, pp. 16. "In taking, then, a full and comprehensive view of the moving incidents of the present epoch, together with the wholesome tendency of these stirring events, it would seem that *a more fitting memorial of these times and magnificent spectacle* could not be transmitted to posterity than that which might be called into existence in England *by the arts assisting*, with the full sanction, and as it were at the bidding, of the world, in celebrating the birth of *our immortal Shakespeare*." Signed A. W. H.]

Proposal for the Transfer to America, in 1852, of Selections from the Great Exposition of the Works of All Nations about to be held in London in 1851.
G. Woodfall and Son, Printers, Angel Court, Skinner Street, London.
[Circulated gratuitously. W. y. 8vo, pp. 8. Mr. J. Jay Smith, the projector, brought letters of introduction from the American Secretary of State, but the proposal was dropped.]

Provident Society at Northampton, v. Rules.

Publication Officielle. Industrie de Toutes les Nations La Grande Exposition de Londres de 1851 sous le patronage du Prince Albert, avec une Description de l'Edifice, etc.
Bruxelles. J. Geruzet, Editeur, Longue Rue de l'Ecuyer. G. Stapleaux, Editeur, Rue de la Montagne, 51. 1850.
[Price 1 franc. Royal 8vo, pp. 23, with a View of the Building. Contains a short description of the Arrangements, with the classification announced, and the general conditions.]

Public Meetings in Agricultural Villages. The Great Exhibition of the Works of Industry of All Nations, to be opened in Hyde Park, London, on the 1st day of May, 1851. President: H. R. H. The Prince Albert, K. G., &c., &c., &c.
[Without Publisher's or Printer's name, or year. Printed for gratuitous circulation. 8vo, p. 1. A letter signed R. Andrews, and dated Southampton, May 10th, 1850. Mr. Andrews was the then Mayor of Southampton.]

Public Testimonial to the Acting Members of the Executive Committee of the Great Exhibition.
[Without Publisher's or Printer's name, or year. 4to, pp. 3. With a second circular of resolutions, and a third circular inviting co-operation.]

Pudelnärrische Reise nach London im Jahre 1851 zur Industrie-Ausstellung aller Nationen im Glaspalast. Von J. W. Christern. Mit einem Reisemarsch.
Leipzig, 1851. Verlag von Ignaz Jackowitz.
[Price 7½ sgr. 8vo. pp. 36, with an engraving of the Building. Dialogues in a humorous style, between persons of different nationalities, travelling together to the Exhibition.]

°Pulchinello's Industrial Exhibition 1851.
London : W. Strange, 21 Paternoster Row. Price only Threepence.
[W. y. 4to, pp. 16. A collection of facetious engravings.]

°Pulchinello's Panorama of London in 1851.
London : G. Vickers, 28 & 29 Holywell Street, Strand. Price Threepence.
[W. y. 4to, pp. 16. Facetious engravings.]

Punch, v. Crystal Palace, Intercepted Letters—Records of the Great Exhibition.

Punch's Comic Guide to the Exhibition, showing how to see Everything that is in London, as well as a great deal that is not. An immense number of comic engravings.
London.—Printed by W. S. Johnson, 60, St. Martin's Lane, Charing Cross. Sold by all Booksellers.
[W. y. 4to, pp. 16.]

N

Pusey, Philip, *v.* Reports by the Juries.

Puzzles, *v.* Crystal Labyrinth—To the Great Exhibition—Crystal Palace seen from Kensington Gardens—Crystal Palace Puzzle—Exhibition Puzzle—Gleanings from the Exhibition—View of the Building.

Queen's Commission for the Exhibition of 1851 (The).
London :—Printed by George Barclay, Castle Street, Leicester Square.
[W. y. Circulated gratuitously. 8vo, pp. 12. A reprint from the London Gazette of the Warrant, dated 3rd day of January, 1850, under which Her Majesty's Commissioners acted.]

Queen's Warrant, *v.* London Gazette.

Querschnitte von hundert Holzarten, umfassend die Wald- und Gartenbaumarten, so wie die gewöhnlichsten ausländischen Boskethölzer Deutschlands. Zur Belehrung für Forstleute, Landwirthe, Botaniker, Holztechnologen, herausgegeben von Professor Dr. H. Nördlinger, Revierverwalter zu Kirchheim u. T.
Stuttgart und Tübingen. J. G. Cotta'scher Verlag. 1852.
[Price R 4. 20 sgr. 16mo, 18 pp. of text, and 100 species of wood pasted on paper, in a box. This collection of specimens, cut in thin tablets, is intended as a sort of text or class-book for foresters, with directions for preparing similar specimens.]

Rambling Inspiration (A) over Ackermann's Pictures of the Crystal Palace. By F. W. N. Bayley.
Ackermann & Co., 96, Strand.
[W. y. Printed for gratuitous circulation. A 4to sheet.]
These pictur'd ripenings from the Tree of Art,
Pouring their juices in her sparkling chalice,
Gleam to their task, and glory in their part
Of showing to the world
Our CRYSTAL PALACE !]

Randoing, M. J., on Woollen and Worsted Goods, *v.* Travaux.

Ranelagh Club. The Mechanics' Home for 1851, Ranelagh-Road, near Cubitt's Pier, on the Middlesex side of the River Thames. Accommodation for One Thousand persons.
[Without Publisher's or Printer's name, or date. Two prospectuses, folio and 4to, circulated by Mr. Thomas Harrison.]

*Rapport du Délégues a Londres pour la Commission Centrale Suisse. Division B. Machines par M. D. Colladon.
[Inserted as Professor Colladon announced privately that it would be published about the same time as this Catalogue.]

Rapport sur l'Industrie du papier blanc, Présenté dans la séance du 26 Novembre 1851, par MM. V. Journet et A. Rieder, délégués par la Société industrielle à l'Exposition universelle de Londres.
[W. y. 8vo, pp. 32. " Mulhouse—.impr. de P. Baret." Circulated gratuitously. No distinct title.]

Rapport sur l'Industrie du Papier pour Tentures, lu à la Société-industrielle de Mulhouse, séance du 27 Août 1851, par M. Jean Zuber fils, Ancien Président de la Société.
Mulhouse. Impr. de P. Baret.
[W. y. 8vo, pp. 33. M. Zuber treats his subject first historically, second statistically, thirdly of the commercial laws which govern the trade in each country, and of the degree of perfection to which the trade has arisen under the various laws.]

Rau, Dr. Karl H., *v.* Amtlicher Bericht—Landwirthschaftlichen Geräthe (Die).

Rawlins', Bailey, Expanding View of the Great Exhibition—The Nave—
Printed in colors and Published for the Proprietor, By Chas. Moody, 257, High Holborn.
[W. y. Price 7*s.* 6*d.* A telescopic View, *v.* also Lane's Telescopic Views.]

Real Exhibitors Exhibited; or an enquiry into the condition of those industrial classes who have really represented England at the Great Exhibition. By the Rev. John Richardson, B.A., Incumbent of St. Barnabas', Manchester.
London : Wertheim and Macintosh, 24, Paternoster Row. 1851.
[Price 2*s.* 12mo, pp. 122. Mr. Richardson devotes his attention to the condition of the Working Classes generally, rather than to any special circumstances connected with the Exhibition.]

Reasons for converting the Crystal Palace into a Winter Garden.
[Without Publisher's or Printer's name, or year. Folio, p. 1.]

Reasons Why the Crystal Palace should not be a permanent Building.
[Vacher & Sons, Stationers, 29, Parliament Street. W. y. Privately circulated. 8vo, pp. 4. The principal reasons assigned by the writer are, the probable expense and the promise that the building should be removed. "Let no tales of broken faith be brought forward, to tarnish the glory and success of the most magnificent spectacle the world has ever witnessed. Beautiful, and ingenious, and well adapted for its purpose as I heartily confess the Edifice to be; it is altogether unfit for a permanent structure." It is signed 'One of the Public,' and dated July, 1851.]

Reciprocity, v. Great Exhibition Essay.

Recollections and Tales of the Crystal Palace. By the Authoress of ' Belgravia ;' ' Temptation, or a Wife's Perils ;' ' Spencer's Cross Manor House,' &c. &c. &c.
London : W. Shoberl, Publisher, 20, Great Marlborough Street. 1852.
[Price 5s. Post 8vo, pp. 150.
"Lo! as I roam o'er this unequalled spot,
Earth and its drearier scenes are all forgot ;
The mighty minds that with resistless will,
Raised the fair temple, seem to haunt it still !
A solemn glory shines along these aisles,
And in the violet-tinted distance, smiles ;
And Peace, with dove-like pinions, seems to brood
Above this swarming, countless multitude."]

Recollections of the Great Exhibition of 1851.
London : Published by Lloyd Brothers & Co., 22, Ludgate Hill, & Simpkin Marshall & Co. Stationers Hall Court. September 1st., 1851.
[Price 3l. 3s., coloured 8l. 8s. W. y. Twenty-five lithographed plates.]

Record (A) of the Great Exhibition of 1851; a Poem by Thomas Colsey.
London : printed and published for the Author, by F. J. Whiteman, 19, Little Queen Street, High Holborn.
[W. y. Price 6d. 12mo, pp. 24. Illustrated with a vignette of the "Grand National Exhibition of 1851." Mr. Colsey was understood to be a person in a very humble station. His feeling in reference to the Exhibition is exemplified in the following lines :—
"The Exhibition is over, the spell is past,
The beautiful vision too sweet to last."]

Records of the Great Exhibition, extracted from Punch.
[Printed by William Bradbury, of No. 13, Upper Woburn Place, in the parish of St. Pancras, and Frederick Mullett Evans, of No. 7, Church Row, Stoke Newington, both in the county of Middlesex, Printers, at their Office in Lombard Street, in the precinct of Whitefriars, in the City of London, and Published by them at No. 85, Fleet Street, in the Parish of St. Brides', in the City of London. Saturday, Oct 4, 1851. Price 6d. Large folio, pp. 8. With 51 Engravings, taken from the weekly numbers of Punch.]

Recueil des Opinions Emises par le Jury Central des Expositions de l'Industrie Nationale de 1844 et de 1849; les Conseils Généraux d'Agriculture, du Commerce et de l'Industrie Réunis à Paris en 1845 et 1850; la Société Royale d'Agriculture de Bordeaux (1846); la Société Royale et Centrale d'Agriculture de France (1847); la Société Séricole à Paris (1847) ; la Société d'Encouragement pour l'Industrie Nationale (1847) ; le Congrès Central d'Agriculture (1847) ; la Chambre de Commerce de Lyon (1848) ; et par la Société d'Encouragement des Arts et Manufactures à Londres (1850). Sur les Avantages de la Race de Vers à Soie Bronski et sur la Qualité de la Soie Produite par cette race.
Paris Imprimerie Centrale de Napoléon Chaix et Cie, Rue Bergère, 20, près du Boulevart Montmartre. 1851.
[Circulated gratuitously with a specimen of the silk. 4to, pp. 23.]

Redding, Cyrus, v. Stranger in London.

Redgrave, R., v. Department of Practical Art—Reports by the Juries.

Reeve, Isaac, A Poem, v. Vision.

°Registered Exhibition Hand Guide to London.
Published by J. Allen, Warwick Lane. Price one penny.
[W. y. P. 1. Drawing of a hand, with a map of London engraved within the outline.]

Reid, Sir William, v. Illustrated London Almanack.

Reis, *v.* Jolige Reis naar de Tentoonstellung te Londen.

Rejected (The) Contributions to the Great Exhibition of All Nations. Collected by Luke Limner, Esq. with the classes in which they will not be found. If the public maintain that many of the articles are not rejected, but still occupy distinguished positions, the collector distinctly states it is no fault of his— They ought to have been.
Printed by Leighton Bros. Seventy *odd* Illustrations. Price one shilling.
[W. y. Oblong 8vo, pp. 8. of illustrations. One of Luke Limner's facetious books.]

Remarks on the Particular Advantages which The Great Exhibition of 1851 is likely to confer on the Tradesmen of the Metropolis. By John Smith, Publican.
[Printed by G. Barclay, 28 Castle St. Leicester Sq. W. y. 8vo, pp. 2. Understood never to have been circulated. Smith was a fictitious name.]

Remembrances of the Great Exhibition. (Second Edition.) A series of views Beautifully Engraved on Steel, from Drawings made on the spot. Including a general History of its Origin, Progress, and Close.
H. Mandeville, *Paris.* Ackerman & Co. & Read & Co. *London.*
[W. y. Price 8s. 6d. plain, 14s. 6d. colored. Oblong 4to. Contains Eleven Engravings of Exterior and Interior.]

Second Series. A Series of ten Departmental Views, Beautifully Engraved on Steel, from Drawings made on the spot. Including a pleasing account of each department.
London: Read & Co., 10, Johnson's Court, Fleet Street; Ackermann and Co., 96, Strand.
[W. y. Price, 8s. 6d. plain, 14s. 6d. colored. Oblong 4to.]

Reminiscence (A) of the Exhibition of 1851.
[Without Publisher's or Printer's name, or date. Royal 8vo, pp. 15. A Poem.
" But, beauteous as the work, 'tis but a cobweb—
A cobweb in its rise, its time, its fall.
'Twas a vision, a brighter never imaged,
Entrancing with its sympathies the soul.
It was a book from which we read
Rich intellectual lessons, and imbibed
The charities of our kind, and this indeed
A priceless benefit How good it were
To reinstate the shrine, resuscitate
Its raptures, and maintain it unimpaired
In fullest splendour, loveliness, and grandeur."
A new Edition was published in 1853 with the imprint of— *London :* Printed & Published by Jones & Causton, 47, Eastcheap, for the Author, A. Edmond. 1853. And contained 18 pp.]

Reminiscences of the Crystal Palace, with a full description of the principal objects exhibited. And a Plan, showing the arrangements of the various Departments; New Edition, illustrated with numerous woodcuts.
London : Geo. Routledge & Co., Farringdon Street. 1852.
[Price 1s. 12mo, pp. viii., 231.]

Reminiscences of the Great Exhibition ; or Annales Facetiarum of 1851.
G. Mann, Cornhill. Dean & Son, Printers, Threadneedle Street.
[W. y. Price 1s. An oblong sheet of colored facetious engravings, with explanations, bound in a square form.]

Removal of the Crystal Palace (The). Fourth Thousand.
Houlston & Stoneman, Paternoster Row; Seeleys, Fleet Street Hamilton & Co., Paternoster Row 1852. Price One Penny.
[12mo, pp. 12. Relates principally to opening the Crystal Palace at Sydenham on Sundays.]

Removal of the Crystal Palace from Hyde Park.
[Without Publisher's or Printer's name, or year. Small 4to, p. 1. Recommending the removal of the Crystal Palace to Battersea Park.]

Rendle, William Edgecumbe, *v.* Shall the Crystal Palace remain.

Report (A) on the Eleventh French Exposition of the Products of Industry. Prepared by the direction of, and submitted to, the President and Council of the Society of Arts. By Matthew Digby Wyatt, architect. 11 Park Street, Westminster, Sept. 1849.

London :

London: Chapman and Hall, 186 Strand; Joseph Cundall, 21 Old Bond Street; and David Bogue, 86 Fleet Street. 1849.

[Folio, pp. 36. Contains a ground-plan. This Report was prepared in accordance with instructions from the Council of the Society of Arts. Mr. Wyatt divided the subject under the following heads: "Firstly—a description of the *present Building*, and generally of the nature of the *present* Exposition. Secondly—A short account of the history of the institution of past *Expositions*, and their connexion with the industrial progression of the country. And Thirdly—An analysis of the official arrangements, their routine, and, in an appendix, copies of public documents connected with the organization of the present and past Expositions."]

Report made to His Royal Highness the Prince Albert, President of the Society of Arts, etc. etc. etc., of preliminary inquiries into the willingness of Manufacturers and others to support Periodical Exhibitions of the Works of Industry of All Nations. By Henry Cole and Francis Fuller, Members of the Council of the Society of Arts.

London: Society of Arts, John Street, Adelphi. 1849.
[Printed for circulation amongst the Members of the Society of Arts. 8vo, pp. 28.]

Report made to His Royal Highness the Prince Albert, President of the Society of Arts, &c. &c. &c., of preliminary inquiries into the willingness of Manufacturers and others to support *periodical Exhibitions of the Works of Industry of all Nations.* By Henry Cole and Francis Fuller, Members of the Council of the Society of Arts.

[Without Publisher's or Printer's name. Dated *London*, October 1849. Printed for circulation amongst the Members of the Society of Arts. Folio, pp. 79.]

Report of a Meeting held at the Mansion-House, London, October 17, 1849, in support of the Great Exhibition of the Works of Industry of All Nations in 1851, under the Presidency of H. R. H. the Prince Albert, K.G., &c. &c. &c. From the Times of October 18, 1849.

London:—Printed by G. Barclay, Castle St. Leicester Sq.
[W. y. 12mo, pp. 16.]

Report of a Meeting of Foremen, Overlookers, & Operatives, held at the Exchange Buildings, Bradford, on the 18th of April, 1850. Henry Forbes, Esq., Mayor, in the chair.

W. Byles, Printer, Observer Office, Kirkgate, *Bradford* [Yorkshire].
[W. y. Circulated gratuitously. 12mo, pp. 12.]

Report of Benj. P. Johnson, Agent of the State of New York, appointed to attend the Exhibition of the Industry of All Nations, held in London, 1851.

Albany: C. Van Benthuysen, Public Printer. 1852.
[Price 75 cents. 8vo, pp. 193. Contains two engravings of the Prize Medal and a Ground-plan of the Building, with the situation of many of the articles exhibited. Is addressed to His Excellency Governor Hunt, and illustrated by several woodcuts.]

[Report of the Number of Vehicles which passed Bow Church, Cheapside, between the Hours of 6 P.M. on Thursday, the 8th day of August, and 6 P.M. on Friday the 9th of August 1850, and the Number of Persons in and with the said Vehicles; also the Number of Foot-Passengers who passed during the same time. and Similar Report taken from Aldgate Church.]

[Without Publisher's or Printer's name, or year. Folio, pp. 2. Information furnished by Mr. Daniel W. Harvey, Chief Commissioner of Police of the City of London, in accordance with a request made by the Executive Committee.]

Report of the Commissioners appointed to inquire into the Cost and Applicability of the Exhibition Building in Hyde Park. Presented to both Houses of Parliament by Command of Her Majesty.

London: Printed by George Edward Eyre and William Spottiswoode, Printers to the Queen's most Excellent Majesty. For Her Majesty's Stationery Office. 1852.
[Folio, pp. vii., 49. The Commissioners, Lord Seymour, Sir William Cubitt, and Dr. Lindley, reported against the Building remaining in Hyde Park. A reply was published by the Committee appointed to secure the Preservation of the Building, *v.* Preservation.]

Report of the Frauds of London, *v.* By Authority.

Report of the Proceedings at the Public Meeting held at the Riding School of the Royal Artillery Barracks, Woolwich, on Tuesday, the 4th of June, 1850, in support of the Great Exhibition of the Works of Industry of All Nations in 1851.

1851. Lieut.-General Sir Thomas Downman, C.B., K.C.H., in the Chair. From the Kentish Independent of June 8th, 1850.

E. Jones, Printer, 'Kentish Independent' Office, *Woolwich.*
> [W. y. Printed for gratuitous circulation. 4to, pp. 12.]

Reports by the Juries. Class XXIX. Miscellaneous Manufactures and Small Wares. Warren de la Rue, F.R.S., Reporter. Professor A. W. Hofmann, F.R.S., Joint Reporter.
> [Without Publisher's or Printer's name, or date. Crown 8vo, pp. 1333-1527. An excerpt from the large Edition of the Reports by the Juries. One hundred copies were printed.]

Reports by the Juries on the Subjects in the Thirty Classes into which the Exhibition was divided. Presentation Copy.

London: Printed for the Royal Commission, by William Clowes & Sons, Stamford Street and Charing Cross. 1852.
> [Crown 8vo., pp. cxx., 868. Contains Report of Viscount Canning—Decisions regarding Juries—Classification of Subjects—Instructions from Council of Chairmen—List of Jurors—Answer of Prince Albert to Chairman of Juries—List of Jury Awards—Reports on Class 1, M. Dufrenoy, pp. 1-36—Class 2, Thomas Graham, pp. 37-50—Class 3, J. D. Hooker, pp. 51-67—Class 4, Richard Owen, pp. 68-166—Class 5, Henry Moseley, pp. 167-191—Class 5a, Joseph Holland, pp. 192-193—Class 6, R. Willis, pp. 194-205—Class 7, I. K. Brunel, pp. 206-207—Class 8, Baron C. Dupin, pp. 209-224—Class 9, Ph. Pusey, pp. 225-242—Class 10, James Glaisher, pp. 243-323—Class 10a, H. R. Bishop, pp. 324-335—Class 10b, E. B. Denison, pp. 336-343—Class 10c, Joseph Henry Green, pp. 344-346—Class 11, Thomas Ashton, pp. 347-349—Class 12, Samuel Addington, pp. 350-361—Class 13, Thomas Winkworth, pp. 362-368—Class 14, William Charley, Grenier Lefevre, pp. 369-373—Class 15, William Prinsep, pp. 374-382—Class 16, J. A. Nicholay, J. B. Bevington, pp. 383-395—Class 17, A. Firmin Didot, C. Whittingham, T. De la Rue, pp. 396-455—Class 18, Edmund Potter, pp. 456-459—Class 19, Richard Birkin, pp. 460-476—Class 20, T. Christy, pp. 477-484—Class 21, Lord Wharncliffe, pp. 485-491—Class 22, W. Dyce, pp. 492-509—Class 23, Duke de Luynes, pp. 511-520—Class 24, Lord De Mauley, pp. 521-537—Class 25, Duke of Argyll, pp. 538-543—Class 26, Professor Roesner, J. G. Crace, pp. 544-552—Class 27, D. T. Ansted, pp. 553-589—Class 28, Edwin Lankester, pp. 590-602—Class 29, Warren de la Rue, A. W. Hofmann, pp. 603-682—Class 30, A. Panizzi, pp. 683-690—Class 30, Supplementary Report, with engravings, Richard Redgrave, pp. 691-749—Index, &c.

Reports by the Juries on the Subjects in the Thirty Classes into which the Exhibition was divided. By Authority of the Royal Commission. In four volumes. Vol. 1. Introductory; Awards; Reports—Classes 1 to 4. Vol. 2. Reports—Classes 5 to 16. Vol. 3. Reports—Classes 17 to 28. Vol. 4. Reports—Classes 29; 30.

London: Spicer Brothers, Wholesale Stationers; W. Clowes and Sons, Printers; Contractors to the Royal Commission. 1852.
> [Imperial 4to. Vol. 1, ccv., 358; Vol. 2, iv., 359 to 870; Vol. 3, iv., 871 to 1332; Vol. 4, iv., 1333 to 1828. Illustrated with 153 Photographs and 3 Colored Lithographic Plates, and with half titles peculiar to this edition. This was the Edition of the Jury Reports prepared for, and presented with, the large edition of the Catalogue and Special Reports to Foreign Governments and Her Majesty's Commissioners.]

Retention of the Crystal Palace, *v.* Preservation.

Reverie (A) about The Crystal Palace. By the Author of 'Proverbial Philosophy.'

G. J. Palmer, Savoy Street, Strand.
> [W. y. Circulated gratuitously. 8vo, 1 p. A Poem signed M. F. T.
> "Dream of splendour, bright and gay,
> Disenchanted all too soon,
> Dimly fading fast away
> Like a half-remembered tune,—"]

Reynaud, Maurice, *v.* Pieces.

Reynolds's New Map of London; and Visitors Guide   One shilling.
> [Without Publisher's or Printer's name, or year. 12mo, pp. 36. Contains a short account of the Exhibition.]

Rhyme (A) for The Close of 'The Great Exhibition.'

From the establishment of Thomas Brettell, Rupert Street, Haymarket, Printer of 'The Hymn for All Nations!' in Thirty Languages.
> [W. y. Circulated gratuitously. 8vo, p. 1. A Poem by "Martin F. Tupper," dated Albury, Guildford. Appeared in two forms. It was also set to music by Miss Lydia B. Smith.
> "Glory to the God of heaven,—
> Peace on earth, tow'rds men good will!
> Now shall honours due be given
> To the best of human skill;"]

Rhyme Book (The) : by Hercules Ellis.

THE POET'S MOTTO.

Whence should the Poet seek the sacred fire,
To kindle in his soul the thought divine?
To what high themes should he attune his lyre,
To crown with immortality his line?
First let him strike the sounding shell,
And to all time the praises tell
Of those, who nobly fought, and fell,
The tyrant's bonds to break ;
Next let him sing in softer strain,
Of those, who wore love's gentle chain,
And proved that wealth and power were vain,
Their constancy to shake:
And ever let the Poet's motto be—
' The liberty of Love, and love of Liberty.'

London: Longman, Brown, Green & Longmans.
Dublin:—Duffy, 11, Wellington Quay. 1851.
[Price 21*s.* Royal 8vo, pp. 712, with an Introduction and Postscript, not paged. Dedicated to the Prince of Wales. The postscript complains of poems not receiving prizes.]

Richard et Lake, *v.* Guide du Voyageur a Londres.

Richardson, Rev. John, *v.* Exhibition London Guide—Real Exhibitors Exhibited.

Richmond, Music at the Dinner at the Castle at, *v.* Selection.

Ricordi a' Forestieri che Visitano la Grand' Esposizione delle Arti in London, l'Anno 1851. Della Scrittura e della Osservanza in Inghilterra del Sabato, O sia Giorno del Signore chiamato comunemeente "la Domenica."
Londra: Stampato per la Società Promotrice della Dottrina Cristiana. Si Vende al suo Depositorio, Great Queen Street, Lincoln's-Inn-Fields; al N. 4, Royal Exchange; al N. 16, Hanover Street, Regent Street; e Presso tutti i Libraj. 1851.
[Price 4*s.* per 100. 12mo, pp. 8. One of the addresses issued by the Society for Promoting Christian Knowledge.]

Rieder, M. A., sur l'Industrie du Papier Blanc, *v.* Rapport.

Rights of Inventors. First Report from the Committee on Legislative Recognition of the Rights of Inventors. Ordered by the Council of the Society of Arts to be Printed, 2nd December, 1850.
London: Published for the Society by Chapman and Hall, 193 Piccadilly ; and Cundall and Addey, 21 Old Bond Street. Price 6*d.*
[W. y. 8vo, pp. 24.]
Second Report—Ordered by the Council of the Society of Arts to be printed, 22nd January, 1851.
[8vo, pp. 16.]
Third Report—Ordered by the Council of the Society of Arts to be printed, 28 January, 1852.
[Circulated gratuitously. 8vo, pp. 12 These papers, in their special title, are called Reports " On the principles of Jurisprudence which should regulate the recognition of the Rights of Inventors."]

Roberts, David, R.A., *v.* Dickensons' Comprehensive Pictures.

Roberts, Henry, *v.* Model Houses.

Rochdale, *v.* Ful.

Rodgers, Charles T., *v.* American Superiority at the World's Fair.

Roesner, Professor, *v.* Reports by the Juries.

Roessler, Commerzienrath, *v.* Amtlicher Bericht.

Roland, Ollivier, *v.* Exposition Universelle de Londres.

Romainville, *v.* Cantata.

Rongeat, A., *v.* Royal Exhibition, Guide through London.

Ross and Son's Great Exhibition Almanac for 1851, Fourteenth year of the Reign of Her Present Majesty. Contents. The Great Industrial Exhibition of all Nations—Eclipses—The Calendar, with the Moon's Changes—Routes for
Viewing

Viewing London in Six Days—Gratuitous Exhibitions—Cab Fares, &c. Entered
at Stationers' Hall.
> *London.* Published by Ross and Son's, 119 & 120, Bishopsgate Street. W Ostell, Printer, Hart
> St., Bloomsbury.
> [W. y. Price 6*d.* 32mo. Contains an "Elevation of the Building," and an account in
> English, French, and German, of the undertaking.]

Rosse, Earl of, *v.* Illustrated London Almanack.

Ross Songster (The).   Price One Penny.
> Printed and Published by H. May, Holywell Street, Strand, *London.*
> [W. y. 24mo. No. 3 contains Songs, entitled "Opening the Palace of Crystal" and
> "The Exhibition of 1851," and No. 5 contains "The Exhibition Prizes, or, Comic Medals,"
> and "Exhibition Lodgers."]

Royal Charter of Incorporation of the Society for the Encouragement of Arts,
Manufactures, and Commerce.   Granted in the tenth year of the Reign of Her
Most Gracious Majesty Queen Victoria, and the 93rd. Session of the Society,
Anno Domini, 1847.
> [Without Publisher's or Printer's name, or year. Circulated amongst members. Sm. 4to,
> pp. 8.]

Royal Exchange (The) and the Palace of Industry; or, the Possible Future of
Europe and the World.   In three Parts.
> 'The Earth is the Lord's, and all that therein is,
> The compass of the world, and they that dwell therein.'
> *London :* The Religious Tract Society; 56, Paternoster Row, and 65, St. Paul's Churchyard. 1851.
> [Price 2*s.* 12mo, pp. 176. Translations will be found under "Bourse," and "Königliche
> Börse." "Philosophers, and politicians, and social economists, are all regarding the great
> event which is just at hand, as constituting the beginning of a new era and of better
> times; and as embodying in itself something like a prophecy of a brightened and improved
> future for the nations." This work also appeared with a new title-page, and with the name
> of Dr. Binney as the Author.]

Royal Exhibition Drawing Slate.
> [W. y., or maker's name. Price 1*s.* A transparent slate, with an exterior view of the
> Exhibition.]

Royal Exhibition Guide through London.   1851.
> I. & J. McRae. *London.*
> [A map, "compiled by A. Rongeat." Has nothing relating to the Exhibition, except an
> exterior view on the cover.]

Royal Exhibition Song Book.   No. 2.
> *London :* T. Goode, 30, Aylesbury Street, Clerkenwell.
> [W. y. Price 1*d.* 24mo. Contains a Song, called "The Wonderful National Grand
> Exhibition."]

Royal Exhibition (The) Knitting, Netting, and Crochet book.   No. 12.   By W.
Carter.
> *London :* Published by J. T. Wood, Holywell Street, Strand. Price One penny.
> [W. y. 24mo. Contains no other reference to the Exhibition than the title.]

Royal Game (The) of the Gathering of the Nations.
> *London :* published by John Betts, 115, Strand. (nearly opposite Exeter Hall).
> [W. y. Price 6*s.*, including a sheet of colored engravings adapted for a child's game.
> The centre compartment is the Building. Small 4to, pp. 23.]

Royal (The) Road to Reading, through the Great Exhibition; In which those who
were too young to visit the Exhibition, may learn to read about it.   Part 1.—
About the Things.   Part 2.—About the Persons.   Part 3.—About the Places.
By the Editor of Pleasant Pages.
> *London :* Houlston and Stoneman;
> *Edinburgh :* Menzies; *Dublin :* J. Robertson; and all Booksellers.
> [W. y. Price 1*s.* Square 18mo, pp. 49, with 17 engravings. A book for young people.]

Royle, Dr. J. Forbes, *v.* Illustrated London Almanack—Lectures—Papers.

Rühlmann, Professor, *v.* Amtlicher Bericht.

Rules of the Northampton and Northamptonshire Provident Society.
> [Without Publisher's or Printer's name, or date. A card.]

Ruskin, John, *v.* Opening of the Crystal Palace.

Russell, J. S., *v.* Special General Meeting.

Russian Section. By Authority of the Royal Commission. Official Catalogue of the Great Exhibition of the Industry of All Nations, 1851.
London: Spicer Brothers, Wholesale Stationers; W. Clowes & Sons, Printers; Contractors to the Royal Commission. City Office, 29 New Bridge Street, Blackfriars.
[W. y., but published in 1851. Price 3*d.* 4to, pp. 27.]

Saintes Ecritures (Les), et le Dimanche en Angleterre, *v.* Aux Etrangers.

Saint-Léon, Arthur, *v.* Fête.

Sala, G. A., *v.* Great Exhibition, Wot is to be—Great Glass House Opened—House that Paxton Built.

Sallandrouze de Lamornaix, *v.* Exposition des Produits, and also Memorandum.

Salvétat, M., on Ceramic Manufactures, *v.* Travaux.

*Samoileff and Sherer on the Cotton Wool and Flax Manufactures.
St. Petersburg.

Sandboys, Visit of Mr. and Mrs., *v.* 1851.

Sartorius, C., *v.* Industrieausstellung in London.

Saunders, F., *v.* Memories of The Great Metropolis.

Saunders, W. J. B., *v.* Palace of Industry, a comprehensive account.

Saxon Section. By authority of the Royal Commission. Official Catalogue of the Great Exhibition of the Industry of All Nations, 1851.
London: Spicer Brothers, Wholesale Stationers; W. Clowes & Sons, Printers; Contractors to the Royal Commission. City Office, 29, New Bridge Street, Blackfriars. Price 3*d.*
[W. y., but published in 1851. Small 4to, pp. 32. The prices of the greater number of the articles are given.]

Schafhäutl, Dr., *v.* Amtlicher Bericht.

Scherer, H., *v.* Londoner Briefe.

Schlüssel zu der grossen Industrieausstellung von E. Heine.
London: Druck von Reynell und Weight, No. 16 Little Pulteney Street, Haymarket.
[Price 8*d.* A sheet, bearing names of articles exhibited, arranged as a sort of ground-plan. There were editions in English and French, *v.* Key, and Guide.]

Schneider, Professor, *v.* Amtlicher Bericht.

Schneitler, Dr. C. F., *v.* Bericht über die Landwirthschaftlichen Maschinen.

Schreiber, F., *v.* Amtlicher Bericht.

Schubarth, Professor B. J., *v.* Amtlicher Bericht—Erster und zweiter Bericht.

Schueler, Dr. Gustav, *v.* Amtlicher Bericht.

Schwanthaler, Ludwig, Friezes of, *v.* Graydon's Crusader Chessmen.

Science in its Relations to Labour. Being a Speech Delivered at the Anniversary of the People's College, Sheffield, on the 25th October, 1853. By Lyon Playfair, C.B., F.R.S. Authorised Edition.
London: Chapman and Hall, 193 Piccadilly. 1853. [Price Three pence.]
[Post 8vo, pp. 24.]

Scotland, Vegetable Products of, *v.* Synopsis.

Sculptors, *v.* Friendly Observations addressed to.

Sculpture from the Great Exhibition of 1851, Lithographed by Louisa Corbaux.
London, printed and published by Stannard and Dixon, 7 Poland St. & Ackermann & Co. 96, Strand.
[W. y. Small folio, 20 plates.]

°Sculpture Plates.
Gilbert, Bride Lane.

Section III.—Manufactures. Catalogue détaillé des Articles Soieries Exposé par 42 Fabriques du Canton de Zurich, Suisse.
[Without Publisher's or Printer's name, or year. 12mo, pp. 13. With the breadth of the silks and their prices, *v.* Catalogue—Switzerland.]

Selby Resolutions, Working Classes, *v.* Important.

Selection of Music at the dinner given by the Council of Chairmen of the Metropolitan Local Commissioners, to the Foreign Commissioners to the Exhibition of All Nations, at the Castle, Richmond, May 20, 1851.
Thomas Harrild, Printer, Silver Street, Falcon Square, *London.*
[W. y. Circulated gratuitously, 8vo, pp. 14.]

Selous, H. C., Picture, *v.* Descriptive Key.

Semaine a Londres (Une) pendant l'Exposition de 1851 renfermant la Description du Batiment de l'Exposition avec deux grands plans officiels, et une jolie Vue du Palais de Cristal le Guide exact et pittoresque de l'Etranger dans Londres et ses Environs. Disposé par journées, et suivi d'Instructions à l'usage du Voyageur et du Répertoire de l'Etranger à Londres contenant la Nomenclature des établissements français, hotels, etc. Monuments et Curiosités, Amusements du soir, etc. Postes, Ambassades, Monnaies un Vocabulaire des mots anglais et des phrases les plus utiles orné d'un beau plan de Londres, très-complet gravé et colorié avec un Index des principales Rues un Tableau de Londres Revue caractéristique et animée des mœurs britanniques ; resumé rapide des impressions et des souvenirs d'un voyage dans la capitale de l'Angleterre par M. J. Bard Chevalier de plusieurs Ordres, Inspecteur honoraire des monuments historiques, etc.
Paris Borrani et Droz, Libraires-Commissionaires Rue des Saints-Pères, 7.
Bruxelles, Ostende, Leipzig, Kiessling et Cᵉ, Libraires.
Londres F. Horncastle 50, Burlington Arcade, Piccadilly P. Rolandi 20, Berners Street, Oxford Street.
[Price 2 francs 50 centimes. Post 8vo, pp. xv., 156. Another copy has a little fuller description of the booksellers. The title is copied from the cover, as there appears to be no inner title. The account of the Exhibition is contained in pages viii.-xv.]

Semper, Gottfried, *v.* Wissenschaft, Industrie und Kunst.

Sermon (A) Preached in The Church of St. George's, Hanover Square, on Sunday Oct. 19, 1851. Being the Sunday after the Closing of the Great Exhibition of The Industry of All Nations. By Henry Howarth, B.D. Rector.
London: John Rodwell, 46 New Bond Street. 1851.
[Price 6*d.* 8vo, pp. 19.]

Sermon on the Exhibition of Art and Industry of All Nations, by the Rev. J. F. Denham, M.A., F.R.S., Rector of St. Mary-le-Strand, Lecturer of St. Bride's, Fleet Street ; Respectfully dedicated to the Inhabitants of the above Parishes ; at the request of many of whom it is now Published ; and nearly as it was delivered in their churches.
London: Published by C. C. Spiller, 102, Holborn Hill. 1851, Price Fourpence.
[8vo, pp. 15. A second edition was published.]

Sermons by the following authors will be found. Aldis, Rev. J.—Allon, Rev. H.—Archer, Rev. Dr.—Aveling, Rev. T.—Beaumont, Rev. Dr.—Binney, Rev. T.—Birch, Rev. Harry—Brock, Rev. W.—Brown, Rev. J. B.—Burnet, Rev. J.—Burrows, Rev. H. W.—Chalmers, Rev. W.—Clayton, Rev. George—Conway, Rev. W.—Cooke, Rev. Dr.—Cox, Rev. Dr.—Croly, Rev. Dr.—Cumming, Rev. Dr.—Davies, Rev. C. T.—Denham, Rev. J. F.—Dixon, Rev. Dr.—Fleming, Rev. Fletcher—Fletcher, Rev. Dr. A.—Flower, Rev. T.—Goode, Rev. D.—Hamilton, Rev. Dr.—Harrison, Rev. J. C.—Higgenson, Rev. E.—Hinton, Rev. J. H.—Howarth, Rev. H.—Hulbert, Rev. D. P. M.—Kennedy, Rev. J.—Leask, Rev. Wm.—Marshall, Thomas L.—Miller, Rev. J. C.—Moore, Rev. D.—Morison, Rev. Dr. John—Noel, Rev. B. W.—Smith, Rev. G.—Stoughton, Rev. J.—Stovel, Rev. C.—Thoresby, Rev. T. E.—Tyerman, Rev. L.—Weir, Rev. J.—Wordsworth, Rev Dr. C.

Sewers, Correspondence with Commissioners of, *v.* Correspondence.

Seyffarth, Dr. Woldemar, *v.* London.

Seymour, Lord, *v.* Report of the Commissioners.

Shakespeare, *v.* Proposal for erecting a Monument to.

Shall the Crystal Palace remain, or shall it not? by William E. Rendle, Plymouth.
London: Bradbury & Evans, 11, Bouverie Street.
Plymouth: Jenkin Thomas, 9, Cornwall Street.
   [W. y., but dated Plymouth, January, 1852. Price 1*s.* 8vo, pp. 21. Printed by Jenkin Thomas, Plymouth. "What! Destroy a Building that has proved to be the wonder and admiration of millions of all the Inhabitants from all Climes and from all Nations? It remains for the Public to say, if it shall be demolished or not, for Lord John Russell has stated in the most emphatic way, *that the Public voice must decide the question.*"]

Shall we keep the Crystal Palace and have Riding and Walking in all Weathers among Flowers—Fountains—and Sculpture? By Denarius.
London: John Murray, Albemarle Street. 1851. Price Sixpence.
   [8vo, pp. 15. "The first condition in carrying out these views is, that the great principle of the Exhibition itself shall be applied to any future uses to be made of the building, namely, the self-supporting and self-managing principle. The success of the Exhibition itself is mainly due to the adoption of this feature; and no one can doubt that the Exhibition would have been far less popular and far less successful if it had been carried out by the Government instead of the public themselves."]

Shall we Spend £100,000 on a Winter Garden for London, or in Endowing Schools of Design in Birmingham, Manchester, Sheffield, Belfast, Glasgow, Leeds, &c. &c.? A letter to the Right Hon. the President of the Board of Trade. By Francis Fuller, member of the Executive Committee of the Great Exhibition; Chairman of the Council of the Society of Arts, for 1849–50.
London: John Ollivier, 59, Pall Mall. 1851. Price Sixpence.
   [8vo, pp. 20. "What will 100,000*l.*, sunk in a Winter Garden, do towards cultivating those arts of design, that taste in colour in which our artificers and manufacturers are manifestly deficient? *What will it do towards encouraging and rewarding humble merit?*"]

Sharp, Granville, *v.* Gilbart—Prize Essay.

Sharp's New London Songster; being a Collection of the newest & most favorite Songs of the Day. N°. 11. Price 1*d.*
London: published by James Pattie, Shoe Lane, Fleet Street.
   [W. y. Post 8vo. Contains "The Exhibition of 1851," and "The National Exhibition."]

Shaw, George, *v.* Lectures [Glass].

Sheepshanks, Rev. R., on "the Calumnies of Mr. Babbage" in his book entitled The Exposition of 1851, *v.* Letter to the Board of Visitors.

Sheffield, *v.* Address of the Local Commissioners.

Sherer on Cotton Wool and Flax Manufactures, *v.* Samoileff.

Short Statement (A) of the Nature and Objects of the proposed Great Exhibition of the Works of Industry of All Nations, Appointed to take place in London in 1851, and of its interest to all classes of the people.
Printed and Sold by Harrison & Son, 45, St. Martin's Lane, *London*, at ½*d.* each, in parcels of 25 copies, at 6*d.*, and in parcels of 100 copies at 1*s.* 6*d.*—Sold by all Booksellers and Stationers in the United Kingdom.
   [W. y. 8vo, pp. 7.]

Shrapnel, Captain N. Scrope, *v.* Stradametrical.

Sightseers, Parliamentary Report on, *v.* Tower of London.

Sights of London, and How to See Them; being a complete Visitors' Guide to the Metropolis for 1851. By William Collier. Containing a description of the Theatres, Exhibitions, Museums, Gardens, Literary and Scientific Societies, Curiosities and Principal Public Buildings, with their situation and terms of admission.
London: Published by Vickers, 28 & 29, Holywell Street; and sold by all Booksellers in town and country. Price Twopence.
   [W. y. Post 8vo, pp. 32, with an engraving of the Exhibition Building on the cover. Pages 1–3 contain an account of the Crystal Palace.]

Simpson, William, *v.* Souvenir.

Singapore, Articles collected by Local Committee of, *v.* Indian Archipelago.

* Six discours prononcees en Angleterre dans les Reunions publiques par M. C. Dupin.

Skiñs, J. A. Nicholay on, *v.* Historical Account of.

Slate, *v.* Royal Exhibition Drawing Slate.

Slight Sketch (A) of the Manipulatory Processes in Electro-Metallurgy, Glass, and Papier Mache Manufacture, Steel Pen and Button Making, Brassfounding, Coining, &c. With the list of Manufactories to be visited. Printed for private gratuitous distribution among the visitors to Birmingham on the 19th of June, 1851.

> *Birmingham:* Printed at M. Billing's Steam-Press, Newhall Street.
> [12mo, pp. 28. "The writer of this is one of those who recognise the dignity of labour, and is proud to think that the working men and women of England have at length had assigned to them that position which they are entitled to by their works. He is proud to think that this position is the result of the labours of the Royal Commission and those of the Executive Committee of the Exhibition of the Industry of all Nations; and on their visit to the town on this the 19th day of June, 1851, to receive from a community, whose united labours form in the aggregate no unimportant part of the Hyde Park Exhibition, some token of their gratitude for services conferred, he dedicates to them this brief sketch of some of the processes gone through in the manufactories to be visited."]

Sling and a Stone for the Great Exhibition, *v.* John Bull—Mirror of the Time.

Small Contribution (A) to the Great Exhibition of 1851. By J. C. H. Freund, M.D.

> ' Prüfe Beides und wähle das Rechte.'

> *London:* Groombridge and Sons, Paternoster Row. 1851. Price One Shilling.
> [8vo, pp. 40. This pamphlet was apparently a reply to "The Philosopher's Mite." "The Exhibition will prove neither dangerous to the country nor to your popularity; decidedly the reverse: and the beneficial effects resulting from it, with respect to art and science, education and religion, and the political and social institutions, will be incalculable, and be felt far beyond the time of all who now censure or praise it." It was addressed to Prince Albert.]

Smith, John, *v.* Remarks.

Smith, John Jay, *v.* Letters—Proposal.

Smith, Rev. G., *v.* Forty-four Sermons.

Smythies, Mrs. Yorick, A poem, *v.* Prince and the People.

Snow, Robert, A Poem, *v.* On the Closing.

Society of Arts, *v.* Constitution of—Copies of Contract with Messrs. Munday—Great Exhibition of Industry, Correspondence with Mr. Drew—Inventors, on the Principles of Jurisprudence—Lectures—Letter from Mr. H. Chester—On the Musical Department of the late Exhibition—On the Origin—Rights of Inventors—Royal Charter of Incorporation—Special General Meeting—Statement of Proceedings.

Society of Arts, Manufactures, and Commerce. Art Manufactures' Institute, with Elementary Drawing Schools, at Bradford.

> *London:*—Printed by G. Barclay, Castle St. Leicester Sq.
> [8vo, pp. 16. Report of a Meeting held at Bradford, Yorkshire, February 2nd, 1852.]

Society of Arts—Mr. Paxton on the origin and details of the Building, *v.* On.

Soieries, Catalogue détaillé, *v.* Section III.

Solly, Edward, *v.* Lectures [Vegetable Substances]—Trade Museums.

Songs, *v.* Ballads—Music—Ross Songster—Royal Exhibition Song Book—Sharp's New London Songster—Yankee Smith's London Comic Songster.

Sonnenthal, J., *v.* Amtlicher Bericht.

Soper, Richard Coltman, Poem by, *v.* England's Lament.

Souvenir of the Great Exhibition, comprised in six authentic coloured Interiors, after drawings by J. McNevin, made expressly for this work. 1. The British department, viewed towards the Transept. 2. The British department, viewed from the Transept. 3. The Foreign department, viewed towards the Transept. 4. The Foreign department, viewed from the Transept. 5. The Transept, from the Grand Entrance. 6. The Transept, towards the Grand Entrance. In Chromography by Messrs. Thomas Picken, William Simpson, R. K. Thomas, and E. Walker.

London:

London: Ackermann and Co., 96, Strand, by appointment to H. M. the Queen, H. R. H. Prince Albert, H. R. H. the Duchess of Kent, and the Royal Family. Price—in Chromography, £2 2*s.* ; Extra coloured, £3 3*s.*, the Series.
[W. y. Royal Folio, pp. 6.]

Sovereign of All! Hymn for the Queen, and Welcome to All Nations: A Contribution to the Great Exhibition of 1851. Dedicated to Joseph Paxton, Esq. By an Exhibitor.

London: Nisbet & Co., Berners Street, Oxford Street: Sold by J. Mason, 66, Paternoster Row, and all Booksellers. The Profits will be devoted to the aid of the Ragged Schools. Price Fourpence. Hayman, Carvosso, and Co., Printers, 5, Whitefriars Street, Fleet Street.
[W. y. Post 8vo, pp. 8. Printed in gold, with coloured borders. It was also set to music by Mr. L. H. Lavenu.

" Here let perpetual concord dwell
Clear as this Crystal Shrine,
With grateful love all bosoms swell,—
' My heart beats true to thine.'
Be this a Temple to Thy praise !
All nations learn the strain ;
Their tribute to Jehovah raise,
And hail VICTORIA's reign."]

Spare the Crystal Palace!! An Appeal to the Public on its behalf.

' A rare Pavilion, such as Man
Saw never since Mankind began ! ' *Thackeray.*

London: Gilbert, Paternoster Row.
[W. y. Post 8vo, pp. 7. " Would it not be sacrilege to destroy a marble column of the ruins of Athens? Is it less so to break up this beautiful structure, fraught with even diviner recollections, and consecrated by a thousand associations? " It is signed Philanthropos.]

Special General Meeting of the Society of Arts, February 8, 1850, with regard to the Great Exhibition of Industry.

[Without Publisher or Printer's name, or date. 4to, pp. 2. A circular advocating Mr. Whishaw's claims. " For private circulation only, unless Mr. Russell's statement is made public," *v.* Statement of Proceedings.]

Spectator, an Article from, *v.* Cosmopolitan Exhibition.

Speech of His Royal Highness Prince Albert, at the Grand Banquet at the Mansion House, on Thursday, March 21st, 1850.

Sold by Horatio Owen, Bookseller, Stationer, and Newspaper Agent, Falcon Square.
[W. y. Price 6*d.* Quarto, p. 1.]
[Ditto, in another form, in gold letters, on blue paper, and with an ornamental border.]
[W. y. Price 1*s.* Royal Folio, p. 1.]
[Ditto, in French.]
[Ditto, in German.]
[Ditto, in Italian.]
[Ditto, in Arabic.]
[Ditto, in Turkish.]

Speech of R. Cobden, Esq., M.P. Exhibition of the Industry of All Nations, 1851. Meeting of the Borough of Marylebone.

John Dale, Printer, Thornton's Buildings, Bradford, Yorks.
[W. y. Circulated gratuitously. Royal 8vo, pp. 4.]

Spooner's Perspective View of the Western Nave of the Great Exhibition; with the Crystal Fountain, Silk Trophy, Seeley's Fount^n. Coalbrook Dale Dome, &c. &c.

London: Published by William Spooner, 379, Strand, Septr. 23. 1851.
[Price 7*s.* 6*d.* Small 4to. One of the expanding views for young people.]

S. S., *v.* Farewell Lines.

Stanley, on the Exhibition, *v.* Lord [Present Earl of Derby].

Statement of Proceedings preliminary to the Exhibition of Industry of All Nations, 1851.

Vacher & Sons, 29, Parliament Street.
[W. y. Circulated gratuitously. Folio, pp. 12.]

Statement of the Nature and Objects of the proposed Great Exhibition, *v.* Short.

Statistical Chart of the Great Exhibition. Showing at a view the number and class of visitors on each day, and the receipts at the doors. Presented to the Subscribers of the Weekly Dispatch, January 4, 1852.
<blockquote>Printed in Colours with Moveable Types, and by Steam, at Vizetelly & Company's Offices, Peter-borough Court, 135 Fleet Street, London.—From Designs by Corporals J. Mack and A. Gardener, of the Royal Sappers and Miners. And Published with the sanction of the Royal Commis-sioners, by R. J. Wood, at the 'Weekly Dispatch' Office 139 Fleet Street, London.
[Price 6d. A large sheet, with an engraving of the exterior. See also Memorial of the Great Exhibition and Illustrated London News Grand Panorama.]</blockquote>

Statuary, *v.* Friendly Observations to Sculptors—Gallery of Art—Gems of Art.

St. Clair, William, Poem by, *v.* Great Exhibition of 1851.

Stein, Baurath, *v.* Amtlicher Bericht.

Steinbeis, Dr. Von, *v.* Amtlicher Bericht.

Stephenson, Roberts, *v.* Great Exhibition, its Palace and Contents.

Stodart. Miss M. A., Poem by, *v.* Close of the Great Exhibition.

Stone the First at the Great Glass House. To be completed in Six Stones.
<blockquote align="center">' 'Tis all a libel; Paxton, Sir, will say.'—Pope.</blockquote>
<blockquote>London: William Edward Painter, 342, Strand, Printer; and all Booksellers. Price Sixpence.
[W. y. 12mo, pp. 28. The only part ever published. " From Bubbles, great and small, may we be delivered! And from the evil effects of none so much as from those of the great bubble of 1851—that Great Bubble which has been blown over the Upas Tree of Competition!"]</blockquote>

Stoughton, Rev. J., *v.* Forty-four Sermons—Palace of Glass.

Stovel, Rev. C., *v.* Forty-four Sermons.

Stradametrical Survey of London (The), Part I. Containing the mean distances, with their relative cab fares, from all the principal streets, squares, or places in London, to the Great Exhibition, and the several Railway Termini in the Metropolis. By Captain N. Scrope Shrapnel, late 3rd Dragoon Guards.— Entered at Stationers Hall.
<blockquote>London: William Grigg, 183, Regent Street. 1851.
[Price 2s. 6d. 18mo, pp. ii., 101.]</blockquote>

Stranger in Hyde Park, *v.* To a Stranger.

Stranger in London (The); or Visitor's Companion to the Metropolis and its Environs, with an Historical and Descriptive Sketch of the Great Exhibition. By Cyrus Redding.
<blockquote>London: Henry G. Bohn, York Street, Covent Garden. 1851.
[Price 2s. Post 8vo, pp. viii., 287. With Illustrations. The account of the Exhibition is contained in pp. 238-268. The outside cover bears the Title of London and the Exhibition.]</blockquote>

Strangers' Guide to London and its Environs (The), for 1851; being the year of the Great Exhibition of the Works of Industry of All Nations: containing full particulars of all the Public Buildings, Parks, Palaces, Gardens, Government Offices, Churches, Chapels, Meeting-Houses, Hospitals, Literary and Scientific Institutions, Places of Amusement, (Open Gratuitously); Theatres, Concert and Assembly Rooms, Ball Rooms, Exhibitions, Panoramas, Dioramas, Cycloramas, Cosmoramas, Picture Galleries, Bazaars, Arcades, Museums, Promenades, Streets, Bridges, Markets, Fairs, Monuments, Barracks, Baths, and Wash-houses, Hotels, Taverns, Coffee Houses, Steam Boats, Piers, Hackney Coach and Cab Fares, Railway Stations, &c.: also, important facts relating to the Great Fire of London, in 1666: together with an account of the Crystal Palace, erected for the World's Fair; and everything interesting, or worth seeing in this modern Babylon; &c., &c. Compiled from authentic sources, By Hugh C. Gray.
<blockquote>London: Elliot, New Oxford Street; Vickers; Dipple, Holywell Street; And Sold at all Steam-Boat Piers and Railway Stations throughout the Kingdom. Price Twopence. Entered at Stationers' Hall.
[W. y. 12mo, pp. 32; with an engraving. Only the first two pages contain an account of the Crystal Palace.]</blockquote>

Street Songs, *v.* Ballads.

Strengthening the Bonds of Peace, *v.* Placards.

Strutt, J. G., *v.* Tallis's History of the Crystal Palace.

Substances used as Food, as exemplified in the Great Exhibition. Published under the Direction of the Committee of General Literature and Education, appointed by the Society for Promoting Christian Knowledge.

> *London :* Printed for the Society for Promoting Christian Knowledge; sold at the Depository, Great Queen Street, Lincoln's Inn Fields; 4, Royal Exchange; and 16, Hanover Street, Hanover Square; and by all Booksellers.
> [W. y. Price 2*s.* 8*d.* Square 18mo, pp. iv., 347.]

Suggestions addressed to the Producers and Manufacturers of France. By M. Charles Dupin. Translated and Published by the Westminster Local Committee. 1850.

> *London :* Printed by T. Brettell, Rupert Street, Haymarket.
> [8vo, pp. 18.]

Suggestions for a Crystal College or New Palace of Glass, for combining the Intellectual Talent of All Nations; or a Sketch of a Practical Philosophy of Education. By W. Cave Thomas, Master of the North London School for Drawing and Modelling.

> ' I seize this, as I shall every other opportunity, to advocate that system of education which regards the training of all the faculties.'—*Address to the Students of the North London School, May* 1850.

> *London :* Dickenson Brothers, 114, New Bond Street, and Marchant Singer & Co., 1, Ingram Court, Fenchurch Street. 1851.
> [Price 2*s.* 8vo, pp. 63. "It may be gathered from the more frequent allusions of the press to the subject of Art Education for the Masses, and also from the private discussions of individuals concerning the merits of the various art-manufactures lately exhibited, that 'The Exhibition of Industry of all Nations' has awakened the public mind to the importance of schools for the development and education of taste. There may be some however, who witnessed the honourable position which British articles of taste maintained in the Crystal Palace, who would rest content with the present state of things. We must confess ourselves not of the number."]

Sullivan, William K., *v.* Journal of Industrial Progress.

Sunday School Teacher, *v.* What I thought.

Sutton, Leslie, *v.* Fate of Crystal Palace.

S. V., *v.* Deux Lettres Sans Adresse

Switzerland. Manufactures, Section III. Catalogues of Classes XIV., XVI., and XVIII. of the Exhibition in London.

> *St. Gall :* Printed by Scheitlin & Zollikofer. 1851.
> [8vo., pp. 14. Title taken from cover. The prices are generally affixed to the articles. *v.* also Catalogue—Section III.]

Synopsis of the Vegetable Products of Scotland, Forming a Descriptive Account of the collection exhibited at the Great Exhibition of the Industry of All Nations. By Peter Lawson & Son. Seedsmen and Nurserymen to the Highland and Agricultural Society of Scotland

> ' God said, Behold, I have given you every herb bearing seed, which is upon the face of all the earth, and every tree, in the which is the fruit of a tree yielding seed.'—*Genesis* i. 29.

> *Edinburgh :* Private Press of Peter Lawson & Son. 1851.
> [The separate divisions were given away during the time of the Exhibition. Since that time the work has been published in one volume, price 10*s.* 6*d.* Small 4to. Division 1, " Plants cultivated for their Farinaceous seeds, together with their straw or haulm," pp. 138; Division 2, " Plants cultivated for their Herbage and Forage," pp. 128; Division 3, " Plants chiefly cultivated for their Roots," pp. 64; Division 4, " Plants cultivated for their uses in the Arts and Manufactures," pp. 72; Appendix, "List of Fruit Trees," pp. 83. A detailed account of vegetable products of Scotland in the Exhibition. " The desire has been to render clear and accessible to the many thousands who may congregate at this Great Industrial Exhibition of all Nations, a knowledge of the leading characters of those plants, which are, by art or culture, rendered subservient to the wants of man."
> ANOTHER EDITION was published in 1852, headed " The Lawsonian Collection. Synopsis of the Vegetable Products of Scotland in the Museum of the Royal Botanic Gardens of Kew. By Peter Lawson and Son." Dedicated to Sir William Jackson Hooker, with a view of Messrs. Lawson's house at Edinburgh. Pp. xx. Division 1, pp. 138; Division 2, pp. 128; Division 3, pp. 64; Division 4, pp. 80; Division 5, " Plants cultivated for their Timber,
> Bark,

Bark, &c.," pp. 72; Appendix, pp. 83. The collection shown in 1851 by Messrs. Lawson was at the close " presented to the Royal Commissioners, and, under subsequent arrangements with the British Government, deposited in the Royal Botanic Gardens of Kew."]

Synopsis, Robert Hunt, v. Companion to Official Catalogue—Guide du Catalogue.

Tabular and Descriptive Lists of Articles, from Malwa, Khyrpoor, Cutch, and the Territories under the Government of Bombay, which have been forwarded to the East India House by the Central Committee at Bombay, for the Grand Exhibition of 1851. Arranged after the Classification of H. M.'s Commissioners, published in February 1851.

Bombay. Printed for Government, at the Bombay Education Society's Press, 1851.
[Circulated gratuitously. 8vo, pp. 51. The prices of the articles are added.]

Tait's Edinburgh Magazine. February, 1852. No. CCXVIII. Vol. XIX. Fiat Justitia.

Sutherland and Knox, *Edinburgh ;*
Simpkin, Marshall, and Co., *London;* and John Robertson, *Dublin.* 1852. Price One Shilling.
[Imperial 8vo. Contains an article, pp. 99–107, on " The Health of the Metropolis during the Year of the Great Exhibition by the Author of ' The Philosopher's Mite.' " Afterwards printed separately, v. Health.]

Tales of the Crystal Palace, v. Recollections.

Tallis's History and Description of the Crystal Palace, and the Exhibition of the World's Industry in 1851 ; illustrated by beautiful Steel Engravings, from original drawings and daguerreotypes, by Beard, Mayall, etc., etc. Dedicated to H.R.H. Prince Albert, K.G., etc., etc., etc.

Printed and published by John Tallis and Co., *London* and *New York.*
[Price 2*l.* 8*s* W. y. 4to, 3 Volumes, vol. 1, pp. iv., iii., 268; vol. 2, iii., 262; vol. 3, ii., 110. The Title-pages of Volumes 2 and 3 bear the words " Edited by J. G. Strutt, Esq. ;" and " Printed and published by the London Printing and Publishing Company, London and New York."]

Tallis's Illustrated London ; in commemoration of the Great Exhibition of All Nations in 1851. Forming a complete Guide to the British Metropolis and its environs. Illustrated by upwards of Two Hundred Steel Engravings from Original Drawings and Daguerreotypes. With Historical and Descriptive Letter-press, by William Gaspey, Esq. Vol. 1. [Vol. 2]

John Tallis and Company, *London* and *New York.*
[W. y. Price £1. Post 8vo, Vol. 1, pp. vii., 320. Vol. 2., pp. vii., 304. Pages 273–304 of Vol. 2 contain an account of the Exhibition, illustrated by several engravings.]

Taunton Cabinet (The). A Reprint from the ' Somerset County Herald.' March 22, 1851.
[Printed by W. Bragg, and Son, Herald Office, 34, Parade, *Taunton.* W. y. 8vo, pp. 7. A description of a carved cabinet sent from Taunton to the Exhibition.]

Telescopic Views, v. Interior—Lane—Rawlins—Spooner—View.

Temperance & Peace, Reign of, J. S. Buckingham, v. Earnest Plea.

Temperance Cause, Thomas Beggs, v. Exhibition and the People.

Tempest Prognosticator, Merryweather, v. Essay on.

Temple of Truth (The) ; its wonders—its worshippers—and its Witnesses. A Great Exhibition Tract.
[Ward, Paternoster Row. Nisbet and Co. 21, Berners Street, Oxford Street; and all Booksellers. 1*d.* each, or 7*s.* per 100. W. y. 12mo, pp. 12.]

Ten Centuries of Art. Its progress in Europe from the 9th to the 19th Century. With a glance at the Artistic works of Classical Antiquity, and concluding considerations on the probable influence of the Great Exhibition, and the present state and future prospects of Art in Great Britain. By Henry Noel Humphreys, Author of the ' Illuminated Books of the Middle Ages,' ' Ancient Coins and Medals,' ' The Coinage of England,' &c.

London : Grant and Griffith, St. Paul's Churchyard. 1852.
[Price 1*l.* 8*s.* 4to, pp. 118, with numerous colored Plates. " The international Exhibition will be repeated, and that at no far distant period ; and its next advent will be a still

more

more effective promoter of the true interests of the real producers of the wealth of all countries. But the next time its management must be no little private matter—no affair of a small clique of well-intentioned, but unsuitable gentlemen, supported by a few noble lords, and enlivened by the uniforms of a few military men. No! such a meeting is necessarily a truly democratic and industrial fête, and must be managed entirely by the people. It will be so next time, and it will then be seen whether the founders of the feast will be excluded from the honours of their own festival, and the banquet of their own providing."]

Tennant, James, *v.* Lectures [Gems]—Engravings, Precious Stones.

Tentoonstelling (De) der Nijverheid van alle Volken te Londen, door Dr. S. Bleekrode, Hoogleeraar in de Natuur- en Wiskundige Wetenschappen aan de Koninklijke Akademie te Delft. Geschiedenis en Beschrijving der Tentoonstelling; Voortbrengselen uit de drie Natuurrijken; Beweegkrachten en Werktuigen; Burgerlijke-, Water- en Scheepsbouwkunde; Wapenen. Met Houtsnê-Figuren. Tweede Vermeerderde Uitgave, met Uitvoerig Register.
'S Gravenhage, Gebroeders Belinfante. 1853.
[Price 12*s.* Royal 8vo, pp. vi., 530. A republication of a series of articles, contributed to the Sunday edition of the "Algemeen Handelsblad," from May 1851 to May 1852. "It is from London that the industrial movement has received a new impulse. Albion has given it a tendency which till now was unknown in the history of mankind. By this undertaking, Great Britain will have revealed the greatness of her power to the whole world."]

Texier, Edmond, *v.* Lettres sur L'Angleterre.

Thalaba Academicus, *v.* Great Foreign Bazaar—Great Humbug of 1851—Great Job of 1851—Whig Attorney's Great-iron-glass-foreign-Bazaar.

°Theology and Morality (The) of the Great Exhibition, as set forth in certain leading Articles which have lately appeared in 'The Times' and 'Record' Newspapers. By a Spiritual watchman of the Church of England.
'Here is Britain Row, the French Row, the Italian Row, the Spanish Row, the German Row, where several sorts of vanities are to be sold. But, as in other fairs, some one Commodity is the chief of all the fair, so the Ware of Rome and her merchandise is greatly promoted in this fair.'—*Bunyan's* 'Pilgrim's Progress'—'Vanity Fair.'
London: William Edward Painter, 342, Strand. 1851. Price Sixpence.
[8vo, pp. 19.]

This is the Great Exhibition of the Idleness of All Nations—which may be carried away for One Shilling
Mann Cornhill-Dean & Son Printers
[W. y. Square 18mo. A long sheet of facetious engravings folded. A number of the engravings appear to have been used in another work, which will be found under Now Open.]

Thomae, Dr., *v.* Bericht über die englische Landwirthschaft.

Thomas, R. K., *v.* Souvenir.

Thomas, W. Cave, *v.* Suggestions for a Crystal College.

Thoresby, Rev. T. E., *v.* Forty-four Sermons.

Thoughts on the Crystal Palace, and other Poems. By Caroline Patston, Peterborough.
London: Houlston & Stoneman, Paternoster Row.
Peterboro: Clarke. 1854.
[Price 6*d.* 12mo, pp. 48. The first poem is "Thoughts on the Great Exhibition." Others are on the Crystal Palace.
"My poor weak fancy ne'er can trace,
The beauties of this wondrous place—
The consciousness of human art.
Who doth this knowledge then impart?"]

Timbs, John, *v.* Year Book.

Times (The) v. the Exhibition of 1851. (From the Daily News of July 16th, 1850.)
[Wm. Byles, Printer, Observer Office, Kirkgate, *Bradford.* W. y. Royal 8vo, p. 2. A reply to an article in the "Times," threatening an application for an injunction against Prince Albert on account of the proposed erection of the Building in Hyde Park, reprinted from the "Daily News."]

Times, *v.* Extracts from—Great Exhibition, Times Reprint.

Tiny Exhibition Catalogue, *v.* By the authority of the Inventors.

Tit for Tat, for Juvenile Minds; with large additions of Prose and Verse for more mature intellects, in advocacy of Peace Principles.

London: William and Frederick G. Cash, (Successors to Charles Gilpin,) 5, Bishopsgate Street Without.

William Irwin, *Manchester.* 1853.

[Price 2s. 12mo, pp. viii., 140. Dedicated to "Britain's Beloved and Honoured Queen, with her Royal Consort, Prince Albert, as a small token of the Author's high appreciation of the distinguished patronage so gracefully and liberally accorded to the Wonder and Delight of our Age, that Temple of Concord, the Crystal Palace in Hyde Park." Pp. 25-30 and 71-72 contain articles and verses relating to the Exhibition. The Author, Mr. John Harris, a Quaker, records his name in the book.]

To a Stranger in Hyde Park.

The Religious Tract Society, Instituted 1799. 56, Paternoster Row, and 65, St. Paul's Church-yard. [Price 3s. per 100.]

[W. y. 12mo, pp. 12. A tract, with a view of the building. A translation, *v.* A l'Etranger.]

Toespraak (Eene) aan Vreemdelingen, bij het bezoeken der Groote Tentoonstelling van Kunsten, in Londen, 1851. De Heilige Schrift en de Sabbath in Engeland.

Londen: Gedrukt voor het Genootschap ter Bevordering van Christelijke Kennis, te Londen; Great Queen Street, Lincoln's-Inn-Fields; 4 Royal Exchange; en 16 Hanover Street, Regent Street. 1851.

[Price 1d., or 7s. per 100. 12mo, pp. 12. One of the addresses issued by the Society.]

To Her Majesty's Commissioners for the Exhibition, 1851.

[*London:* Printed by Levy, Robson, and Franklyn, Great New Street, Fetter Lane. W. y. 12mo, pp. 23. Letters Reprinted from the Devonport Telegraph, signed Richard Burnet, and dated April 8th, 1850. The first of these letters was published in March, 1841, "in order to stimulate the members of the Devonport Mechanics' Institute to get up an Exposition of Arts; and the second was addressed to the subscribers of the British Association in the autumn of the same year. * * * I now reprint them, in the hope that they may contain some points which otherwise might escape the notice of Her Majesty's Commissioners, and more particularly the few sentences upon the exhibition of *tools*, to which the most minute attention should be paid."]

To His R. H. Prince Albert, the Royal Commissioners, and the Executive Committee of the Industry of All Nations.

Printed at M. Billing's Steam-Press Offices, 74, 75, and 76, Newhall Street, *Birmingham.*

[W. y. Folio, p. 1. Address from a Meeting of the Clerks and Workpeople in the employ of Mr. R. W. Winfield, of the Cambridge Street Works, Birmingham, dated 19th June, 1851. "The Exhibition of 1851 is, however, but one great history of Industry, written by Labour, on Metals, on Stone, on Clay, on Silk, and on Cotton, bound up in Iron, Glass, and Timber, and as supplying a page in the volume, we are emboldened to approach you, for in that assemblage of all that is useful, rich, and rare, it is proved that indeed 'all is the gift of Industry—rich power.' For the first time the varied Skill, Talent, and Industry of England and Englishmen have been rendered apparent to themselves and to the world; Labour has been elevated by collecting together its results; the whole is replete with instruction, to this and all succeeding generations; it presents and will present a spectacle unsurpassed in moral grandeur in the history of the Universe."]

Tolpatsch, *v.* Meister.

To-morrow! The Results and Tendencies of National Exhibitions deduced from strict historic Parallels; developing a Uniform Law of peculiar interest at the present time. By Historia.

London Saunders and Otley, Conduit Street. 1851.

[Price 1s. 6d. 8vo, pp. iv., 67. "We may remark that this narrative of Babel has never, in the history of the world, had a similarity or a repetition till this vision of '51 floated before us; and perhaps it may still be thought that the resemblance is somewhat imperfect,—we will therefore take it up again in the beginning."]

To the Exhibitors at the Great Exhibition of the Industry of All Nations.

Sumfield & Jones, Printers, King's Head Court, Holborn Hill.

[Folio, pp. 2. Dated May 1851, and signed an Exhibitor. "A great wrong has been done you. A gross and unmerited indignity has been offered to you. You were excluded from a scene of which you would have been the most fitting witnesses, and which but for your mighty intellects had not been witnessed by any. A national scandal!"]

Another Edition.

[Without Printer's name. Printed as a broadside, with slight alterations.]

Another.

[Without Publisher's or Printer's name, or date, giving the names of the Committee. A copy of the Protest, and a broadside calling on Exhibitors to sign it.]

To the Great Exhibition of All Nations and the Funny People going there 1851. A Puzzle Price 1s.

W Roxbrough 9 Aldgate, City, London.

[12mo, in a case.]

Tour (Eine) nach London und Paris im Sommer 1851 von Dr. F. W. Ghillany.
Nürnberg, Verlag von Bauer und Raspe (Julius Merz) 1853.
> [Price R 3. 12mo, 3 vols, pp. xiv. 260; vii. 293; viii. 427. A book of travels, with a description of a visit to the Crystal Palace. The author is of opinion that the most remarkable English contributions were to be found in the engine-department; but he cannot help feeling some misgivings about the alarming increase of machinery, tending to supersede useful human labour. In the preface, he testifies candidly to the "dryness" of his remarks on the Industrial Exhibition.]

Tower of London, &c. Return of the number of Visitors to the Armouries and the Jewel House in the Tower of London; to the Apartments at Hampton Court; to Westminster Abbey; to St. Pauls Cathedral; to the British Museum, the National Gallery, the Vernon Gallery, the Geological Museum, and the Museum of Ornamental Art, in each of the years 1850, 1851, 1852, and 1853. (Mr. Hume.) Ordered, by The House of Commons, to be Printed, 24 January 1855. 21. Under 2 oz.
> [Folio. A Parliamentary Return, giving details as to the amount of sight-seeing in 1851 as compared with the previous and two following years.]

Tracts for the Million. No. VII. The Great Exhibition of 1851.
> [Thompson and Davidson, Printers, 19, Great St. Helens, *London.* W. y. 8vo, pp. 4. "Notwithstanding these certain indications of injury to Native Industry, a class of men still insist upon the advantages of Free-trade. But, let it not be forgotten that these very men are the most active in their support of the Great Exhibition of 1851! * * * Be then earnest—be resolute—be energetic in moving Her Gracious Majesty to dissolve the present Parliament, so that PROTECTION may once more be afforded to you. If you will but do this, you need not fear the consequences of the Great Exhibition of 1851—IT WILL NEVER TAKE PLACE !"]

Trade Museums, their Nature and Uses considered in a letter addressed, by permission, to H. R. H. the Prince Albert, K.G. Etc. Etc. Etc. By Edward Solly, F.R.S. G.S. & L.S. Hon. Member of the Royal Agricultural Society of England, Hon. Professor of Chemistry to the Horticultural Society, Lecturer on Chemistry in the Hon. E. I. C. Military Seminary at Addiscombe, and Secretary to the Society for the Encouragement of Arts, Manufactures, and Commerce.
London: Longman, Brown, Green, and Longmans. 1853.
> [Price 6d. 8vo, pp. 15. "There is little doubt that the idea occurred to many of those who visited the Great Exhibition, and who studied the people who came to see, as well as the things that were collected together, that a permanent exhibition of useful products, displaying at once the productions of nature and the results of human industry, and contrasting the resources of different countries, would be extremely interesting, and what is more, extremely useful."]

Tradesmen of the Metropolis, *v.* Remarks.

Travaux de la Commission Française sur l'Industrie des Nations, publiés par ordre de l'Empereur.
Paris. Imprimerie Impériale. 1854.
> [8vo. The Reports in each of the Classes are paged separately. This work is to be completed in 8 volumes, but Vols. 4, 5, and 6, price £1 10s., only are published up to this date (10th of April, 1855). Vol. 4, containing " Hommage a l'Empereur," by Baron C. Dupin—Reports on Jury 11, M. Mimerel, pp. 64—Jury 12, M. J. Randoing, pp. 38—Jury 12 and 15, Second Part, M. Bernaville, pp. 216—Jury 13, M. Arlès-Dufour, pp. 15—An Appendix on Classes 11, 12, and 13, Baron C. Dupin, pp. 30—Jury 14, M. Legentil, pp. 64—Jury 15, M. Maxime Gaussen, pp. 22. Vol. 5, containing Jury 16, M. Fauler, pp. 50—Jury 17, M. Ambroise Firmin Didot, pp. 128—Jury 18, M. Persoz, pp. 74—Jury 19, M. Felix Aubry, pp. 158—Jury 19, M. Chevreuil, pp. 100, including the correspondence relative to the omission, in the list of the awards, of the fact that the Council Medal voted for the Gobelin Tapestry was partly awarded for the invention of the Chromatic system after which the Tapestry is colored—Jury 20, M. Bernoville, pp 88. Vol. 6, containing Jury 21, M. F Le Play, pp. 74 —Jury 22, M. Goldenberg, pp. 158, with engravings—Jury 23, M. Le Duc de Luynes, pp. 262—Jury 24, M. E. Péligot, pp. 58—Jury 25, M. Salvétat, pp. 135.]

Trip (The) to the Great Exhibition, of Barnabas Blandydash and Family. By 'Uncle Joseph.'
> 'All the world's a stage, and all the men and women merely players.'—*Shakespere.*
London: Published by Houlston and Stoneman, Paternoster Row. 1851.
> [Price 2d. 12mo, pp. 28. A tale.]

Troup, George, *v.* Art and Faith.

Tunstall, James, *v.* Address of the Bath Local Committee.

Tupper, Martin Farquhar, v. Appeal—England's Welcome—Grand Exhibition—Hymn for All Nations—Last Call—Reverie—Rhyme for the Close.

Turkish Section, v. Catalogue of.

Turner, Joseph, v. Echoes of the Great Exhibition.

Turner, R. & T., v. Crystal Palace, its Architectural History.

Twining, Thomas, Jun., on Industrial Colleges, v. Notes.

Two Premiums of Fifty Pounds each, for Essays on China and the Eastern Archipelago, in connexion with the objects of the Great Exhibition, Offered by Mr. W. Parker Hammond, London.

> [Without Publisher's or Printer's name, or date. 8vo, pp. 4. A prospectus.]

Tyerman, Rev. L., v. Forty-four Sermons.

Typographique, Etablissement de M. Paul Dupont, v. Notice concernant.

Uncle Joseph, v. Trip to Great Exhibition.

Uncle Nimrod's Visits, v. Aunt Mavor.

United States, Proceedings of the Central Committee of the, v. Proceedings.

Unity of the Place (The), with its correlative claims : Thoughts suggested by the Great Exhibition. By John Morison, D.D., LL.D.

> London : W. F. Ramsay, 11, Brompton Row. And 20, Paternoster Row. 1851.
> [Price Sixpence. 12mo, pp. 23. A sermon.]

Universal Brotherhood, a poem, v. Exhibition, 1851.

Urinals, On Establishment of, v. Correspondence.

Useful Arts (The) : Their Birth and Developement. Edited for the Young Men's Christian Association, By Samuel Martin, Minister of Westminster Chapel, Westminster. Second Edition.

> London : James Nisbet and Co. Berners Street ; Hamilton, Adams, and Co. Paternoster Row. 1851.
> [Price 3s. 6d. 12mo, pp. xvi., 415. With numerous engravings. Pages 1-44 contain an account of the Exhibition. "The Great Exhibition will, we believe, act upon society with such corrective, directive, and impulsive powers as the following :—1. The inventor, the manufacturer, and the artisan, will be raised in social estimation and position. With a most mischievous exclusiveness, the heroes of the nation have hitherto been raised from the army and navy. Yet men of war have not built up, although they have protected, the wealth and well-being of the country. James Watt and Fulton, Arkwright and Cartwright, have done more for us than the leaders of all our battles ; yet the honours of the nation are not put upon their heads, neither have the resources of the country ministered to their wants. We build their sepulchres, but we have not spread a table for them while they could eat bread. Yet who so worthy of a dukedom as our leader in the annihilation of space and in the safe and speedy intercourse of man with man ? What lords so real, and therefore so noble, as the men who can take spinning and weaving from the human fingers, and accomplish it by a power which to a pair of human hands is as 266 to one ? Who so truly constitute nobility and aristocracy as those whose skill gives advantage to the industry of our empire, and whose productions promote the comfort and welfare of the race ? Could the court of a sovereign be better graced, than by the men who, in promoting and elevating the industry of the people, lay deep and wide the foundations of national prosperity, social order, and true patriotism ?"]

Vaillard, Adolphe, v. Palais de Cristal ou les Parisiens a Londres.

Varrentrapp, Professor, v. Amtlicher Bericht.

Vates Secundus, v. Great Exhibition wot is to be.

Vehicles, Number passing Bow Church and Aldgate, v. Report of.

Verdon, Rev. T. K. de, v. Crystal Palace of Industry [a poem].

Verhandlungen der eidgenössischen Expertenkommission für die 1851 in London abgehaltene Gewerbeausstellung.

> Bern. Buchdrukerei von Rudolf Jenni. 1854.
> [Price 15 sgr. pp. viii., 120. "The productions of Swiss industry have given the proof, which was intended, that a lasting progress of industry cannot be secured by protection ; nor has the practical result been wanting, many customers, who formerly bought only in English and French markets having since resorted to Swiss ones." The reporter regrets,
>   that

that certain productions of Swiss dairies had not obtained admission at the Crystal Palace. It contains a list of the Swiss exhibitors to whom medals were awarded or who were honourably mentioned.]

Verres, Vitraux et Cristaux, G. Bontemps, v. Examen Historique.

Vers a Soie Bronski, v. Recueil des Opinions sur.

Verses for 1851, In commemoration of The Third Jubilee of the Society for the Propagation of the Gospel. Edited by the Rev. Ernest Hawkins.

London: George Bell, 186, Fleet Street ; Hatchard & Son, Piccadilly. 1851.
[Price 3s. 12mo, pp. iv., 146. The references to the Exhibition are rather exceptional than otherwise. A second edition of this work appeared under the title 'Jubilee Year.'

" The world is keeping holiday,
With banners flaunting proud ;
And ye cannot hear the trumpets bray,
For the voice of Babel's crowd !
The world is keeping holiday,
The world of trade and hire ;
And a crystal vault lets in the ray
On the merchandise of Tyre."]

Viebahn, Dr. Geo. W. von, v. Amtlicher Bericht.

Vienna Imperial Printing Establishment, v. Brief Survey of.

View of the Building.
[Price 3s. A puzzle.]

View of the Great Exhibition Telescopically arranged.
[An expanding view.]

Views, Departmental, of the Great Exhibition, v. Remembrances.

Vision (The) ; or the Spirit of the Great Industrial Exhibition, 1851. A Poem, by Mr. Isaac Reeve, M.C.P., Author of 'The Olive Branch,' 'Not One Lash,' 'Intellect of Woman,' etc.

' Leaving its shell, all beautiful,
Let us consider what the SPIRIT is,
That reigns within and consecrates its walls.' *See Page* 31.

' Most earthly monarchs think that they do well,
When their *own* subjects' welfare they consult ;
But he, who, with his *people's* good, connects
Th' *amelioration* of the *world at large*,
Approaches nearest to the attributes,
The loveliest attributes of *Deity*.' *See Page* 43.

Κλῦτε φίλοι· θεῖος μοι ἐνύπνιον ἦλθεν Ὄνειρος. Ἰλιάδος, β 56.

Published by Houlston and Stoneman, Paternoster Row ; to be had of all Booksellers, Or of Mr. Reeve, Chase Lodge, *Hounslow*.
[W. y. Price 1s. 12mo, pp. iv., 60. The Introduction says : "In this little Poem, the Author has not attempted to give any description of the specimens displayed in the Great Exhibition. * * * His object is a different and a far higher one. As it is the duty of religious instructors to bid their auditors look, from the glorious beauties of nature, up to the still more glorious God of nature ;—so it has been the Author's wish to induce all who visit the Crystal Palace, while their eyes are dazzled with the radiance, and surprised by the ingenuity, delighted with the elaborate art, and ravished with the exquisite beauty, of the objects that surround them, to elevate their minds to a contemplation of the enlightened liberality and benevolent motives, with which the Great Spirit of Spirits inspired the Royal Authors of this most magnificent scheme."]

Visit (A) to the Great Exhibition. By one of the Exhibitors.
London:—Cundall and Addey, 21, Old Bond-Street ; and all Booksellers and Newsmen. 1851.
[Price 6d. Small 4to, pp. 32. With numerous engravings of articles exhibited.]

Visitor's Aid, Accommodation Society, v. Grand Exhibition.

Visitor's Companion, v. Stranger in London.

Visitor's Map of London (The). With 271 References to Public Buildings, and other places of Interest, including an Easy Plan of Measuring Distances, to regulate Cab Fares, &c. Constructed as a Guide for Visitors of All Nations. Price 1s. Coloured.
London: Cradock & Co., 48, Paternoster Row.
[W. y. A map in a case. 18mo.]

Visitors to Public Buildings, Parliamentary Report on, v. Tower of London.

Visit to England, v. Frenchman's Visit.

Visit to London during the Great Exhibition (A) : showing the Visitor, at one glance, What to See, and How to See It, at a Small Expense, in Six Days. Also, a Complete List of Railway, Omnibus, Steamboat, and Coach Fares, their Starting-points, and the Places passed in their Routes ; the Best Coffee Houses and Taverns to put up at, etc. To which are appended Excursions Around London, including Kew Gardens, Richmond, Hampton Court, Windsor, Greenwich, Woolwich, Gravesend, Etc. Embellished with an Engraving. Accompanied by a Full Description of Mr. Paxton's Building, the Objects to be Exhibited, Expense of Visiting, Etc.
>*London* : Henry Beal, 3, Shoe Lane, Fleet Street.
>[W. y. Price 4*d*. 12mo, pp. iv., 56. Pages 5-11 contain an account of the Exhibition.]

Vitraux, Verres et Cristaux, G. Bontemps, *v*. Examen Historique.

Vogel, Dr. Carl, *v*. Wunder (die) des Glaspalastes.

Voices from the Workshop on the Exhibition of 1851. Price One Penny. Entered at Stationers' Hall.
>*London* : 8, George Street, Euston Square.
>[Working Printers, 4A, Johnson's Court, Fleet-street. W. y. A large broadside, containing poems headed " Britannia and Genius, on the Exhibition of 1851," "Song of the Pirates preparing for the Exhibition of 1851," '' Britannia, Genius, Justice," and " National Anthem for 1851." Also an Allegorical Engraving of " Britannia supplicating Justice to protect Inventive Genius."]

Volks-Kalender für das Jahr 1852, *v*. Weber.

Volpe, Girolamo, *v*. Il Giglio e l'Ape.

Volz, *v*. Zeitschrift für die gesammte Staatswissenschaft.

º Voyage a Londres avant l'ouverture de l'Exposition de 1851, Lettres ou Impressions par M. Jules Boyer.
>*Paris*, Imprimerie et Lithographie de Paul Dupont, Rue de Grenelle-Saint-Honoré, 45. 1851.
>[Circulated gratuitously. 8vo, pp. 58. Lithographed. Letter IV. describes and criticizes the Building, then in progress of construction, and other letters treat of subjects connected with the Exhibition. One hundred copies only were printed.]

Waagen, Professor G. F., *v*. Amtlicher Bericht.

Wade, James, *v*. Memorial.

Walker, E., *v*. Souvenir—Engravings on Paper.

Walker, Samuel, *v*. Notes on Woollen Manufactures.

Walk through the Crystal Palace (A).
>The Religious Tract Society, instituted 1799 ; 56, Paternoster Row, and 65, St. Paul's Churchyard.
>[W. y. Price 2*s*. per 100. 12mo, pp. 8, with a woodcut. "We invite our readers to join with us in walking through the building and viewing the novel scene in some of its plain and obviously religious bearings."]

Wallis, George, *v*. Art Journal Prize Essay—Future Uses of the Crystal Palace.

Wanderings in the Crystal Palace. By Robert Franklin, Author of the ' Miller's Muse,' &c.
>*London* : Houlston & Stoneman, 65, Paternoster Row.
>[W. y. 8vo, pp. 24. The author, who resided at Barton-on-Humber, says in his Preface, " Not holding worldly possessions—to become a contributor, and fulfil my heart's best wishes towards it in this respect—I was resolved to sing the praises of its great projectors, contributors, &c.
>>" Contributors to this imposing scene,
>>From distant lands where oceans roll between,
>>Rich was the freight your gallant vessels bore,
>>We bid you welcome to our friendly shore ;
>>You give your time, your wealth, and works sublime,
>>To grace Old England at this happy time."]

Wanderings (The) of Mrs Pipe & Family to view The Crystal Palace   Designed & Etched by Percy Cruikshank. Price 1*s*. plain & 2*s*. 6*d*. colored.
>Published by W. Spooner, 379, Strand, *London* May 5th. 1851.
>[Oblong. 9 sheets of engravings, with letter-press descriptions.]

Ward, James, *v*. Great Exhibition of 1851—World in its Workshops.

Warren, Samuel, *v*. Giglio e l'Ape—Lily and the Bee.

Washington, Captain, Naval Architecture, *v.* Lectures.

Watch and Clock Trade, Report of a Meeting, *v.* Circular.

Water Closets, On Establishment of Public, *v.* Correspondence.

[Waterline Portraits of Her Majesty and Prince Albert, and View of the Building.]
Thos H Saunders *London*
[W. y. One large sheet of tinted paper.]

Watts, Thomas, Aerial Pontoon Railway Suspension Bridge, *v.* Description.

W., C. T., a Poem, *v.* Crystal Hive.

Weale's London in 1851, *v.* London Exhibited.

Wealth of the World in its Workshops, *v.* Great Exhibition or.

Weber's Volks-Kalender für das Jahr 1852.
Leipzig, Verlag von J. J. Weber.
[Pp. 137–148 Die Weltausstellung in London. Price 12½ sgr. Post 8vo, with Illustrations. Contains an account of the Exhibition, preceded by a brief glance at previous undertakings of the same kind, with several woodcuts of the palace and its contents.]

Wedding, Professor W., *v.* Amtlicher Bericht.

Weekes, Henry, A.R.A., On the Fine Arts, *v.* Prize Treatise.

Weigert, S., *v.* Amtlicher Bericht.

Weir, Rev. J., *v.* Forty-four Sermons.

Weld, C. R., *v.* Exposition of 1851.

Welsh Account of the proposed Exhibition, *v.* Mynegiad.

Wereld-Tentoonstelling. Het Nijverheids Paleis te Londen; Bevattende eene korte Geschiedenis van den Oorsprong en den Voortgang des Glazen Gebouws, benevens eene Beschrijving van de Belangrijkste Werktuigen bij het Optrekken Gebezigd. Met vele Houtsnêe- en Steendrukplaten. Ten behoeve van allen die de Tentoonstelling Bezoeken, of die zich eene Herinnering aan dit Kunstgewrocht willen Bewaren. Vrij naar het Engelsch.
Haarlem, A. C. Kruseman. 1851.
[Price 3s. 6d. Small 4to, pp. 55, with Illustrations. A history of the Crystal Palace, with a description, and diagrams, of some of the machines used in the various stages of its erection. "The exhibition is not to be a contest with weapons, not a waste of power and wealth, caused by hostile passions and destruction, but is to show all that is admirable, beautiful, and precious, gathered in one gigantic cornucopia of glass, which by its abundance shall at the same time give proof of the richness, the industry, the genius, and the taste of the present world."]

Wesley, S. Sebastian, *v.* Hymn for All Nations.

West, Edward, *v.* Hymn.

Westminster and Foreign Quarterly Review (The). No. 104. and No. 89. For April, 1850. No. 109. and No. 94. For July, 1851.
London : G. Luxford, Whitefriars,' Street.
Edinburgh : Adam and Charles Black. *New York :* Wiley and Putnam. *Paris :* Guillaumin, 14, Rue Richelieu. Waterlow and Sons, Printers, London Wall, London.
[Price 6s. each. 8vo. The No. for April, 1850, contains an article (pp. 85–100) entitled "The Industrial Exhibition of 1851." The writer concludes as follows : "The grand objects of the Exhibition, as we regard them, may thus be summed up : 1. To promote brotherhood amongst mankind. 2. To make all cognisant of what each can do for others. 3. To diminish human drudgery by mechanism. 4. To promote art of the higher kind. 5. To show how clothing may best be made by machines, without handicrafty. 6. New preparations of human food." The article (pp. 346–3 ¹4) in the No. for July, 1851, was a summary of the early proceedings in connexion with the Exhibition, and a short account of the various sections. This number was published by Groombridge and Sons, 5, Paternoster Row.]

West of England (The) and the Exhibition, 1851, by Herbert Byng Hall, K.S.F., Author of ' Scenes at Home and Abroad,' ' Highland Sports,' ' Exmoor,' etc., etc. with Illustrations.
London : Longman and Co., Paternoster-Row. 1851.
[Price 14s. Post 8vo, pp. viii., 348. Mr. Hall was one of the representatives of the Royal Commissioners in the West of England. The work, which is illustrated with engravings, has no immediate reference to the Exhibition, but consists of chapters on various localities which he visited. It was printed by W. A. Woodley, Taunton.]

Weyhe, *v.* Amtlicher Bericht.

Wharncliffe, Lord, *v.* Reports by the Juries.

'What have they seen in Thine House?' or Reflections on the Opening of the Great Exhibition. A sermon Preached on Sunday Morning, April 27th, 1851. By Daniel Moore, M.A., Perpetual Curate of Camden District, Camberwell.
London; Kerby & Son, 190, Oxford Street. 1851.
> [Price 6*d.* 8vo, pp. 31. " The scheme would not be human, if it pleased everybody ; and it would not be English, if it did not provide for our national propensity to complain. For myself, I have no extreme feelings upon the subject, either of hope or fear." *v.* also Goode.]

What I saw at the Worlds Fair or Notes of the Great Exhibition, by Mr. Comic-eye. Price 1*s.* 2*s.* 6*d.* col^d. T. Onwhyn Delt.
London Pub by Rock. Brothers & Payne.
> [W. y. An oblong sheet of facetious engravings.]

What is to become of the Crystal Palace? by Joseph Paxton.
London : Bradbury & Evans, 11, Bouverie Street. 1851.
> [Price 1*s.* 8vo, pp. 15. " The Building, I would suggest, should be allowed to remain standing on account of its peculiar fitness to supply a great public want, which London, with its two and a half millions of inhabitants, stands most essentially in need of – namely, a *Winter Park and Garden* under glass." An answer to this pamphlet, by Greville, will be found under " Answer."]

> Another Edition.
> [Price 2*d.* Square 18mo, pp. 16.]

What *is* to be done with the Crystal Palace? Illustrated in 14 proposals (etched on steel) by Percy Cruikshank.
Published by J Clayton & Son 265 Strand *London* 1*s.* plain & 2*s.* col^d.
> [W. y. An oblong sheet of colored facetious engravings.]

What *is* to be done with the Crystal Palace.
> 'Quod Petis—hic est.'
London: Simpkin, Marshall, and Co. Stationers' Hall Court. Price Sixpence.
> [W. y. 8vo, pp. 16. The proposal was to remove the Crystal Palace to a range of heath and downs within a dozen miles of Hyde Park. The spot to be converted into a park, with villas, a racecourse, and the Crystal Palace as a conservatory.]

What I thought of the Crystal Palace; or, the Great Exhibition compared with Holy Writ.
London: G. E. Petter, 102, Cheapside. 1852.
> [Price 1*s.* 18mo, pp. iv., 140. By a Sunday School Teacher. "The subject matter of this little volume was an Address which the author delivered in his Sunday-school."]

What Shall we do with the Glass Palace ? A letter addressed to the Commissioners of the Great Exhibition. By Spiridione Gambardella.
> 'We have now, on the one hand, the eager competition of a vast array of artists of every degree of talent and skill, and on the other, as judge, a great Public, for the greater part wholly uneducated in Art.'—*Speech of Prince Albert.*

London : Charles Westerton, 20, Saint George's Place, Hyde Park Corner; Aylott and Jones, Paternoster Row; and all Booksellers. 1851.
> [Price 1*s.* 8vo, pp. 28. "My Plan is this: I propose—1. That the Crystal Palace shall remain on its present site, to be used among other things as a Temple of Art: one year for Painters, one year for Sculptors. * * * 4. That those artists who are too poor to have a large studio shall be accommodated with room in the Crystal Palace." Mr. Gambardella proposes that money be taken at the doors, which, in his opinion, would be sufficient to pay all expenses, to provide prizes, and to form a permanent fund for the erection of some Temple of Art.]

What's What in 1851 ? A Guide to London, for the Year of the Great Industrial Exhibition, embracing a lucid and comprehensive Epitome of all the leading Places of Importance & Attraction throughout the Metropolis and its Suburbs, and comprising the necessary Information and Instructions to both Natives and Foreigners, with regard to the Exhibition of Industrial Art—Theatres—Hotels—Government Offices—Banks—Assurance Companies—Public Gardens—Parks—Cathedrals—Halls—Palaces—Club Houses—Monuments—Bridges—Railway Stations—Markets—Post Offices—Colleges—Newspapers, and every leading Commercial Establishment catering for the Wants, Luxuries, and Tastes of Connoisseurs. By One who not only knows 'What's What,' but 'Who's Who,' and 'Where's Where.' Entered at Stationers' Hall.
London :

London: Published by Whittaker & Co., Ave Maria Lane; and may be had of all Booksellers·
Price One Shilling
    [W. y. 18mo, pp. VI., 93. The title contains the only reference to the Exhibition.]

Whewell, Rev. W., *v.* Lectures [Bearing of Exhibition on Art and Science].

⁰Whig Attorney's Great-iron-glass-foreign-Bazaar, for the Sham-free-trade-festival,
    in the Dog-days of 1851.
    [Arthur Wallis, Printer, 5, Bartholomews, *Brighton.* W. y. Price one half-penny. 8vo,
    pp. 4. Another version of "The Great Job" with variations. Signed Thalaba.]

Whish, Rev. J. A., *v.* Great Exhibition Prize Essay.

Whishaw, Francis, *v.* Origin of the Great Exhibition—Special General Meeting.

Whitby Philosophical Society, Tempest Prognosticator, *v.* Essay read before.

White, John Bazley, on Cements, *v.* Experiments.

Whittingham, C., *v.* Reports by the Juries.

Wieck, F. G., *v.* Wunder des Glaspalastes.

Wight, Dr. Robert, on the Forest Trees of Southern India, *v.* Proceedings.

Willis, Rev. Robert, *v.* Lectures [Machines and Tools]—Reports by the Juries.

Wilson, Professor John, *v.* Lectures [Agricultural Products and Implements].

Winfield, R. W., Address of Clerks in Employ of, *v.* To His R. H. Prince Albert.

Winkworth, Thomas, *v.* Reports by the Juries.

Winter Garden, *v.* Medical Man—Reasons for converting the Crystal Palace into.

Wissenschaft, Industrie und Kunst. Vorschläge zur Anregung nationalen Kunst-
    gefühles. Bei dem Schlusse der Londoner Industrie-Ausstellung von Gottfried
    Semper, ehemaligem Director der Bauschule zu Dresden. London, den 11.
    October 1851.
    Braunschweig, Druck und Verlag von Friedrich Vieweg und Sohn. 1852.
    [Price 15 sgr. 8vo, pp. 76. An essay written four weeks after the close of the Exhibition.
    It refers principally to English and American matters of art, with the special object of
    throwing out hints for a reform of the system of public instruction in the schools of art
    and design. The author recommends the adoption of a series of lectures similar to that
    given at the Conservatoire des Arts et Metiers at Paris (in the winter half-year 1851-2),
    completed by another course on the application of arts to practical sciences, &c.]

Woche (Eine) in London oder so sieht man die Riesenstadt mit allen ihren
    National-Anstalten und Instituten, öffentlichen Gebäuden, Merkwürdigkeiten
    etc. in sieben Tagen. Nebst historischer und beschreibender Skizze der
    Haupstadt von den frühesten Zeiten bis auf die Gegenwart. Mit 32 Ansichten
    in Stahlstich und 1 Plan von London.
    Leipzig und Dresden, Englische Kunstanstalt von A. H. Payne.
    London, W. Trench, 67 Paternoster Row.
    [Price 15 sgr. 12mo, pp. IV., 78. A guide for visitors to London during the Exhibition.
    The map indicates the spot occupied by the Exhibition building.]

Woodhall, Charles, Visits of Working People from Selby, *v.* Important.

Woodhead, C. S., *v.* Letters.

Woolwich, Meeting at, *v.* Report of.

Wordsworth, Dr. C., Sermon, *v.* On the Great Exhibition.

Working Classes, *v.* Essay—Exhibition and the People—Great Industrial Exhi-
    bition, its importance to—Important to—Leeds Agency for conveyance.

Working Classes Central Committee.
    [Without Publisher's or Printer's name, or date, but issued March, 1850. Three circulars,
    4to and 8vo, containing Resolutions, List of Committee, and Bishop of Oxford's lithographed
    letter.]

Working Man's Papers. Paper 2. The Grand Mistake; or, the Exhibition of
    1851. Its effects Upon the Working Classes; Upon the Shop-keepers; Upon
    Manufacturers; Upon Artizans of every denomination Upon Factory Opera-
    tives. Stagnation of Trade—Reduction of Wages—Increase of Poor Rates.
    By Junius.

Q   *London:*

London: J. James, 44, Holywell Street, Strand and J. Pavey, 47, Holywell Street.
[W. y. 8vo, pp. 16. "In my first paper I stated, that the effect of the Exhibition would be very disastrous to English mechanics of every class, and my predictions, unfortunately, are already coming to pass. I am informed, on good authority, that even now numbers of German carpenters and cabinet-makers are going about to the workshops of London demanding labour. Speaking little or no English, their answer to every question is, 'The Exhibition.' Aye, it is the Exhibition, this fatal Exhibition which has brought them over, and which will yet bring over thousands more. * * * Unless the protectionists return to office, I do not anticipate any increase in the price of food, but I do anticipate wonderfully low wages, wages indeed lower than any which an Englishman would at present stop to take, but which he must come to at last. Hunger, an empty stomach, and famishing little ones, will bring the proudest down. It is, indeed, most astonishing to me, that the manufacturers should so entirely have overlooked the dangerous tendency of the Exhibition."]

Working Men, Advantages to be gained by, *v.* Essay by T. Briggs.

Working Men's Association, Rules of, *v.* Bristol.

Workman (The) and the International Exhibition. (From the Leader, No. 65.)
Holyoake Brothers, Printers, 3, Queen's Head Passage, Paternoster Row.
[W. y. Price ½d., or 6d. a dozen. 12mo, pp. 8. "If the International Exhibition be the means of calling the attention—bestowed so plentifully on industrial products—to the social condition of the producers, it will not pass away without leaving a noble moral behind."]

World-Embracing Faith (A); or, Religious Whispers from the Exhibition of Industry. By Edward Higginson, Minister of Westgate Chapel, Wakefield. Reprinted from the Christian Reformer, June, 1851.
London: E. T. Whitfield, 2, Essex Street, Strand.
Wakefield: Lamb and Heald. 1851. Price Threepence.
[12mo, pp. 23. "The great Industrial Exhibition is, in itself, an event of properly religious interest. Not religious interest in any technical or sectarian sense, but in a sense to reprove all merely sectarian and technical notions of religion."]

World's Fair (The), and the Progress of Truth. A Poem, by Julio Henry Hughes, Comedian.
London: Published by Cawthorn & Hutt, Cockspur Street. 1851.
[Price 3s. Fcap. 8vo, pp. viii., 63.
"The nave in its perspective endlessness,
Or the fair transept with its broad roof curled
O'er-arching highest Trees, therein preserved
Because the People willed it! To all time
This circumstance should be recorded, served
To show a Nation's wish was not a crime
To be resisted and subdued, but soon
As formed was gracefully conceded by
Authority, nor yielded as a boon,
But recognized a right; 'twas Liberty!"]

World's Fair (The); or, Children's Prize Gift Book of the Great Exhibition of 1851. Describing the beautiful inventions and manufactures exhibited therein; with Pretty Stories about the People who have made and sent them; and how they live when at home.
London: Thomas Dean and Son 35, Threadneedle-Street, and Ackermann and Co. 96, Strand.
[W. y. Price 2s. 6d. Post 8vo, pp. 106; with illustrations.]

World's Great Assembly (The).
J. F Shaw, Bookseller, Southampton Row, and Paternoster Row, *London;*
and W. Innes, Bookseller, South Hanover St, *Edinburgh.* London J. & W. Rider, Printers, 14, Bartholomew Close.
[W. y. Price 1d. 24mo, pp. 16. A little tract in favour of the Exhibition; with a religious tendency. "The palace of glass will be much, the wonders it contains will be much, the throng assembled to see it will be much; but be assured of one thing, that, whatever may be the case with our own countrymen, *to all Foreigners England and the English will be the Great Exhibition of* 1851."]

World in its Workshops (The): A Practical Examination of British and Foreign Processes of Manufacture, with a Critical Comparison of the Fabrics, Machinery, and Works of Art contained in the Great Exhibition. By James Ward. Metals, Machinery, and Glass.
A Second Division, "Sculptures, Cabinet-Work, Glass, &c."
London: William S. Orr and Co., Amen Corner, Paternoster Row.
[W. y. Price 1s. each part. 12mo, pp. 284. The two divisions are paged continuously, and contain four engravings. The work treats of the following subjects: "Steel—swords, guns, and pistols—percussion caps—copper, brass, and mixed metals—steel pens—pin-making, and wire-drawing—needles—buttons—plate, Sheffield-plate, and electro-plate—
typography,

typography, lithography, stereotype—machinery, etc.—agricultural implements—glass—sculpture—wood-carving—designs and decorations—painting on glass—paper-staining and paper-hangings—cabinet-work—pianofortes—papier-maché—pottery and porcelain—silks—printed fabrics—carpets—the etceteras of the Exhibition—patents, patent laws." Another work on the same subject will be found under Great Exhibition of 1851, or the Wealth of the World in its Workshops.]

Wornum, Ralph N., on Ornamental Art, *v.* Art Journal Illustrated Catalogue.

Wortley, The Lady Emmeline Stuart, *v.* Honour to Labour—On the approaching Close.

Writing Paper with Illustrative Views.
    Letter paper.
    Note paper.

Wunder (Die) des Glaspalastes. Ein Festgeschenk für die Jugend von F. G. Wieck. Nebst einem Vorwort von Dr. Carl Vogel, Director der allgemeinen Bürgerschule zu Leipzig. Mit 8 bronzirten und 120 in den Text gedruckten Abbildungen.
    Leipzig, Verlag von J. J. Weber, 1852.
        [Price 1 thaler 20 sgr. Royal 16mo, pp. xii, 262. This volume is a book for the young, neither a child's book nor a school book. It is a reading book, in which the pictures and the letterpress are intimately connected.]

Wunderlich, Robert, *v.* Beobachter.

Würtemberg Section. By authority of the Royal Commission. Official Catalogue of the Great Exhibition of the Industry of All Nations, 1851.
    London: Spicer Brothers, Wholesale Stationers; W. Clowes & Sons, Printers; Contractors to the Royal Commission. City Office, 29 New Bridge Street, Blackfriars.
        [W.y., but published in 1851. Price 3*d.* 4to, pp. 19. More detailed than the Illustrated Catalogue, and contains the prices of the articles exhibited.]

Würtemburg, *v.* Comical Creatures of.

Wyatt, Matthew Digby, *v.* Illustrated London Almanack—Industrial Arts—Lectures [Form in Decorative Art]—On Construction of Building—Report.

Wyld's Map of London and Visitor's Guide to the Great Exhibition 1851.
    Published by James Wyld Geographer to the Queen and H.R.H. Prince Albert Charing Cross East (opposite Northumberland Street) *London.*
        [W. y. Price 1*s.* colored, and 6*d.* plain. In 18mo. case. A large sheet, with an engraving of the Crystal Palace, and others. Copies in the French and German Sections will be found under "Nouveau Plan" and "Neuer."]

Yankee and Nigger at the Exhibition, *v.* Chaff.

Yankee Smith's London Comic Songster; a Selection of The Best Comic Songs and Parodies. Price 1*d.* Nos. 28. 32. 37. and 38.
    London: R. Macdonald, 30, Great Sutton St., Clerkenwell.
        [W. y. 24mo. No. 28 contains a Song called the Great Exhibition of 1851. No. 32 contains a Song called the Glass House Exhibition of 1851. No. 37 contains a Song entitled "Wake up, Johnny Bull, or you're safe to be done!" (a Song of the Great National Exhibition), and No. 38 contains "The Cast-Iron Man for the Great Exhibition."]

Yapp, G. W., *v.* Art Education at Home and Abroad.

Year-Book of Facts (The) in The Great Exhibition of 1851: its Origin and Progress, constructive Details of the Building, the most remarkable Articles and Objects exhibited, etc. By John Timbs, Editor of 'The Arcana of Science and Art.'
        'To seize the living scroll of human progress, inscribed with every successive conquest of man's intellect, filled with each discovery in the constructive arts, embellished with each plastic grace of figured surface or of moulded form, and unroll this before the eyes of men, the whole stream of history furnishing its contingent, placing Archimedes, Arkwright, Davy, Jacquard, Watt, and Stephenson side by side,—leaving the instructive lesson to be learned that always lies in the knowledge and example of great things done;—this is, indeed, no mean design, no infelicitous conception.' *Edinburgh Review,* No. CXCII., *October,* 1851.
    London: David Bogue, Fleet Street. .1851. Extra Volume.
        [Price 6*s.* 12mo, pp. iv., 348. With a portrait of Prince Albert. Contains also the official award of the prizes, and the number of visitors to the Exhibition.]

Year 1851 (The).

> Now gone, involved, in ages past away
> Since time on earth, for no one thing will stay
> A floating thought, on what was lately seen;
> And though a fact, yet much more like a dream.

London: T. F. A. Day, 13, Carey Street (Successor to Mr. Hastings.)　1852.
[Price 2s.　8vo, pp. 84.　A Poem.

> " A work was done, the like not known before,
> Which brought us pleasure, and yet something more:
> Proofs undisputed of triumphant skill,
> Each nation's tribute, sent with right good-will,
> In peace conceived, and by a few contrived;
> In splendour lived, and to the end survived.
> A thousand ill forebodings saw no light—
> Mere brainless phantoms, lost in endless night—
> Nor work or workmen in the least disgrace;
> Miscarriage none, in money, time, or place.
> Once set on foot, would not admit of change
> This vast conception, with its ample range,
> In frame and fashion new, no forms to guide,
> Our country's boast, the Prince and People's pride."]

Yorkshire Visitors' Guide (The) to the Great Exhibition, and also to the Principal sights of London.　By the Reporter for the ' Leeds Times.'　(With Additions and Corrections by the Author.)　Price Twopence.

1851:　Printed by Joseph Buckton, 50, Briggate, Leeds, and may be had of all Booksellers and News Vendors in the West-Riding.
　　[12mo, pp. 27.　" It is utterly impossible for the mind of man to conceive the grandeur and magnificence that here await him, or, if he possess a soul capable of emotion, to subdue and keep altogether in abeyance those sensations of awe and wonder, admiration and reverence, which the first view of the interior of this majestic temple will assuredly awaken."]

Younge, Robert, v. Address of the Local Commissioners for Sheffield.

Zeitschrift für die gesammte Staatswissenschaft.　In Vierteljahrs-Heften herausgegeben von Volz, Schüz, Fallati, Hoffmann, Göriz, Helferich, Mitgliedern der staatswirthschaftlichen Facultät in Tübingen, und Robert Mohl: Siebenter Jahrgang.　Viertes Heft.　Achter Jahrgang.　Erstes Heft.　Achter Jahrgang.　Zweites und drittes Heft.

[Grosbritannien und Deutschland auf der Industrie-Ausstellung zu London im Jahre 1851.　Von Volz.　I. Grossbritanniens Colonialschätze.　II. Britische Arbeit.　III. Deutschland zu Grossbritannien.]

Tübingen.　Verlag der H. Laupp'schen Buchhandlung.　1851-2.
　　[Price R 5.10　8vo, pp. 687-727, 107-210, 434-473.　The author gives an account of the principal objects of English industry in the Crystal Palace, arranging them under different heads, such as machinery, metallurgy, mining, raw products, etc.　Speaking of the chemical manufactories at Glasgow, etc., the author is struck by the tallness of some of their chimneys, and finding them above the height of the Egyptian Pyramids and Strasburg cathedral, he says, " Pyramid, church, and chimney, what speaking monuments in the history of mankind! "　In the latter portion of his essay, exclusively devoted to the German articles, he gives utterance to some painful feelings, that with all the excellence of many Austrian, Prussian, and other German productions, no greater amount of well-merited credit accrued to them, as manifestations of *national* skill, whereas the English and French were universally praised as such.　He consequently admonishes his countrymen to strenuous exertions in favour of national unity.]

Zenos, Stephanos O., v. Παγκοσμιος.

Zuber, Jean, sur L'industrie du Papier pour Tentures, v. Rapport.

Zurich, v. Section III.

Zusammenstellung der Einsendungen von Hamburg und den übrigen Staaten Nord-Deutschlands zur Industrie-Ausstellung aller Völker in London.

N.B.—Die Nummern sind nach dem Catalog der Königlich Grossbrittannischen Commission geordnet.

Hamburg: Buch- und Steindruckerei von J. G. Bitter, 1851.
　　[Price 5 sgr.　Long 8vo, pp. 16.　Arranged according to towns and countries, with an alphabetical list of the exhibitors mentioned in the pamphlet.　The prices are affixed in the Hamburg currency.]

LONDON: PRINTED BY W. CLOWES AND SONS, STAMFORD STREET AND CHARING CROSS.